SUBJECT AND PSYCHE:

Ricoeur, Jung, and
the Search for Foundations

Robert M. Doran
Creighton University

University Press
of America™

ACKNOWLEDGMENTS

From PHILOSOPHY OF GOD, AND THEOLOGY, by Bernard
J. F. Lonergan, S.J. Copyright (c) 1973, by Bernard
J. F. Lonergan, S.J. Published by The Westminster
Press. Used by permission.

From METHOD IN THEOLOGY by Bernard J. F. Lonergan, S.J.
(c) 1972 by Bernard J. F. Lonergan . Used by permission
of the Seabury Press.

From COLLECTION: Papers by Bernard Lonergan, S. J.
(c) 1967 by Bernard Lonergan, S. J. Used by permission
of The Seabury Press.

From THE MYTH OF ANALYSIS by James Hillman. (c) 1972
by Northwestern University Press. Used by permission of
Northwestern University Press.

From INSIGHT: A Study of Human Understanding. (c) 1957.
Used by permission of Philosophical Library.

From THE WAY OF ALL THE EARTH by John S. Dunne (c) 1972
by John S. Dunne, C.S.C. Used by permission of Macmillan
Publishing Company.

From EXPERIENCING AND THE CREATION OF MEANING by Eugene
Gendlin (c) 1962 by The Free Press of Glencoe. Used by
permission of Macmillan Publishing Company.

From FREUD AND PHILOSOPHY by Paul Ricoeur (c) 1970 by
Yale University. Used by permission of Yale University Press.

From THE COLLECTED WORKS OF C. G. JUNG, (c) by Bollingen
Foundation, New York. Used by permission of Princeton
University Press.

TABLE OF CONTENTS

Chapter

PREFACE

Our twentieth century is the scene of a breakthrough in the evolution of human consciousness, a movement to a new stage of meaning in which the self-appropriation of interiority becomes the touchstone of the control of meaning. The writings of Bernard Lonergan, I am convinced, have solidified this breakthrough, made it more than merely coincidental, systematized it, given it a secure foothold, integrated it. But Lonergan's work would have no context, no materials to integrate, were it not for the earlier and less successful but nonetheless essential developments that may roughly be included under the rubric of the "turn to the subject." Among these developments has been the discovery and scientific and therapeutic exploration of the psychological depths.

A large part of the work that follows tries to show how Lonergan's analysis of human intentionality allows one to generate categories through which both the human psyche and the science of depth psychology can profitably be understood. The key to my thesis is located in the development of Lonergan's thought from cognitional analysis to intentionality analysis. I accord primary importance to the emergence of a notion of a level of human consciousness distinctly concerned with the issue of value, the notio valoris, the human good. Values are primordially apprehended in feelings, and feelings are ascertainable, identifiable, through symbols. From this clue, I employ

Lonergan's thought to aid me in developing a metascientific understanding of the psychotherapeutic phenomenon. I utilize basic notions of Jungian analytical psychology, while clarifying some ambiguities in Jung's thought with the aid of both Lonergan's intentionality analysis and Paul Ricoeur's philosophy of the symbol. Especially, I propose the need for moving beyond the framework of Jung's implicit metascience at a certain crucial moment both in Jung's thought and in one's exploration of one's own symbolic interiority.

There is also a second moment to my work. Not only does intentionality analysis clarify and correct depth psychological understandings of human subjectivity, but a transformed science of the psyche provides to Lonergan's method a needed complement. This complement can be articulated through a careful analysis of Lonergan's understanding of theological foundations. The very dynamic of Lonergan's thought leads inexorably to a depth psychological analysis that can be integrated with Lonergan's study of human knowledge and human decision. Such an integration greatly expands the foundational resources that are available not only to the theologian but to the critic of culture, the human scientist, and the philosopher as well. The turn to the subject, in every instance--philosophical, psychological, theological--, has been a search for the foundations of a new epoch in the evolution of human consciousness. I only hope my work is a contribution to the one ongoing foundational quest that is, I dare say, the drama of our age.

I have many debts I should confess, but I will limit myself to six acknowledgements. First I must mention the two men most instrumental in mediating the process of self-discovery and personal change that lies behind this work. I had spent seven years on Lonergan's writings before I ever had the pleasure and honor of discussing my own insights with him. But a very happy semester at Regis College in Toronto in the fall and winter of 1973-74 revealed to me a man as gracious and kind as he is perceptive, insightful, and judicious. Lonergan has been, to put it mildly, most encouraging of my efforts and helpful in promoting my confident hope that I might be on to something. Charles Goldsmith, clinical psychologist and chaplain at Deaconess Hospital in Milwaukee, skilfully exercised the delicate maieutic art of introducing me to the symbolic process of my own psychological depths.

Next, I wish to thank three friends with whom I have spent many hours discussing various facets of the problems here treated. It is to Vernon Gregson that I owe the term "psychic conversion," to Sebastian Moore that I am indebted for the insight that brought me beyond Jung's notion of the self, and to Matthew Lamb that I owe thanks for a sharp clarification of the central issue of the interrelationship of theology, philosophy, and depth psychology.

Finally, I wish to express my gratitude to Lorna Rixmann, who typed the final manuscript of this work two years ago and who was readily available again this summer for some needed last-minute alterations.

Three sources which were as yet unpublished when I wrote this manuscript have subsequently been released for publication either in the form in which I made reference to them or in an altered version. Lonergan's "Insight Revisited" has been published in the same form in which it was originally delivered as a lecture to the Jesuit Philosophical Association. It appears in Bernard Lonergan, A Second Collection. edited

v

by William F. J. Ryan, S.J. and Bernard J. Tyrrell, S.J. (Philadelphia: Westminster), pp. 263-278. Sebastian Moore has published under the title, The Crucified Jesus is No Stranger (New York: Seabury) some of the reflections which I met in his Journey Into a Crucifix. Giovanni Sala has summarized the fruit of his research on Lonergan and Kant in an altered version of the paper I employ in Chapter Four. The published paper, "The A Priori in Human Knowledge: Kant's Critique of Pure Reason and Lonergan's Insight," appears in The Thomist, 1976, pp. 179-221.

Robert M. Doran
Marquette University
June, 1977

INTRODUCTION

In the following work I attempt a contribution to the analysis of the evaluating, deliberating, deciding existential subject already begun by Bernard Lonergan, and an elucidation of what this contribution has to do with the foundations of theology. I use as my key sentence the following statement from Lonergan's Method in Theology: "Besides the immediate world of the infant and the adult's world mediated by meaning, there is the mediation of immediacy by meaning when one objectifies cognitional process in transcendental method and when one discovers, identifies, accepts one's submerged feelings in psychotherapy."[1] I attempt to understand the second mediation as aiding the self-appropriation of the existential subject in much the same way as the first aids that of the cognitional subject. In my first chapter, I show that such a context for understanding psychotherapy is at least implicit in Method in Theology. In the second, third, fourth, and fifth chapters I use Lonergan's thought to aid me in generating appropriate categories for understanding this second mediation of immediacy by meaning. Finally, in the sixth chapter, I state the function of this psychic self-appropriation in relation to the foundations of theology.

While I have made use of the writings of Carl Gustav Jung to elucidate the process of psychotherapy, the present work cannot be taken

---

[1]
Bernard Lonergan, Method in Theology (New York: Herder and Herder, 1972), p. 77.

1

as a thorough statement of Jung's relevance to theology or of the theological pertinence of Jungian analysis. Such a statement, I believe,
must take the form of an analysis and critique of Jung's phenomenology
of the psyche. I do not undertake this task here, nor do I present any
alternative phenomenology. Both of these tasks are reserved for a future
work. In the present study, my interest is method, especially theological
method. I seek to generate explanatory categories connecting psychotherapy with the self-appropriation of the existential subject and
establishing this process as foundational for theology. I am doing
neither depth psychology nor systematic theology, but theological method.

The statement I have cited from Lonergan places on the same level
of discourse the work to which Lonergan has devoted his entire career as
teacher, scholar, and author, and another movement of self-appropriation
achieved in a very different context. It makes these two movements somehow of equal footing, at least in that each is a mediation of immediacy
by meaning.[2] What is the significance of this equivalence? In particular,

---

[2]
    The same equivalence is expressed in Lonergan's very recent and
as yet unpublished paper, "Prolegomena to the Study of the Emerging
Religious Consciousness of Our Time." I quote: "My book, Insight, is
an account of human understanding. As a book, it is an outer socio-
cultural factor providing expression and interpretation of events named
insights. But at the same time it is inviting the reader to self-discovery, to performing in and for himself the illustrative insights set
forth in successive chapters, to adverting to what happens in himself
when the insights occur and, no less, to what is missing when they do not
occur, until eventually as is hoped he will be as familiar with his own
intelligence in act as he is with his ocular vision.
    "What can be done for insights, can also be done for feelings.
Feelings simply as felt pertain to an infra-structure. But as merely
felt, so far from being integrated into an equable flow of consciousness,
they may become a source of disturbance, upset, inner turmoil. Then a
cure or part of a cure would seem to be had from the client-centered
therapist who provides the patient with an ambiance in which he is at
ease, can permit feelings to emerge without being engulfed by them, come
to distinguish them from other inner events, differentiate among them,

what is its significance for the question of method, for philosophy

understood as self-appropriation, and for theology? And what is its

significance for depth psychology itself?

Paul Ricoeur cites with approval the insight of Maurice Merleau-
Ponty to the effect that a philosophy which starts from an infinite

curiosity, from an ambition to see everything, "must subject its own

problematic to the unsettling questions of the body, of time, of inter-

subjectivity, of the consciousness of things or the world, where being

is now 'all around (consciousness) instead of laid out before it . . .

oneiric being, by definition hidden.'"[3] I will start from the cogni-

tional analysis of Lonergan as the philosophy which begins from an

infinite curiosity, rather than, as Ricoeur and Merleau-Ponty, from the

phenomenology of Edmund Husserl. At my own risk, I will wager that this

will be a head start. My wager is encouraged by the fact that for

Lonergan being is precisely never laid out before consciousness. Being

is always a task, a struggle with the flight from understanding. May

we follow this lead and further the work of self-appropriation begun by

Lonergan's intentionality analysis? May we show that the movement of

---

add recognition, bestow names, gradually manage to incapsulate within
a supra-structure of knowledge and language, of assurance and confidence, what had been an occasion for disorientation, dismay, dis-
organization." Pp. 5-6. Here, rather than speaking of the mediation
of immediacy, Lonergan talks of raising "an infra-structure of insights
as discoveries or of feelings as felt" to "a supra-structure of
insights as formulated in hypotheses or of feelings as integrated in
conscious living." P. 6.

3
    Paul Ricoeur, Freud and Philosophy, translated by Denis Savage
(New Haven: Yale, 1970), p. 418, quoting from Merleau-Ponty's Preface
to A. Hesnard, L'Oeuvre de Freud et son importance pour le monde moderne
(1960), p. 8.

self-appropriation instituted by Lonergan extends to the second
mediation of immediacy by meaning? Does this extension in such a context open upon an appropriation of the dynamics of the moral and
religious consciousness which can sublate an intellectually self-
appropriating consciousness? In moving to the psychotherapeutic hermeneutic and dialectic of the symbol, does not the existential subject
achieve a unity-in-differentiation of three previously disparate and
separate disciplines--philosophy, theology, and depth psychology?[4]--and
in this differentiated unity discover new foundations? These are my
questions.

Thus in one sense I do not start simply from Lonergan's cognitional analysis but from the new problematic raised by his recent
explorations of the evaluative level of intentional consciousness, of
the existential subject, of dialectic and foundations.[5] I start from
his cognitional analysis as from a secure, massive, and in its

---

[4]
Just what I mean by this unity-in-differentiation can only be
spelled out in Chapter One, in the context of a discussion of
Lonergan's notion of method. My clue is the interrelation of philosophy and theology argued in Lonergan's Philosophy of God, and Theology
(Philadelphia: Westminster, 1973). My present work is an attempt to
interrelate depth psychology with philosophy and theology on the basis
of the same notion of method that allows Lonergan to move toward a
unity-in-differentiation of the philosophy of God and the theological
functional specialty, systematics. As Lonergan argues that the
separation but not the distinction between philosophy and theology
should be abolished, so I will want to maintain that depth psychology
is neither philosophy nor theology but methodologically related to both
in the context of the self-appropriation of foundational subjectivity.

[5]
This problematic is carefully studied by F. E. Crowe, "An
Exploration of Lonergan's New Notion of Value," unpublished paper
written for the Lonergan Institute held at Boston College in June,
1974.

essentials irrevocable achievement of the human mind's knowledge of
itself. I start from his explorations of value, dialectic, and foundations as from a problem, and attempt to further, if just so slightly,
a resolution of that problem by pointing to one direction I believe its
resolution may take. I begin with the assumption, then, that there is
no going back on Chapters 11, 12 and 13 of Insight[6] nor on the cognitional structure of theological method derived from the understanding
of understanding. I do not attempt to detail this achievement by means
of a repetition nor to argue for its conclusiveness. There is simply
no substitute for subjecting one's own cognitional activity to the
rigorous critique of Insight and for discovering for oneself the essentials of the answers to the triad of questions: what am I doing when I
am knowing? why is that knowing? what do I know when I do that? I
accept Lonergan's answers to these questions as correct, and his elaboration of an operational notion of method on the basis of these
answers as valid. I wish to move with Lonergan, then, into the exploration of the evaluating, deliberating, deciding subject and to attempt
a contribution to the elucidation of what, in Lonergan's schema, is the
fourth level of intentional consciousness.[7]

In the course of my explorations, I have also arrived at the
beginnings of a depth psychological or, more precisely, archetypal
appreciation of Lonergan's secure epistemological and methodological

---

6
Bernard Lonergan, Insight: A Study of Human Understanding
(New York: Philosophical Library, 1957).

7
For a statement of the levels of consciousness, see below,
pp. 43-44.

achievement and at an understanding of its potential therapeutic value.
A sufficiently penetrating scrutiny of the fourth level of intentional
consciousness may reveal, I believe, that an elaboration of the semantics of human desire is the meaning of a philosophy understood as self-
appropriation. That the phrase, the semantics of desire, is borrowed
from Paul Ricoeur's brilliant study of Freudian discourse[8] is no
indication that I intend to render a psycho-analytic interpretation of
Lonergan's writings. If anything, it would be far more accurate to say
that I am pointing to a re-interpretation of the psychoanalytic and
analytical psychological movements of Freud and Jung, from the standpoint of a philosophy of self-appropriation, from the standpoint of
method; that method, then, provides a horizon for understanding both
Freudian and Jungian discourse and for locating in being the strange
worlds their discoveries open for us. Nonetheless the relationship is
reciprocal. The world opened to method by depth psychology affects
method's understanding of itself. For depth psychology as praxis is
given something of an equivalence with cognitional analysis as praxis,
and so, just as cognitional analysis illuminates the truth of depth
psychology, depth psychology reveals the archetypal significance of cognitional analysis. If we follow Ricoeur's lead in extending our notion
of desire beyond Freud's explicit understanding of it, if we use Jung to
help us follow this lead, and if, with Ricoeur and Jung, we interpret
the teleological dimension of desire as an orientation to becoming ever
more conscious, then the struggles into which one is plunged by reading

---

[8] Paul Ricoeur, op. cit., pp. 5-7, 160, 255, 271, 294, 322, 363, 375, 381, 386.

Lonergan's work take on an explicitly archetypal dimension, perhaps the most primal archetypal dimension. For Lonergan engages one without mercy in the conflict immanent in human desire itself between the intention of being and the flight from understanding, between the desire to know and the desire not to know. It is this struggle which Ricoeur finds at the heart of the Oedipal drama. I will ask whether this discovery does not call for a new understanding of psychotherapy from its origins. I find, in addition, a different solution to the same struggle in the drama of Orestes and within this drama locate the current archetypal situation of method and the archetypal significance of the new directions in Lonergan's explorations of the fourth level of intentional consciousness. Method, on the basis of its resolute and heroic decision in favor of understanding and self-transcendence, is Orestes before his vindication by Athena. The second mediation of immediacy by meaning, when conducted on the basis of the first, and so when engaged in as appropriation at the fourth level of intentional consciousness, will free psyche to be wisdom and to vindicate. For at this level of the existential subject deciding for himself what he is going to make of himself, psychic energy and intentionality may become one, may join in a functional unity.

There is a further achievement of philosophy as self appropriation on which I take my stand. It is the achievement of Paul Ricoeur, who has opened reflective philosophy upon the indispensable requirement of investigating the discoveries of depth psychology and of being instructed and changed by them, even while engaging in debate with their proponents. Ricoeur's study of Freud has affected my understanding of philosophy almost as much as has Lonergan's Insight. Both thinkers have effected a transformation in the direction of "greater concreteness on the side of

the subject,"[9] in the domain of "the pulsing flow of life."[10] Moreover, while for Ricoeur this greater concreteness has meant that
philosophy must become a hermeneutic and dialectic of symbols, for
Lonergan it means that "the very possibility of the old distinction
between philosophy and theology vanishes."[11] Starting from this twofold move, I wish to take one further step in the direction of greater
concreteness. Beyond the conclusions of Ricoeur's dramatic engagement
with psychoanalytic explorations and Lonergan's proposals to interrelate philosophy and theology on the basis of the subject-as-subject
even while preserving a difference in respective methods, I want to
suggest the functional unity-in-difference of philosophy, theology,
and depth psychology in the movement of self-appropriation. Converging
contributions to this movement now stand ready to be joined in a single
but differentiated process of foundational subjectivity. The key to
this unity-in-difference is the understanding of self-appropriation as
the elaboration of the semantics of human desire.

My attempt to move further in the direction of greater concreteness will eventually involve a more detailed study of the analytical
psychology of Carl Jung than I am able to undertake in this work. This
future study will be conducted from a standpoint similar to that which

---

[9]
Bernard Lonergan, op. cit., p. xxv.

[10]
Ibid., p. xix.

[11]
Bernard Lonergan, "Dimensions of Meaning," in Collection:
Papers by Bernard Lonergan, edited by F. E. Crowe (New York: Herder
and Herder, 1967), p. 266. Note that Lonergan is speaking of the old
distinction, not of all distinction.

governs Ricoeur's study of Freud, and with a similar question as to Jung's pertinence for a philosophy of self-appropriation. The differences in my study of Jung from Ricoeur's study of Freud will be at least twofold: my philosophical master is Lonergan, and my interest in Jung originates from analytic experience. The latter experience is at the basis of the proposal defended later in the present work that Jung's psychology may feature in our reflection as opening the subject upon the teleological movement of symbolism in much the same way as Freud's reveals its archeological dimensions. In the present work, I will review Ricoeur's reading of and debate with Freud and place my own reading of and debate with Jung within this already well-established context. My debate with Jung will be both epistemological and psychological. Kantian presuppositions prevented Jung from giving an adequate account of what he was about, of its relation to the concerns of the philosopher and the theologian, and of the ontological reference and import of his statements about the human psyche. These difficulties I hope to correct in the present work. Furthermore, though, a phenomenology of the psyche would show that Jung needlessly shortcircuits the teleology of psyche, by reason of his epistemological confusion, and so ultimately traps psychic unfolding in an intrapsychic erotic cul de sac, in an eternal return, in a perpetually recurring psychic still-birth. The absence of a clear notion of cognitional self-transcendence prevents Jung from vigorously accenting the dynamism to self-transcendence immanent in the psyche itself. There is a kind of love that is beyond the wholeness of the mandala. It has something to do with the negotiation of the archetype, Father, and it is simultaneously realized and symbolized in the Crucified, where archeology and teleology, origin and destiny, alpha and omega, meet as nowhere else. In a future study, I will show that the psychology of Jung breaks down when it is time to meet the Father. But so, perhaps, does all psychology unless psychic process is sublated into the movement of existential subjectivity to the authenticity of self-transcendence. It is Lonergan's invitation to this movement, then, that provides our total context.

I hope I may be forgiven a brief account of the personal quest for meaning which has brought me to the position here offered. It has been a journey guided by a complex foundational question. The general contours of the question were first framed by the slow growth of the persuasion that the paths of thought opened up by Lonergan and by Martin Heidegger were somehow of comparable foundational significance for authentic living, for genuine reflection on that living, and for theology in particular. For nearly a decade I have been in search of a horizon which would allow these two paths, seemingly so very different—the one mysterious, poetic, and elusive, the other forged by a formidable and authoritative intellect—their proper due. Such a horizon was not to be achieved, I was convinced, by a theoretical dialectical interplay of the respective positions of Heidegger and Lonergan. There is a sense in which this would be contrary to the very nature of their thought, which in each case opens upon a personal adventure of exploration and understanding. The solution would have to be found in accepting the invitations of both and in negotiating the corresponding conflict. And so I was in search of a horizon where my understanding could issue in an articulate utterance embodying the meeting of these two paths of thought and their mutual interest and qualification.

The quest was furthered by my study of Paul Ricoeur's philosophy of symbol, by his understanding of the hermeneutic enterprise as an exploration demanded by the very exigencies of philosophic rigor. I came to suspect that perhaps here, in the realm of symbolic utterance, I would find the key to unlocking a mystery of opposites; that the horizon so carefully sought might be opened up by a symbolic coniunctio of the archetypal significances of these two delicately forged ways of being human; that I would find these two procedures which I experienced within myself to be themselves archetypally compensatory and complementary to one another; that perhaps both Lonergan and Heidegger were themselves figurae, embodiments of the profoundest archetypal significance, and that the resolution of my question was to be found in the realm of symbolism.

Thus, in reading both Lonergan and Heidegger, the subject is plunged into struggles of archetypal significance. Lonergan's work to date is, I believe, a cumulative and ever more self-conscious retrieve of a path Western man chose to take at some fateful moment in the past. In the reading of Insight, and especially, I believe, of its first thirteen chapters, the subject finds himself engaged in the archetypal struggle of the desire to understand with the flight from understanding. This struggle provides the deepest archetypal meaning of the dramas of both Oedipus and Orestes. The flight from understanding, archetypally understood, is an unknowing betrayal or primal murder of the father and an undifferentiated incestuous relationship with the mother, undifferentiated despite its protestations of wanting to know. The desire to know, the recognition and acceptance of logos, the acknowledgment of the intention of being, on the other hand, is--again in archetypal

terms--a vindication of the father's primal authority and a resolute
though expeditious slaying of the archetypal mother, followed by the
dreadful flight from the feminine powers at their darkest until one
is finally vindicated by woman as wisdom, by Athena, by Anima-Sophia,
who has been set free by one's resolute choice to understand. She is
the archetypal embodiment of the dynamism of psyche itself toward
self-transcendence. Neither Western man nor method has yet secured
her blessing in any lasting fashion. We are Orestes without Athena,
fleeing the Furies. Heidegger is in search of this blessing, but pre-
maturely. We must first go the whole way with Lonergan in an appropriation and resolute defense of the Western option before exploring the
road not taken. The way opens upon this new exploration by the extension of self-appropriation into the home of psyche, where science
joins wisdom. It is this coniunctio that Lonergan is in search of in
his new reflections on value, feeling, and the symbolic. His is not
a premature search; the blessing should be given, the decision vindicated.

     In a psychotherapeutic process that was basically Jungian, I
then began to travel through the labyrinthine paths of psyche, meeting
some of the various figures of what I believe Edmund Husserl may have
been reaching for in his notion of the system of the concrete a
priori.[12] I found, first, that such an experience allows, in a singular
way, the unfolding of a meaningful contingency,[13] the arrival of a

---

12
     Edmund Husserl, Cartesian Meditations, translated by Dorion
Cairns (The Hague: Nijhoff, 1960), par. 39.

13
     Paul Ricoeur, op. cit., p. 381.

"passive genesis of meaning" and of its active appropriation,[14] the laying bare of the "Cogito that founds in proportion as it lets be,"[15] the inching toward a post-critical immediacy in which the primal Word is simply heard and understood as the dream is lived forward, its logos enfleshed. I discovered, too, that depth psychology is no personalistic affair, that it is the discovery and delineation of the "unity of the race of man, not only in its biology but also in its spiritual history," that it is the archeological digging of "the deep, very deep well of the past," so as to lay bare the very foundations of a science of the human roots of revelation.[16]

But I still did not have a unified horizon. I was still assembling its elements. A first, partial, and completely unexpected resolution of my question was given as I began what was initially to be a study unpacking the Heideggerian roots of Rudolf Bultmann's theological categories. My avenue into Heidegger this time was through Kant und das Problem der Metaphysik.[17] I came to believe that Heidegger's relentless retrieve of the lost imagination from the first edition of the Critique of Pure Reason, the transcendental Einbildungskraft as instituting primordial time, was the opening upon a unified field of

---

14
   Ibid., p. 380.

15
   Ibid., p. 278.

16
   Joseph Campbell, The Masks of God, vol. I: Primitive Mythology (New York: Viking Press, 1970), pp. v, 5, and 7.

17
   Martin Heidegger, Kant und das Problem der Metaphysik (Frankfurt am Main: Klostermann, 1951).

understanding. For I knew then that there was a further dimension
to the foundational domain of the existential subject than that which
had been cleared by Lonergan, that this domain was time, the imaginally instituted horizon of interiority, and that, while its dimensions
had been and are still being reconstituted in Heidegger's meditations,
a sublation of the depth psychological phenomenon into the foundational
quest embodies these dimensions in the archeological-teleological
unity-in-tension of a living symbolic process, thus providing an inner
space correlated with primordial time. I then postulated that the
process cosmology of Alfred North Whitehead might perhaps be reinterpreted as a cosmology of this inner space, of the imaginal, and that
its relevance to external space could only be determined by the joint
researches of those physicists and depth psychologists exploring the
phenomenon of synchronicity, of the unus mundus imaginalis et physica.[18]

Finally, the coupling of my analytic experience with the making
and directing of the Ignatian Exercises and my good fortune of associ-
ating and collaborating with Sebastian Moore as he molded a series of
meditations from a similar coupling[19] has convinced me that the
exploration of the imaginal based in large part on the principles of

---

[18]
See for example Marie-Louise von Franz, Number and Time:
Reflections Leading toward a Unification of Depth Psychology and
Physics, translated by Andrea Dykes (Evanston: Northwestern
University Press, 1974). My proposed interpretation of Whitehead is
still in the order of a postulate. It may turn out to be little more
than a "bright idea."

[19]
Sebastian Moore, Journey into a Crucifix, unpublished manuscript.

Jung may become a way to the discovery of the Crucified as Lord and
Savior. From this discovery one may proceed to the establishment of
the equivalence of certain depth psychological and theological categories and place the entire psychotherapeutic phenomenon into its
ultimately most adequate context, that of the discernment of spirits,
thus providing proper limits for the otherwise limitless treadmill of
self-analysis.[20] In Lonergan's words, "Man can reach basic fulfillment,
peace, joy, only by moving beyond the realms of common sense, theory
and interiority into the realm in which God is known and loved."[21]

With reference to my original question, then, the coniunctio
oppositorum is a matter of the fullness of appropriation, of the
totality of the mediation of immediacy. Nor is this a matter of
Hegelian overambition, for not only is this totality only asymptotically
approached but also our question is not one of the mediation of totality
but of the totality of the mediation of what in itself is always finite,
imaginally constituted by the dimensions of time, namely, the immediacy
of the subject as subject to the world mediated by meaning, constituted
by meaning, motivated by value.

-----

[20]
See Ira Progoff, The Death and Rebirth of Psychology
(New York: McGraw Hill Paperbacks, 1973) for a discussion of the
significance of the work of Otto Rank in emphasizing the necessity of
a "soul beyond psychology." A more profound treatment of Rank is
offered by Ernest Becker, The Denial of Death (New York: The Free
Press, 1973), a book which, if taken as seriously as it deserves to be,
should mark the beginning of a new stage of psychological thought.

[21]
Bernard Lonergan, Method in Theology, p. 84; emphasis
added.

Such is the overall vision. It cannot be explored in its completeness at this point. In fact, only a very few of its features are to be explicated in the following attempt to articulate the meeting of method and psyche. And it is all-important that we begin with method.

CHAPTER I

LOGIC, METHOD, AND PSYCHE

A Contrast

In the Preface to the first edition of his <u>Wissenschaft der</u> <u>Logik</u>, Georg Wilhelm Friedrich Hegel tells us that the movement of <u>Geist</u> is the absolute method of knowing and at the same time the immanent soul of the content of knowledge.[1] For Hegel it is only along a path of the self-construction of <u>Geist</u> that philosophy can become objective and demonstrated knowledge. This path is the phenomenology of mind. It is logic, however, which shows the schema of movement of concrete knowing in its pure essence. Through logic consciousness frees itself in self-reflection from immediacy and engrossment in externality and becomes pure knowing, the knowledge of the pure essence of the schema of movement of <u>Geist</u> in and for itself. Logic, beyond the exhibition of the movement of <u>Geist,</u> is <u>Geist</u> thinking its own essence.

In continuity with the thought of Lonergan rather than with the philosophy of Hegel, I prefer to speak not of logic but of method, not of <u>Geist</u> but of the human subject. Method is, first, the phenomenological

---

[1]
    G. W. F. Hegel, <u>Sämtliche Werke</u>, Bd. IV, <u>Wissenschaft der</u> <u>Logik, Erster Teil: Die Objektive Logik</u> (Stuttgart: Frederick Fromann Verlag, 1965), p. 17.

exhibition of the movement of human subjectivity. Secondly, it is the knowing of the essence of the schema of this movement in and for itself. But as "for itself," it is, thirdly, the self-recovery of human subjectivity, its concrete because self-appropriated recovery. If human subjectivity is recovered with some approximation to its full concreteness, the concrete knowing which occurs in and as a result of this recovery becomes, albeit asymptotically, equal to itself.

Method, then, is not simply the movement of human subjectivity, nor even the knowledge of this movement in itself, but the appropriation of this movement for itself. As such, method is not the Cartesian device correctly deplored by Hans-Georg Gadamer, the "universal procedure for any and every knowledge describable by fixed rules, controllable by set principles, and capable of sealing off the way of knowledge against prejudices and rash assumptions and in general against the unruliness of guesses and flashes of insight."[2] Nor is it, a fortiori, a procedure which excludes moral truth, believed truth, and the provisional from playing a role in human knowing. Finally, far down the line from Descartes, method is not what Lonergan curtly dismisses as "a set of rules to be followed meticulously by a dolt,"[3] or as "a set of recipes that can be observed by a blockhead yet lead infallibly to astounding discoveries."[4]

---

[2] Frederick Lawrence, "Self-Knowledge in History in Gadamer and Lonergan," in P. McShane, ed., Language, Truth and Meaning (Notre Dame: University of Notre Dame Press, 1972), p. 170.

[3] Bernard Lonergan, Method in Theology, p. xi.

[4] Bernard Lonergan, Philosophy of God, and Theology, p. 48.

The notion of method arose for Lonergan in his pursuit of "greater concreteness on the side of the subject."[5] He tells us at the very beginning of his philosophical treatise, Insight:

> Besides the noêma or intentio intenta or pensée pensée. . . , there also is the noêsis or intentio intendens or pensée pensante that is constituted by the very activity of inquiring and reflecting, understanding and affirming, asking further questions and reaching further answers. Let us say that this noetic activity is engaged in a lower context when it is doing mathematics or following scientific method or exercising common sense. Then it will be moving towards an upper context when it scrutinizes mathematics or science or common sense in order to grasp the nature of noetic activity. And if it comes to understand and affirm what understanding is and what affirming is, then it has reached an upper context that logically is independent of the scaffolding of mathematics, science, and common sense. Moreover, if it can be shown that the upper context is invariant, that any attempt to revise it can be legitimate only if the hypothetical reviser refutes his own attempt by invoking experience, understanding, and reflection in an already prescribed manner, then it will appear that, while the noêma or intentio intenta or pensée pensée may always be expressed with greater accuracy and completeness, still the immanent and recurrently operative structure of the noêsis or intentio intendens or pensée pensante must always be one and the same.[6]

This invariant upper context, articulated by Lonergan in his pursuit of greater concreteness on the side of the subject, is what he calls transcendental method.[7]

5

   Bernard Lonergan, Insight, p. xxv.

6

   Ibid., pp. xxvf.

7

   In Lonergan's later work, to be precise, the invariant upper context is not limited to experience, understanding, and judgment or reflection, but includes decision, evaluation, or dialectic. Thus, "the function of method is to spell out for each discipline the implications of the transcendental precepts, Be attentive, Be intelligent, Be reasonable, Be responsible." Philosophy of God, and Theology, p. 48. Thus too, two of the functional specialties of theology are called dialectic and foundations, and they are correlated with the fourth level of intentional consciousness, with evaluation and decision. To understand the movement

I too am seeking greater concreteness on the side of the subject, but with respect, not to the playground of our intelligence which is human conception, but to the playground of our desires and fears which is human imagination.[8] So it is that I propose with the aid of Lonergan's intentionality analysis to further the task of disengaging the structure-in-process of human subjectivity by concentrating on the complex of imagination and disposition. This complex has been the subject of scientific investigation at least since the origins of psychoanalysis in the work of Sigmund Freud. I wish to suggest that a concrete disengagement of this structure-in-process would be a further contribution to the articulation of transcendental method. Transcendental method is the self-conscious articulation of the structure-in-process of the human subject as cognitional and existential. The latter dimension calls for a sublation of psychic analysis into intentionality analysis, and it is this sublation whose contours I wish to articulate in the present work. If intentionality analysis provides the basic context of a transcendental method, the analysis of the psychic dimensions of the existential subject provides

---

to the notion of the good as a separate notion from the intelligent and the reasonable is, in my estimation, the key to any discussion of the "later Lonergan." In addition, Lonergan's treatment of dialectic and foundations, joined of course with his seminal insight of functional specialties, is the key to understanding Method in Theology. The inclusion of evaluation in the invariant upper context of the movement of human subjectivity turns cognitional analysis into intentionality analysis.

8
    See Bernard Lonergan, Insight, p. 8: "Just as imagination is the playground of our desires and fears, so conception is the playground of our intelligence."

a kind of transcendental aesthetic: the clarification of the moral
and religious consciousness capable of sublating an intellectually
self-appropriating consciousness. The core of this transcendental
aesthetic as religious would be the experience of the Crucified. In
my future study of the phenomenology of the psyche, I will argue that
this dimension of the transcendental aesthetic has been captured in
great detail in the meditations of Sebastian Moore.[9] Meanwhile, I

---

[9]
Sebastian Moore, Journey into a Crucifix. Whatever is claimed
to be transcendental must, if the claim is correct, be a constituent
feature of the infrastructure of subjectivity which I will call immediacy.
The function of transcendental method will be to articulate this infrastructure, to mediate it by meaning. The function of the aesthetic dimension of method will be to articulate the moral and religious dimensions of
this infrastructure insofar as these affect the human psyche. To display
the experience of the Crucified as a constituent feature of a transcendental aesthetic is to complement the argument of the last chapter of
Insight that the problem of evil is met only by an absolutely supernatural solution. It is at this point that my phenomenology of the
psyche will diverge sharply from Jung's. For then, "human perfection
itself becomes a limit to be transcended" and "the humanist viewpoint
loses its primacy, not by some extrinsicist invasion, but by submitting
to its own immanent necessities. For if the humanist is to stand by the
exigencies of his own unrestricted desire, if he is to yield to the demands for openness set by every further question, then he will discover
the limitations that imply man's incapacity for sustained development,
he will acknowledge and consent to the one solution that exists and, if
that solution is supernatural, his very humanism will lead beyond itself." Bernard Lonergan, Insight, p. 728. In Ernest Becker's words,
"Absolution has to come from the absolute beyond." The Denial of Death,
p. 173. Jungian psychology is an attempt to integrate evil psychically in a manner quite parallel to Hegel's attempt to integrate it
speculatively. As Kierkegaard provided one of the death blows to the
absolute system, so the work of a man like Becker mercilessly destroys
any claims to totalitarianism on the part of the psycho-therapeutic
profession.
To argue for the constituent function of the Crucified in the transcendental religious infrastructure of the psyche, to identify what Jung
called the Self with Jesus as Victim of human history, raises enormous
theological problems, of course. I am not ready to deal with these yet.
To display this identity as Sebastian Moore has done, however, provides
a twofold contribution to the dialogue of world religions: it aids the
Christian participants in this dialogue to clarify the distinctiveness

must be content with stating that depth psychology and the imaginative resources which it sets free can reveal to the already methodical consciousness a manifold of data which from the standpoint of intentionality analysis is purely coincidental. The critically informed appropriation and articulation of this manifold can provide the reflective thinker with a needed complement to the horizon afforded by Lonergan's disengagement of the intentionality of human consciousness.

My decision to utilize Lonergan's term, method, rather than Hegel's, logic, to characterize the knowing of the schema of movement of the human subject, is not arbitrary. It reflects a profound difference between Lonergan's position and my own, on the one hand, and what Hegel has bequeathed to us on the other. For, no matter how the term, logic, has been used in the history of philosophy--and it has had several meanings, among which Hegel's appears unique--it refers to a movement other than that which will give us what we need. The key to the difference lies in the notion of the <u>control of meaning</u>. Logic either is, or functions in aid of, a movement on the part of thought which seeks a control of meaning in terms of system.[10] Logic is a

---

of Christianity, and it prevents the legitimate theology of the anonymous Christian posed by Karl Rahner from being shifted by theological laziness and superficiality out of the transcendental base from which Rahner's argument proceeds to a categorial base whose term is, not the convergence of world religions, but religious indifferentism.

10
    In <u>Philosophy of God, and Theology</u>, Lonergan makes the decisive contrast between logic and method one between a static and a dynamic viewpoint. While the logic he refers to is a deductivist logic other than Hegel's logic, and while one certainly cannot with impunity call Hegel's viewpoint static, the positive relations Lonergan posits between logic and method are quite valid and must be brought into our present discussion. "Like the mortician, the logician achieves a steady state only temporarily. The mortician prevents not the ultimate but

constituent feature of the emergence of <u>logos</u> from <u>mythos</u>, of theoretically differentiated consciousness from the undifferentiated or,
in psychoanalytic terms, from "the unconscious." The early struggles
of this movement are represented in the pre-Socratic philosophers and
its first secure triumph in the Socratic maieutic. Hegel achieved an
understanding of this movement as essentially dialectical, an

---

only the immediate decomposition of the corpse. In similar fashion
the logician brings about, not the clarity, the coherence, and the
rigor that will last forever, but only the clarity, the coherence, and
the rigor that will bring to light the inadequacy of current views and
thereby give rise to the discovery of a more adequate position.

"The shift from the static to the dynamic viewpoint relativizes
logic and emphasizes method. It relativizes logic. It recognizes to
the fullest extent the value of the clarity, coherence, and rigor that
logic brings about. But it does not consider logic's achievement to
be permanent. On the contrary, it considers it to be recurrent. Human
knowledge can be constantly advancing, and the function of logic is to
hasten that advance by revealing clearly, coherently, and rigorously
the deficiencies of current achievement.

". . . It is method that shows the way from the logically clear,
coherent, and rigorous position of today to the quite different but
logically clear, coherent, and rigorous position of tomorrow." Pp.
47f. Logic and method are said to enter into "a higher functional
unity." P. 48. Lonergan lists four inadequacies of a position that
takes its stand on logic and does not think of method, the last of
which at least is applicable <u>mutatis mutandis</u> to a discussion of Hegel.
"For the man who knows his <u>logic and does not</u> think of method, the
term 'system' will have only one meaning. Systems are either true or
false. True system is the realization of the deductivist ideal that
happens to be true and, in each department of human knowledge, there
is only one true system. But when method is added to the picture,
three notions of system are distinguished. There is the mistaken
notion of system that supposes that it comprehends the eternal veri-
ties. There is the empirical notion of system that regards systems
as successive expressions of an ever fuller understanding of the relevant data and that considers the currently accepted system as the best
available scientific opinion. Finally, there is system in the third
sense that results from the appropriation of one's own conscious and
intentional operations." P. 49. The first notion of system may be
said to seek a control of meaning in terms of system. The second at
least implicitly takes its stand rather on method than on logic. The
third regards the self-appropriating subject as maieutic.

identification of it with the dialectic of reality itself, and an articulation of logic in relation to this dialectic process.

But a control of meaning in terms of system is precisely what we do not need, what we cannot any longer assimilate, what we would have to regard as relative, as of itself without proper grounding.[11] What is needed is the self-appropriating recovery of human interiority, and this is other than a control of meaning through system. It is, I believe, a second movement of historical Western mind, and our age marks its at times excruciatingly painful beginning. It is not the movement from _mythos_ to _logos_ but the movement from _logos_ to _methodos_. Method in its fullness, I submit, is an interiorization of _both logos_ and _mythos_. Its first step is the interiorization of _logos_ through cognitional analysis. But the dynamism urging such interiorization will move beyond cognition to evaluation and, in this move, to psyche, and can then release a cumulative and ever more universal progress to an appropriated second immediacy on the part of the subject-as-subject. This immediacy entails both a methodical consciousness instructed through intentionality analysis and a post-critical symbolic consciousness, the self-articulated unfolding of which would be a transcendental aesthetic. The transcendental aesthetic is, in a sense, the culmination rather than, as with Kant, the beginning of reflective philosophy. The progress to such an

---

11
    I am not saying that we do not need system, but that we cannot accept a control of meaning in terms of system (except, of course, in terms of the third notion of system mentioned by Lonergan in the quotation in the previous footnote--but this notion of system is the fruit, not of logic, but of method).

immediacy would pass beyond the self-appropriation of the cognitional subject to the self-appropriation of the existential subject. This latter movement in its fullness calls for psychic self-appropriation. The fulfilment of this movement for each individual and for the cosmos would be eschatological, the poetic enjoyment of the truth about man and God. The movement to a transcendental aesthetic is a complement to the movement initiated by heeding Lonergan's call to method. For "the key to method is . . . the subject as subject. . . . To do 'method' calls . . . for a release from all logics, all closed systems or language games, all concepts, all symbolic constructs to allow an abiding at the level of the presence of the subject to himself."[12]

Hegel came very close to, and yet remained qualitatively removed from, assuming responsibility for the transition from _logos_ to _methodos_, from a control of meaning in terms of system to an interiorization of system and a progressive advance to the fullness of second immediacy. It is his ambition of an absolute system that marks the end of the first movement of historical Western mind, the movement of the emergence of _logos_ from _mythos_. The frustration to which this ambition was doomed, perhaps most keenly and certainly very quickly sensed by Soren Kierkegaard, signalled the need for a transition to a second movement of historical Western mind.

Nonetheless, because of a psychological recapitulation of phylogenesis by ontogenesis, the emergence of _logos_ from _mythos_ must and will be repeated in individuals. So too may be the ambitioning of absolute

---

12
Frederick Lawrence, _op_. _cit_., p. 203.

knowledge and the recognition of the inevitable frustration of such an
ambition. At this point, the individual reflective thinker will be
prepared to make his own unique contribution to the second movement of
historical Western mind--provided, of course, that the disappointment
of his frustrated ambition is not equated with a despair over truth.
Perhaps no thinker can contribute to this second movement without
having first experienced the suffering of the frustration of the first.
The frustration will take the form of what Lonergan calls an inverse
insight: the point is that there is no point. In this case, there is
no point to the absolute knowledge anticipated by the ambitions of
logos.

Why, then, do we say that Hegel came so close to realizing the
transition from logic to method? The reason is that there is a very
definite sense in which he affirmed the pivotal presupposition of the
second movement: authentic subjectivity is objectivity, the only
objectivity.[13] That Hegel is qualitatively still so distant from the
transition is due, however, to his understanding of subjectivity. "Das
Logische ist seine (man's) eigentümliche Natur selbst."[14] Thus he
could not but misinterpret objectivity. And a misunderstanding of
objectivity entails a counterposition on reality. "Nur in seinem
Begriffe hat etwas Wirklichkeit."[15]

---

[13]
"Objectivity is the fruit of authentic subjectivity, of being
attentive, intelligent, reasonable, and responsible." Bernard Lonergan,
Philosophy of God, and Theology, p. 49. "Subjective doesn't mean anything distinct from objective; it's the source of objectivity." Ibid.,
p. 66.

[14]
G. W. F. Hegel, op. cit., p. 21.

[15]
Ibid., p. 46.

For Carl Jung, Hegel divined a fundamental psychological truth but did not understand it as psychological. This truth is at least roughly glimpsed in the following sentence from Jung: "A wholeness, of which he (the individual ego) is a part, wants to be transformed from a latent state of unconsciousness into an appropriate consciousness of itself."[16] For Jung, Hegel was "a psychologist in disguise who projected great truths out of the subjective sphere into a cosmos he himself had created."[17] It might be said that, if method mediates both _logos_ and psyche, it mediates _both_ Hegel's insistence on objectivity, missed by Jung because of the latter's psychological immanentism, because of his inability to appreciate the self-transcending movement of psyche itself from unconscious to conscious, darkness to light, _mother to father, and_ Jung's insistence on the psychological features of all philosophic thinking, overlooked by Hegel because of a concern not to fall into psychologism.[18]

But surely we cannot claim, can we, that the science of psychology is then to be adopted as the foundation of this second movement of historical Western mind? No, we cannot claim this. At least we cannot do so with reference to any existing psychology, for no current

---

16
C. G. Jung, "Paracelsus as a Spiritual Phenomenon," _Alchemical Studies, Collected Works_ Vol. 13 (Princeton: Bollingen Series XX, 1967), par. 221, p. 180.

17
C. G. Jung, "On the Nature of the Psyche," _The Structure and Dynamics of the Psyche, Collected Works_ Vol. 8, par. 358, p. 169.

18
I am indebted to Rev. Matthew Lamb, Theology Department, Marquette University, for this formulation.

psychological doctrine or praxis is methodologically aware enough of its conditions, its foundations, and its term. No such doctrine or praxis has engaged in adequate philosophical reflection on its own procedures and knowledge. But I can and do claim that the foundation of the second movement of historical Western mind is in part psychological. There is an underlying unity-in-differentiation of philosophy, theology, and depth psychology, which is to be located in the transcendental infrastructure of the subject-as-subject. This infrastructure is immediacy. It is mediated in different ways: philosophically through intentionality analysis, psychologically in psychotherapy, theologically in an objectification of religious conversion. All three mediations feature in the foundations of theology. The meaning of a reference to a second movement of historical Western mind is grounded in the functional unity-in-differentiation of these three mediations.

The cognitive foundations of this second movement of historical Western mind—a movement prepared by the anthropological shift in modern philosophy, by the development of modern scientific and scholarly methods, by Marxism and psychoanalysis, and by existential philosophy—are laid by Lonergan in Insight and Method in Theology. Lonergan's cognitional theory, coupled with his increasing later insistence on historicity and the constitutive function of meaning, afford the first truly foundational key to the concrete mediation of theory and praxis and thus to an advance to an appropriated second immediacy. For Lonergan has opened up for us the fact that the foundations of reflective thought lie in the self-appropriation of the reflective thinker. It is self-appropriation that constitutes the emerging unity-in-differentiation of philosophy, depth psychology, and theology.

The Subject as Control of Meaning

The Call for a New Maieutic

The call for a new control of meaning has been issued by Lonergan in his 1965 lecture, "Dimensions of Meaning,"[19] and the nature of the answer to this call as the self-appropriation of the subject-as-subject is specified in his 1968 lecture, "The Subject."[20] The former lecture begins with a distinction between immediacy and the world mediated by meaning. The distinction meets the objection of the uncritical realist that meaning is, after all, a quite secondary affair, that what counts is the reality that is meant. The objection would be quite weighty, Lonergan argues in effect, if the very stuff of human living were the reality encountered by the infant. But since we develop beyond infancy, such realism finds itself involved in something of an oversight.

> . . . As the command and use of language develop, there comes a reversal of roles. For words denote not only what is present but also what is absent, not only what is near but also what is far, not only the past but also the future, not only the factual but also the possible, the ideal, the ought-to-be for which we keep on striving though we never attain. So we come to live, not as the infant in a world of immediate experience, but in a far vaster world that is brought to us through the memories of other men, through the common sense of the community, through the pages of literature, through the labors of scholars, through the investigations of scientists, through the experience of saints, through the meditations of philosophers and theologians.[21]

---

[19]
F. E. Crowe, ed., Collection: Papers by Bernard Lonergan (New York: Herder and Herder, 1967), pp. 252-267.

[20]
Bernard Lonergan, The Subject (Milwaukee: Marquette University Press, 1968).

[21]
Bernard Lonergan, "Dimensions of Meaning," p. 253.

Meaning as act, then, consists not merely in experiencing but also in understanding and usually in judging and evaluating. The larger world mediated by meaning is thus constituted by human acts of understanding, affirming or denying, and evaluating. And it is this larger world, constituted by meaning, that is the real world in which we live out our lives. Moreover, not only is it a world known through our acts of meaning; it is also made and transformed by means of these same acts, and the transformation is not restricted to nature but extends to man himself.

> . . . The difference produced by the education of individuals is only a recapitulation of the longer process of the education of mankind, of the evolution of social institutions and of the development of cultures. Religions and art-forms, languages and literatures, sciences, philosophies, the writing of history, all had their rude beginnings, slowly developed, reached their peak, perhaps went into decline and later underwent a renaissance in another milieu. And what is true of cultural achievements, also, though less conspicuously, is true of social institutions. The family, the state, the law, the economy are not fixed and immutable entities. They adapt to changing circumstances, they can be subjected to revolutionary change. . . . All such change is in its essence a change of meaning--a change of idea or concept, a change of judgment or evaluation, a change of the order or the request.[22]

It is where meaning is constitutive that man's freedom and responsibility are greatest. It is precisely here that the existential subject emerges, the subject "finding out for himself that he has to decide for himself what he is to make of himself."[23] It is at this level of constitutive meaning, too, that "individuals become alienated from community, that communities split into factions, that cultures

---

22
  Ibid., p. 254.

23
  Ibid., p. 255.

flower and decline, that historical causality exerts its sway."[24]

Lonergan then proposes the notion of the control of meaning. Just as changes in understood and accepted meanings are at the root of social and cultural changes, so "changes in the control of meaning mark off the great epochs in human history."[25] We find the classical expression of the effort to control meaning in Socrates' insistence on universal definitions that apply omni et soli. The Socratic maieutic makes plain that there are at least two levels to meaning, the primary and spontaneous level reflected in ordinary language and a secondary level in which a reflexive movement leads us to say what we mean by ordinary language. Moreover, says Lonergan, the movement of mind in fourth-century Athens represents a line of cleavage dividing two historical epochs. Cultures and civilizations without such a maieutic, no matter what their achievements in the practical affairs of life, are penetrated, surrounded, and dominated, in their routine activities and in the profound and secret aspirations of the heart, by myth and magic. This is "a malady to which all men are prone. Just as the earth, left to itself, can put forth creepers and shrubs, bushes and trees with such excessive abundance that there results an impenetrable jungle, so too the human mind, led by imagination and affect and uncontrolled by any reflexive technique, luxuriates in a world of myth with its glories

---

24
   Ibid.

25
   Ibid., p. 256.

to be achieved and its evils banished by the charms of magic."[26]   The
Socratic maieutic, then, represents an epochal or axial shift in the
control of meaning, a shift that gave rise to classical culture.   The
features of classical culture are perhaps most clearly highlighted in
the notion of science put forth in Aristotle's Posterior Analytics.
Science is "true, certain knowledge of causal necessity,"[27] and the
fact that there are many things in the world that are not necessary but
contingent means that the universe is split between necessity and contingency, and the human mind between science and opinion, theory and
practice, wisdom and prudence.

> Insofar as the universe was necessary, it could be known scienti-
> fically; but in so far as it was contingent, it could be known
> only by opinion. Again, in so far as the universe was necessary,
> human operation could not change it; it could only contemplate it
> by theory; but in so far as the universe was contingent, there
> was a realm in which human operation could be effective; and that
> was the sphere of practise. Finally, insofar as the universe was
> necessary, it was possible for man to find ultimate and change-
> less foundations, and so philosophy was the pursuit of wisdom;
> but in so far as the universe was contingent, it was a realm of
> endless differences and variations that could not be subsumed
> under hard and fast rules; and to navigate on that chartless sea
> there was needed all the astuteness of prudence.[28]

The major point of this 1965 lecture is that the classical culture resulting from this Greek mediation of meaning has passed away;

---

[26]
   Ibid., p. 258.   The reflexive technique introduced by
Socrates is an insistence on logos in preference to mythos. It is a
championing of the cause of differentiated consciousness vis-a-vis
what certain depth psychological systems have called the unconscious.

[27]
   Ibid., p. 259.

[28]
   Ibid., p. 260.

that the multiplicity and complexity of thought-forms and techniques
that has replaced it leave us bewildered, perplexed, and anxious;
and that a new control of meaning is needed, a new maieutic. The
change can be seen most clearly in the field of science. While the
classical notion maintained science to be true, certain knowledge of
causal necessity,

> . . . modern science is not true; it is only on the way towards
> truth. It is not certain; for its positive affirmations it
> claims no more than probability. It is not knowledge but hypo-
> thesis, theory, system, the best available scientific opinion of
> the day. Its object is not necessity but verified possibility .
> . ., not what cannot possibly be otherwise, but what in fact is
> so. Finally, while modern science speaks of causes, still it is
> not concerned with Aristotle's four causes of end, agent, matter,
> and form; its ultimate objective is to reach a complete explanation
> of all phenomena, and by such explanation is meant the determi-
> nation of the terms and intelligible relationships that account
> for all data.[29]

Thus instead of contrasting science and opinion, we speak of
scientific opinion. For the differentiation of theory and practice, we
substitute a continuum from basic research to industrial activity.
Rather than the notion of philosophy as the search for changeless ulti-
mates, we find our philosophers concerned with such matters as the
authenticity of the existential subject and the hermeneutic of cultural
phenomena. This extension of philosophy into concrete living "curtails
the function formerly attributed to prudence. . . . The old-style pru-
dent man, whom some cultural lag sends drifting through the twentieth
century, commonly is known as a stuffed shirt."[30]

29
    Ibid., pp. 259f.

30
    Ibid., p. 261.

The classically oriented science of man, which focused on the essential, necessary, and universal, has given way to an interest in "all the men of every time and place, all their thoughts and words and deeds, the accidental as well as the essential, the contingent as well as the necessary, the particular as well as the universal."[31] The classical science of man is seen to be an arbitrary standardization obscuring man's nature, constricting his spontaneity, sapping his vitality, and limiting his freedom.

> To proclaim with Vico the priority of poetry is to proclaim that the human spirit expresses itself in symbols before it knows, if ever it knows, what its symbols literally mean. It is to open the way to setting aside the classical definition of man as a rational animal and instead, defining man with the cultural phenomenologists as a symbolic animal or with the personalists as an incarnate spirit.[32]

Lonergan summarizes the modern rediscovery of myth in depth psychology and of intersubjectivity and the body in phenomenology, only to conclude that "the psychologists and phenomenologists and existentialists have revealed to us our myriad potentialities without pointing out to us the tree of life, without unraveling the secret of good and evil. And when we turn from our mysterious interiority to the world about us for instruction, we are confronted with a similar multiplicity, an endless refinement, a great technical exactness, and an ultimate inconclusiveness."[33]

---

[31] Ibid., p. 262.

[32] Ibid., p. 263.

[33] Ibid., p. 264.

There is still the individual's moment of profound existential crisis, then, "when we find out for ourselves that we have to decide for ourselves what we by our own choices and decisions are to make of ourselves."[34] Definitions and doctrines are qualified to the point of relativism and skepticism by our knowledge of their histories and adventures of development and decline. Authorities too, are historical beings and so require commentary, interpretation, exegesis. The emerging modern mediation of meaning is one

> . . . that interprets our dreams and our symbols, that thematizes our wan smiles and limp gestures, that analyzes our minds and charts our souls, that takes the whole of human history for its kingdom to compare and relate languages and literatures, art-forms and religions, family arrangements and customary morals, political, legal, educational, economic systems, sciences, philosophies, theologies and histories.[35]

But while countless scholars and scientists devote themselves to this task of understanding meaning, the individual is on his own when it comes to judging meaning and to deciding. "There is far too much to be learnt before he could begin to judge. Yet judge he must and decide he must if he is to exist, if he is to be a man."[36]

The call for a new maieutic could not be issued more clearly and persuasively. It can be developed, Lonergan judges, only by those "big enough to be at home in both the old and the new, painstaking enough to work out one by one the transitions to be made, strong enough

---

34
   Ibid.

35
   Ibid., pp. 265f.

36
   Ibid., p. 266.

to refuse half-measures and insist on complete solutions even though
(they) have to wait."[37]

The Cognitional Subject as Maieutic

In his 1968 lecture, The Subject, Lonergan explores further the
dimensions of the new maieutic and points to the contributions he has
already made to its articulation. If in "Dimensions of Meaning," he had
stated that the crisis of our age is rooted in the immaturity of the
modern culture that replaced classical culture, in The Subject he roots
that immaturity in the neglect of the subject and of the vast labor
involved in knowing him. The subject is twofold: he is a knowing
subject and he is an existential subject, a deciding, evaluating subject. Modern culture's knowledge of the knowing subject is restricted
by philosophic issues that render him a neglected, truncated, and immanentist subject, and the remedy to this tragic state of affairs consists
essentially in the affirmation of the correct positions on knowing,
being, and objectivity, an affirmation rendered possible only by a
personal philosophic experience of conversion.

Contemporary philosophy itself does not neglect the subject, of
course. Rather, it emphasizes him. But the very emphasis points to and
is a reaction against a previous neglect conditioned by at least three
factors: a fascination with the objectivity of truth; Aristotelian and
modern rationalist notions of science and pure reason; and the metaphysical doctrine of the soul.

---

[37]
Ibid., p. 267.

Lonergan, to be sure, has no quarrel with the objectivity of truth, but here as throughout his work he impugns fascination with such objectivity. It is true that once truth is attained it can be contradicted only by falsity. But truth nonetheless resides only in the subject, in the self-transcendence achieved in his true judgment.

> Intentionally it goes completely beyond the subject, yet it does so only because ontologically the subject is capable of an intentional self-transcendence, of going beyond what he feels, what he imagines, what he thinks, what seems to him, to something utterly different, to what is so. Moreover, before the subject can attain the self-transcendence of truth, there is the slow and laborious process of conception, gestation, parturition. But teaching and learning, investigating, coming to understand, marshalling and weighing the evidence, these are not independent of the subject, of times and places, of psychological, social, historical conditions. The fruit of truth must grow and mature on the tree of the subject, before it can be plucked and placed in its absolute realm.[38]

A fascination with the objectivity of truth would neglect this process of its emergence in the subject. In Catholic circles, such one-sidedness marks the old catechetics and the old censorship as well as the theological embarrassment of manual theologies with their syllogistic demonstrations of the mysteries of faith.

> What God reveals is a truth in the mind of God and in the minds of believers, but it is not a truth in the minds of non-believers; and to conclude that the mysteries of faith are truths in the mind of God or in the minds of believers in no way suggests that the mysteries are demonstrable. But this simple way out seems to have been missed by the theologians. They seem to have thought of truth as so objective as to get along without minds.[39]

38
Bernard Lonergan, The Subject, p. 3. For the dynamics of the achievement of truth in judgment, see Insight, cc. 9 and 10.

39
Ibid., pp. 4f.

Secondly, in Aristotelian science and rationalism, conclusions are held to follow necessarily from self-evident premises. If this is the case, the road to truth would seem to be "not straight and narrow but broad and easy. There is no need to be concerned with the subject. No matter who he is, no matter what his interests, almost no matter how cursory his attention, he can hardly fail to grasp what is self-evident and, having grasped it, he can hardly fail to draw conclusions that are necessary."[40]

Thirdly, in Thomist circles there has been defended a metaphysical account of the soul which applies one and the same method to the study of plants, animals, and men, a method which moves back from objects to acts, from acts to potencies, from potencies to habits, and from habits to the essence of the soul. The science of man remains the same whether one is awake or asleep, a saint or a sinner, a genius or an imbecile. But the study of the subject is not a study of the soul. Its concern is with consciousness, with the operations of consciousness, and with their center, not in the soul but in the self. The study of the subject "discerns the different levels of consciousness, the consciousness of the dream, of the waking subject, of the intelligently inquiring subject, of the rationally reflecting subject, of the responsibly deliberating subject."[41] The same distinction occurs in the 1964 paper, "Existenz and Aggiornamento:"

---

[40] Ibid., p. 6.

[41] Ibid., p. 8.

> Of the human substance it is true that human nature is always the same; a man is a man whether he is awake or asleep, young or old, sane or crazy, sober or drunk, a genius or a moron, a saint or a sinner. From the viewpoint of substance, those differences are merely accidental. But they are not accidental to the subject, for the subject is not an abstraction.[42]

These three factors, then, have resulted in the philosophic neglect of the subject. But beyond the neglected subject, who does not know himself, there is the truncated subject, who is unaware of his ignorance of himself and so concludes that what he does not know does not exist. The grossest philosophic reflections of such double ignorance, for Lonergan, are found in behaviorism, logical positivism, and pragmatism. More subtle is the procedure of conceptualism, a style of philosophic thought which cuts across many lines. Conceptualism results from the "apparently reasonable rule of acknowledging what is certain and disregarding what is controverted." Such a procedure fastens on the concept and overlooks the act of understanding with its "triple role of responding to inquiry, grasping intelligible form in sensible representations, and grounding the formation of concepts."[43] Conceptualism is marred by an anti-historical immobilism which cannot account for the development of concepts; by an excessive abstractness that is more concerned with the abstraction of the universal from the particular than with the grasp of a unity or pattern in sense data, images, and symbols; and by an abstract concept of being, least in connotation and greatest in denotation, rather than by a

---

42
  In F. E. Crowe, ed., Collection, p. 241.

43
  Bernard Lonergan, The Subject, p. 9.

concrete notion of being as the desire to know, which intends the unknown in questions, partially discovers it in answers, presses on to fuller knowledge in further questions.

> The neglected subject, then, leads to the truncated subject, to the subject that does not know himself and so unduly impoverishes his account of human knowledge. He condemns himself to an anti-historical immobilism, to an excessively jejune connection between abstract concepts and sensible presentations, and to ignorance of the proleptic and utterly concrete character of the notion of being.[44]

The subject who does not know his knowing does not know that his knowing involves an intentional self-transcendence. Thus he may come to claim that his knowing is merely immanent. At the root of this claim there lies an inadequate notion of objectivity for which the notions of "object" and "objective" are correlates of picture-thinking. An object is something one looks at and objectivity is seeing all there is to be seen and nothing that is not there. For such thinking, the intention of questioning and the understanding of intelligible unity as possibly relevant to data cannot themselves be looked at, and so they must be "merely subjective." The same holds for concepts and judgments, which proceed respectively from direct and reflective understanding. Picture-thinking thinks in visual images and "visual images are incapable of representing or suggesting the normative exigences of intelligence and reasonableness and, much less, their power to effect the intentional self-transcendence of the

---

44
 Ibid., p. 12. "By a conceptualist I mean a person that is a keen logician, that is extremely precise in his use of terms, and that never imagined that the meaning of terms varied with the acts of understanding that they expressed." Philosophy of God, and Theology, p. ix.

subject."[45] Thus the Kantian position on knowing is ultimately
rooted in the notion of "object" as what one looks at in sensitive
intuition, which alone is immediately related to objects and must
mediate the relation to objects of understanding and judgment. The
value of judgments for such a position is no more than the value of
intuition, and since intuitions reveal not being but phenomena, judgments are confined to a merely phenomenal world. They are not knowledge of the real. The alternative to such a notion of the immanence
of knowledge, however, can be discovered only by an appropriation of
the exigences of human intelligence and human reasonableness which
generate a process of knowledge moving from the experiential objectivity of data to the terminal objectivity of judgments with its
sharp distinction between what we feel, imagine, or suppose, and
what we know. This alternative is available only to a subject who
knows himself better than does the neglected or truncated subject,
who knows himself well enough "to discover that human cognitional
activities have as their object being, that the activity immediately
related to this object is questioning, that other activities such as
sense and consciousness, understanding and judgment, are related
mediately to the object, being, inasmuch as they are the means of
answering questions, of reaching the goal intended by questioning."[46]
The genesis of such self-knowledge, however, "is not a matter of
finding out and assenting to a number of true propositions (but) a

---

45
   Bernard Lonergan, The Subject, p. 16.

46
   Ibid., p. 18.

matter of conversion,"[47] of intellectual self-appropriation,
achieved through the "basic discipline" of cognitional analysis.[48]

The Existential Subject as Maieutic

I believe it would be correct to say that intellectual self-
appropriation, the self-knowledge of the subject in his intention of
being as a knower, is the first and indispensable step in the development of the new maieutic. It is the step I am assuming in the
present work, the maieutic of the first thirteen chapters of Insight.
For Lonergan as for myself, however, while this extraordinarily
delicate and subtle procedure is necessary, it is not sufficient.
For the subject is not only a knower but also a doer, an existential
subject who deliberates, evaluates, decides, and acts, and by his
actions changes not only the world of objects but also, and more important, himself.

> Human doing is free and responsible. Within it is contained
> the reality of morals, of building up or destroying character,
> of achieving personality or failing in that task. By his own
> acts the human subject makes himself what he is to be, and he

---

47
Ibid.

48
"The basic discipline, I believe, is not metaphysics but cognitional theory. By cognitional theory is meant, not a faculty psychology that presupposes a metaphysics, but an intentionality analysis
that presupposes the data of consciousness." Bernard Lonergan, Philosophy of God, and Theology, p. 33. "Metaphysics is prior if you consider that what you're studying is fully known objects. In other words,
it's dealing with objects. When you start out that way, you have no
way of critically justifying your metaphysics. You can critically
justify it if you derive it from a cognitional theory and an epistemology. And you can critically justify the cognitional theory by
finding it in yourself: the terms of the theory are found in your own
operations, of which you are conscious and which you are able to identify in your own experience, and the relations connecting the terms are

does so freely and responsibly; indeed, he does so precisely because his acts are the free and responsible expressions of himself.49

The existential subject in his role of self-constitution is not to be understood according to the older schemes of intellect and will, of speculative and practical intellect or pure and practical reason, and of theory and praxis. "None of these distinctions adverts to the subject as such and, while the reflexive, self-constituting element in moral living has been known from ancient times, still it was not coupled with the notion of the subject to draw attention to him in his key role of making himself what he is to be."50 The new schema in which he can be understood is very well known to Lonergan students, but it is so basic both to Lonergan and to this present work that I quote in full the articulation given it in this 1968 lecture. It is a schema of distinct but related levels of consciousness, the highest level being that of the existential subject, of the subject as agent.

> We are subjects, as it were, by degrees. At a lowest level, when unconscious in dreamless sleep or in a coma, we are merely potentially subjects. Next, we have a minimal degree of consciousness and subjectivity when we are the helpless subjects of our dreams. Thirdly, we become experiential subjects when we awake, when we become the subjects of lucid perception, imaginative projects, emotional and conative impulses, and bodily actions. Fourthly, the intelligent subject sublates the experiential, i.e., it retains, preserves, goes beyond, completes it,

---

to be found in the dynamism relating one operation to the other." Ibid., p. 60.

49
  Bernard Lonergan, The Subject, p. 19.

50
  Ibid., p. 20.

when we inquire about our experience, investigate, grow in understanding, express our inventions and discoveries. Fifthly, the rational subject sublates the intelligent and experiential subject, when we question our own understanding, check our formulations and expressions, ask whether we have got things right, marshal the evidence pro and con, judge this to be so and that not to be so. Sixthly, finally, rational consciousness is sublated by rational self-consciousness, when we deliberate, evaluate, decide, act. Then there emerges human consciousness at its fullest. Then the existential subject exists and his character, his personal essence, is at stake.[51]

The metaphor of levels of consciousness denotes a relationship of sublation, according to which a lower level is retained but also transcended and completed by a higher. Lonergan speaks of the sublation of waking consciousness by intelligence, of experience and intelligence by judgment, and of experience, understanding, and judgment by deliberation and action. The key to our notion of psychic self-appropriation will involve extending this process of sublation so that the level of dreaming consciousness is sublated by experience, intelligence, judgment, and action. The notion of sublation enables Lonergan to speak of the distinction and functional interdependence of the levels of consciousness. A further unity is provided "by the unfolding of a single transcendental intending of plural, interchangeable objectives."[52] These objectives are approximately identical with the Scholastic transcendentals, ens, unum, verum, and bonum. Thus:

51
   Ibid., pp. 20f. Ernest Becker, The Denial of Death, has captured the terror sometimes experienced in the full emergence of the subject as existential. Of value to our discussion is that it is within such a context that Becker discusses psychotherapy.

52
   Bernard Lonergan, The Subject, p. 22.

What promotes the subject from experiential to intellectual consciousness is the desire to understand, the intention of intelligibility. What next promotes him from intellectual to rational consciousness, is a fuller unfolding of the same intention: for the desire to understand, once understanding is reached, becomes the intention of the right intelligible. Finally, the intention of the intelligible, the true, the real, becomes also the intention of the good, the question of value, of what is worth while, when the already acting subject confronts his world and adverts to his own acting in it.[53]

The notion of value, which is this highest, existential level of consciousness, is something other than the particular good of the satisfaction of individual appetite and the good of order which ensures for a given group of people the regular recurrence of particular goods. "It is by appealing to value or values that we satisfy some appetites and do not satisfy others, that we approve some systems for achieving the good of order and disapprove of others, that we praise or blame human persons as good or evil and their actions as right or wrong."[54] The notion of value is further explained by comparing it with the notion of being:

Just as the notion of being intends but, of itself, does not know being, so too the notion of value intends but, of itself, does not know value. Again, just as the notion of being is the dynamic principle that keeps us moving toward ever fuller knowledge of being, so too the notion of value is the fuller flowering of the same dynamic principle that now keeps us moving toward ever fuller realization of the good, of what is worth while. . . . Just as the notion of being functions in one's knowing and it is by reflecting on that functioning that one comes to know what the notion of being is, so also the notion or intention of the good functions within one's human acting and it is by reflection on that functioning that one comes to know what the notion of good is. Again, just as

---

53
Ibid., pp. 22f.

54
Ibid., pp. 23f.

the functioning of the notion of being brings about our
limited knowledge of being, so too the functioning of the
notion of the good brings about our limited achievement
of the good. Finally, just as our knowledge of being is,
not knowledge of essence, but only knowledge of this and
that and other beings, so too the only good, to which we
have first-hand access, is found in instances of the good
realized in themselves or produced beyond themselves by
good men.[55]

The existential subject, then, not only freely and responsibly makes himself what he is, but also makes himself good or evil and his actions right or wrong. The notion of value is a transcendental principle of appraisal and criticism giving rise to instances of the good in choices and actions. The determination of the good is "the work of the free and responsible subject producing the first and only edition of himself."[56] This is why ethical systems are also so vague about what it is to do good. We do better to turn to examples about us, to stories, to the praise and blame of others' conversations, and to our own sense, now of elation, now of shame, with respect to our own actions. However it may be that we come to know the good, Lonergan's concern is with the subject, and with the primacy of the subject as existential, as becoming good or evil. It is with respect to the existential subject that we may turn to reflection on the body, on image and feeling, symbol and story, on intersubjectivity, companionship, collaboration, friendship and love. It is also the existential subject who brings into being, maintains, and transforms the world mediated by meaning. This world objectifies

---

55
  Ibid., pp. 25f.

56
  Ibid., p. 27.

the choices of existential subjects.

The primacy of the existential, finally, does not eliminate the pertinence of the questions concerning knowing, the real, and objectivity. On the contrary it reinforces their crucial importance in many ways, not least of all with respect to the question of God's existence, omnipotence, and goodness.

> It is . . . no accident that a theatre of the absurd, a litera-ture of the absurd, and philosophies of the absurd flourish in a culture in which there are theologians to proclaim that God is dead. But that absurdity and that death have their roots in a new neglect of the subject, a new truncation, a new imma-nentism. In the name of phenomenology, of existential self-understanding, of human encounter, of salvation history, there are those that resentfully and disdainfully brush aside the old questions of cognitional theory, epistemology, metaphysics. I have no doubt, I never did doubt, that the old answers were de-fective. But to reject the questions as well is to refuse to know what one is doing when one is knowing; it is to refuse to know why that is knowing; it is to refuse to set up a basic semantics by concluding what one knows when one does it. That threefold refusal is worse than mere neglect of the subject, and it generates a far more radical truncation.[57]

In so far as the doubt extends to objective knowledge of God's exis-tence, omnipotence, and goodness, it entails a skepticism about the value of God's world. If man alone then is good, he is alien to the rest of the world; and if "he renounces authentic living and drifts into the now seductive and now harsh rhythyms of his psyche and of nature, then man is alienated from himself."[58]

The only alternative, however, to the neglected or truncated or immanentist or alienated subject lies in cognitional and existential

---

57
  Ibid., pp. 32f.

58
  Ibid., p. 32.

self-appropriation. Psychic self-appropriation is obviously to take place within the context of existential self-appropriation. The articulation of the dynamics of cognitional and existential self-appropriation constitutes the new maieutic. More precisely, the self-appropriating subject is the new maieutic, the only viable control of meaning in modern culture. No finer instrument of cognitional self-appropriation has been provided than Lonergan's Insight. But, I believe, the dynamics of existential self-appropriation can be given further refinement. The context has been set by Lonergan, but it is toward the further refinement that the present work heads, under the rubric of an attempt to extend interiority analysis to the level of the psyche. One must first go all the way with Lonergan beyond the cognitional subject to the existential subject before asking the question of the contribution of depth psychology to the new maieutic. For it is Lonergan who has provided the context and essential structure of a viable control of meaning for our age.

The Existential Subject as Moral and Religious

A further concretion of the necessary and fundamental context of our problem is provided in Lonergan's treatment of moral and religious conversion in Method in Theology. These two conversions, along with the philosophic conversion of intellectual self-appropriation, provide the criteria for the discrimination of psychic process involved in the self-appropriation of the existential subject. Lonergan's discussion of these two conversions is the beginning of the further refinement referred to above and sets the immediate context for our discussion of the psyche.

The Problem of Ethics in Insight

Mention must be made of the treatment accorded ethics in
Insight, both for the sake of highlighting the greater concreteness
of the discussion of the existential subject in Lonergan's later
writings, and in order to help us situate more fully the context of
our present problematic. In "Insight Revisited," Lonergan states a
difference in his later work which accounts for its greater concreteness in the treatment of the moral subject.

> In Insight the good was the intelligent and reasonable. In
> Method the good is a distinct notion. It is intended in
> questions for deliberation, Is this worth while? Is it truly
> or only apparently good? It is aspired to in the intentional
> response of feeling to values. It is known in judgments of
> value made by a virtuous or authentic person with a good cons-
> cience. It is brought about by deciding and living up to one's
> decisions. Just as intelligence sublates sense, just as
> reasonableness sublates intelligence, so deliberation sublates
> and thereby unifies knowing and feeling.[59]

There is no contradiction in this later notion of the good from the
earlier one, but there is, I believe, a very important development in
the articulation of the good as a distinct notion from the intelligent
and reasonable. What is highlighted is real self-transcendence in the
making of being and constitution of the world as distinct from cognitional self-transcendence in the knowing of being. This distinction
is far from absent in Chapter 18 of Insight, but the emergence of the
existential subject is now granted a primacy not fully accorded it in
the earlier work. Furthermore, and of special concern to the present

---

59
Bernard Lonergan, "Insight Revisited," paper for discussion
at the thirty-fifth annual convention of the Jesuit Philosophical
Association, College Jean-de-Brebeuf, Montreal, pp. 16-17.

work, the positive function of feelings vis-a-vis the existential subject, their transcendental significance as the locus of the primordial apprehension of value, and the role of symbols as a way of certifying affective development or decline, are all granted much greater explicit significance in Method in Theology. What is of lasting value from the discussion of ethics in Insight is preserved in this later discussion, but significant new features are introduced which further concretize our understanding of the emergence of the existential subject. The criterion of moral authenticity shifts from an emphasis on the intelligent and reasonable to an ascending scale of values certifying the extent of the subject's self-transcendence.

It seems important, nonetheless, to mention the context of ethical decision as this is presented in Insight. After the establishment of a method of ethics, of an ontology of the good, and of the fact of man's essential freedom and responsibility, there is a discussion of the problem of effective freedom. "Is an ethics possible in the sense that it can be observed? Is man condemned to moral frustration? Is there a need for a moral liberation, if human development is to escape the cycle of alternating progress and decline?"[60] What renders these questions so acute is the fact that certain conditions must be met if the dynamic structure that is man's essential freedom is to find an operational range within which to exercise itself. These conditions are fourfold. First, there are

---

60
Bernard Lonergan, Insight, p. 595.

limitations placed upon effective freedom by external constraint.
"Whatever one's external circumstances may be, they offer only a
limited range of concretely possible alternatives and only limited
resources for bringing about the enlargement of that range."[61]
Secondly, effective freedom is limited by one's psychoneural state
in several ways: by inadequately developed sensitive skills and
habits, and by the anxiety, obsessions, and other neurotic phenomena
resulting from the scotosis responsible for a disproportion between
intellectual and psychic development. Thirdly, "the less the development of one's practical intelligence, the less the range of
possible courses of action that here and now will occur to one."[62]
Finally, effective freedom is dependent on a particular quality of
antecedent willingness, which alone keeps one open to various
possible courses of action. As long as one's antecedent willingness
defines only a more or less narrow pattern of routine, as long as
one's dynamism to moral self-transcendence is less radical than the
dynamism of the desire to know toward cognitional self-transcendence,
one's effective freedom will suffer restriction.

> In brief, effective freedom itself has to be won. The key
> point is to reach a willingness to persuade oneself and to
> submit to the persuasion of others. For then one can be per-
> suaded to a universal willingness; so one becomes antecedently
> willing to learn all there is to be learnt about willing and
> learning and about the enlargement of one's freedom from
> external constraints and psychoneural interferences. But to
> reach the universal willingness that matches the unrestricted

---

61
   Ibid., p. 622.

62
   Ibid., p. 623.

desire to know is indeed a high achievement, for it consists not in the mere recognition of an ideal norm but in the adoption of an attitude towards the universe of being, not in the adoption of an affective attitude that would desire but not perform but in the adoption of an effective attitude in which performance matches aspiration.

Finally, if effective freedom is to be won, it is not to be won easily. Just as the pure desire to know is the possibility but not in itself the attainment of the scientist's settled habit of constant inquiry, so the potency, will, is the possibility but not in itself the attainment of the genuine person's complete openness to reflection and to rational persuasion. Clearly, this confronts us with a paradox. How is one to be persuaded to genuineness and openness, when one is not yet open to persuasion?[63]

The incompleteness of man's intellectual and volitional development is the radical root of the restriction of man's effective freedom called by Lonergan moral impotence. Moral impotence is measured by "a gap between the proximate effective freedom he actually possesses and, on the other hand, the remote and hypothetical effective freedom that he would possess if certain conditions happened to be fulfilled."[64] This moral impotence is neither grasped with perfect clarity nor totally unconscious.

For if one were to represent a man's field of freedom as a circular area, then one would distinguish a luminous central region in which he was effectively free, a surrounding penumbra in which his uneasy conscience keeps suggesting that he could do better if only he would make up his mind, and finally an outer shadow to which he barely if ever adverts. Further, these areas are not fixed; as he develops, the penumbra penetrates into the shadow and the luminous area into the penumbra while, inversely, moral decline is a contraction of the luminous area and of the penumbra. Finally, this consciousness of moral impotence not only heightens the tension between limitation and transcendence but also can provide ambivalent materials for reflection; correctly interpreted, it brings home to man the fact that his

---

63
  Ibid., pp. 623f.

64
  Ibid., p. 627.

living is a developing, that he is not to be discouraged by his failures, that rather he is to profit by them both as lessons on his personal weaknesses and as a stimulus to greater efforts; but the same data can also be regarded as evidence that there is no use trying, that moral codes ask the impossible, that one has to be content with oneself as one is.[65]

Not only does society both reflect and heighten this tension and ambivalence, but also there is a threefold bias to common sense leading us to expect "that individual decisions will be likely to suffer from individual bias, that common decisions will be likely to suffer from the various types of group bias, and that all decisions will be likely to suffer from general bias."[66] General bias opposes the detachment and disinterestedness required for self-transcendence in knowing and doing.

More or less automatically and unconsciously, each successive batch of possible and practical courses of action is screened to eliminate as unpractical whatever does not seem practical to an intelligence and a willingness that not only are developed imperfectly but also suffer from bias. But the social situation is the cumulative product of individuals and group decisions, and as these decisions depart from the demands of intelligence and reasonableness, so the social situation becomes, like the complex number, a compound of the rational and irrational. Then if it is to be understood, it must be met by a parallel compound of direct and inverse insights, of direct insights that grasp its intelligibility and of inverse insights that grasp its lack of intelligibility. Nor is it enough to understand the situation; it must also be managed. Its intelligible components have to be encouraged towards fuller development; and its unintelligible components have to be hurried to their reversal.[67]

65
   Ibid.

66
   Ibid., p. 628.

67
   Ibid., pp. 628f.

It is this social compound of the intelligible and the absurd that constitutes the materials for further practical insights, the conditions for further reflection, and the reality to be modified by further decisions. But:

> Just as there are philosophies that take their stand upon the positions and urge the development of the intelligible components in the situation and the reversal of the unintelligible components, so too there are counter-philosophies that take their stand upon the counter-positions, that welcome the unintelligible components in the situation as objective facts that provide the empirical proof of their views, that demand the further expansion of the objective surd, and that clamour for the complete elimination of the intelligible components that they regard as wicked survivals of antiquated attitudes. But philosophies and counter-philosophies are for the few. Like Mercutio, the average man imprecates a plague on both their houses. What he wants is peace and prosperity. By his own light he selects what he believes is the intelligent and reasonable but practical course of action; and as that practicality is the root of the trouble, the civilization drifts through successive less comprehensive syntheses to the sterility of the objectively unintelligible situation and to the coercion of economic pressures, political forces, and psychological conditioning.68

There is a tension between limitation and transcendence inherent in all development. But as this tension is conscious in man, it is intensified to the point of desperation by the outer conditions and inner mentality prevalent in social decline. The intelligence, reasonableness, and willingness of man proceed from the unfolding of a single transcendental intending of truth and value to be realized by self-transcending cognitional and existential subjectivity. Nonetheless, while these potentialities for effective freedom can integrate psychic, organic, chemical, and physical manifolds, they also "stand in opposition and tension with sensitive and intersubjective attachment,

---

68
Ibid., p. 629.

interest, and exclusiveness, and . . . suffer from that tension a
cumulative bias that increasingly distorts immanent development, its
outward products, and the outer conditions under which the immanent
development occurs."[69] The root of the problem lies in man's inherent
incapacity for sustained development. This incapacity is radical,
affecting every issue, for it is inherent in the very dynamic structure of cognitional, volitional, and social activity. It is permanent,
for both development and tension pertain to the very nature of man.
This incapacity does not lie in the physical, chemical, organic, and
sensitive manifolds which can be integrated by intelligence, reasonableness, and willingness, but in the very dynamic structure of the
integrating components. This incapacity is not radically social;
rather, it results in the social surd and "receives from the social
surd its continuity, its aggravation, its cumulative character."[70]
This incapacity is not to be met by the discovery of a correct philosophy, ethics, or human science, nor a fortiori by a benevolent despotism that would enforce a correct philosophy, ethics, or human
science. The problem of man's incapacity for sustained development
does not reside in some theoretical realm, but takes its dimensions
from the very dimensions of human history. Its only solution can be
a higher integration of human living even than that provided by man's
intelligence, reasonableness, and genuine willingness. This solution
must begin with people as they are, it must acknowledge, respect,

---

69
  Ibid., p. 630.

70
  Ibid., p. 631.

and utilize their intelligence, reasonableness, and freedom, but it must replace an incapacity for sustained development with a capacity for sustained development without eliminating the tension inherent in all development.

I shall return to the problem of this necessary higher integration of human living after discussion of Lonergan's treatment of moral and religious conversion in Method in Theology.

Moral Conversion

The development of the discussion of morality from Insight to Method in Theology lies principally, as we have seen, in the emergence of a distinct notion of the good. Parallel with this development is a consideration very important to our present discussion. When the good is the intelligent and reasonable, everything psychic is a lower manifold to be integrated by knowledge. When the good is a distinct notion, however, and when it is correlated with a fourth level of intentional consciousness, feelings and their symbolic constitution become at least under one aspect a coincidental manifold from the standpoint of intelligent and reasonable consciousness. Their integration and that of the psyche into the dynamism of conscious intentionality toward real self-transcendence becomes the function, not of knowing, but of deliberating. "Just as intelligence sublates sense, just as reasonableness sublates intelligence, so deliberation sublates and thereby unifies knowing and feeling."[71]

---

[71] Bernard Lonergan, "Insight Revisited," p. 17.

Moral conversion, then, is a shift of the criterion of one's decisions and choices from satisfactions to values.[72] Values and potential satisfactions are both apprehended in feelings, particularly those feelings called intentional, those arising out of perceiving, imagining, or representing particular objects. Such objects may be, on the one hand, agreeable or disagreeable, satisfying or dissatisfying, or, on the other hand, truly worth while or not worth while. The two classifications do not coincide, for what is agreeable may not be worth my while and what is worth my while may be such that it can be pursued only at the cost of self-denial. But the sufficient criterion of the difference lies not here, for what is agreeable may also be worth my while, and what is disagreeable may indeed be also worthless. The difference is located rather in the measure of self-transcendence toward which our response carries us. "Response to value both carries us towards self-transcendence and selects an object for the sake of whom or of which we transcend ourselves. In contrast, response to the agreeable or disagreeable is ambiguous."[73] The same criterion of self-transcendence enables the construction of an ascending scale of values: vital (health and strength, grace and vigor); social (the good of order, conditioning the vital values of the whole community); cultural (the discovery, expression, validation, criticism, correction, development, and improvement of the meanings mediating men's worlds and of the values motivating their performance);

72
Bernard Lonergan, Method in Theology, p. 240

73
Ibid., p. 31.

personal (the person in his self-transcendence, as loving and being loved, as originator of values in himself and in his milieu); and religious (the self-transcendence experienced in and flowing from religious conversion).[74]

The movement from basic moral conversion to moral goodness entails discovering and rooting out one's biases, developing one's knowledge of human reality and potentiality--one's own and that of others--in concrete situations, continually scrutinizing one's intentional feeling-responses to value and their implicit scales of preference, listening to criticism and protest and remaining ready to learn from others. This moral growth obviously entails the development of feelings, which may be reinforced by advertence and approval or curtailed by distraction and disapproval. Such action on one's feelings will modify one's spontaneous scale of preferences. Thus feelings are related not only to their objects and to one another but also to the subject as subject. "They are the mass and momentum and power of his conscious living, the actuation of his affective capacities, dispositions, habits, the effective orientation of his being."[75] This description is particularly apt for those feelings which are "so deep and strong, especially when deliberately reinforced, that they channel attention, shape one's horizon, direct one's life."[76]

74
  Ibid., pp. 31f.

75
  Ibid., p. 65.

76
  Ibid., p. 32.

The <u>transcendental significance of feelings</u> lies in the
fact that they are the locus of the primordial apprehension of
value. Lonergan thus discusses feelings as mediating consciousness
at its fullest, the consciousness of the existential subject. We
have already seen that value, as what I intend when I ask whether
this or that object or possible course of action is truly or only
apparently good, is part of the dynamism of conscious intentionality,
just as much a part as the intelligible intended in questions for
understanding and the truth intended by questions for reflection.
The apprehension of value and of potential satisfaction in feelings
initiates the process of questions for deliberation which promote
the conscious subject from the rational to the existential level of
consciousness, where the individual decides for himself what he is
going to make of himself, where he takes a stand reflecting his dynamic orientation to the authenticity of self-transcendence. This
dynamic orientation as transcendental notion provides the criterion
of one's performance as existential subject. A person who would consistently affirm and choose what is truly good would have achieved
the self-transcendence which is the authentic realization of his
conscious intentionality. Obviously, such sustained authenticity
demands that feelings be "cultivated, enlightened, strengthened, refined, criticized and pruned of oddities."[77] In this way, "the development of knowledge and the development of moral feeling head to
the existential discovery of oneself as a moral being, the

---

[77]
 <u>Ibid</u>., p. 38.

realization that one not only chooses between courses of action but also thereby makes oneself an authentic human being or an unauthentic one. With that discovery, there emerges in consciousness the significance of personal value and the meaning of personal responsibility. One's judgments of value are revealed as the door to one's fulfillment or to one's loss."[78] The apprehension of value in feelings initiates the process to these existentially significant judgments of value. The feelings in which potential satisfactions and values are apprehended range everywhere from "the initial infantile bundle of needs and clamors and gratifications" to "the deep-set joy and solid peace, the power and the vigor, of being in love with God." In the measure that one has been brought to this summit, "values are whatever one loves, and evils are whatever one hates. . . . . Then affectivity is of a single piece. Further developments only fill out previous achievement. Lapses from grace are rarer and more quickly amended."[79]

Such moral self-transcendence is equated with what Abraham Maslow calls self-realization and which he finds in less than one percent of the adult population. Judgments of value occur, then, not only within a context of developing knowledge, refinement of feeling, and an ascending scale of preferences, but also within a context determined by neurotic need, by the refusal of change, by rationalization, bias, ideology, and by what Max Scheler calls ressentiment.

---

[78] Ibid., pp. 38f.

[79] Ibid., p. 39.

"So one may come to hate the truly good, and love the really evil.
Nor is that calamity limited to individuals. It can happen to
groups, to nations, to blocks of nations, to mankind. It can take
different, opposed, belligerent forms to divide mankind and to menace
civilization with destruction."[80] The individual bias of the egoist,
the group bias of the class, and the general bias of common sense
which demands that theoretical premises conform to and support supposed matters of fact, are all at the root of the neglect of the
precepts demanding fidelity to the transcendental notions. Such neglect is the basic form of human alienation, while a doctrine justifying such alienation is the basic form of ideology. One is alienated
to the extent that he disregards the dynamism of his spirit with its
imperatives, Be attentive, Be intelligent, Be reasonable, Be responsible,
and consequently fails to promote himself or allow himself to be promoted to the authenticity of self-transcendence. One is the victim of
the mystification of ideology to the extent that he justifies this
inauthenticity.

Now, as it is within the context of the treatment of value
that Lonergan discusses feelings, so it is within the same context
that he mentions psychotherapy. The relation of feelings to the imperative of fidelity to the transcendental notions is such that "to take
cognizance of them makes it possible for one to know oneself, to uncover
the inattention, obtuseness, silliness, irresponsibility that gave rise
to the feeling one does not want, and to correct the aberrant

_____

80
   Ibid., p. 40.

attitude"[81]--and, we might add, conversely, to uncover the feeling

that gave rise to the inattention, obtuseness, silliness, irres-

ponsibility one does not want. Not to take cognizance of one's

feelings is to leave them in "the twilight of what is conscious but

not objectified" known in psychotherapy as the unconscious.[82] Then

there results a misconception of what one spontaneously is, a con-

flict between the self as conscious and the self as objectified.

Psychotherapy, then, is an appropriation of one's feelings analogous

to the appropriation of one's attending, inquiring, understanding,

conceiving, and affirming effected through the cognitional analysis

of Insight, so much so as to be a second mediation of immediacy by

meaning.[83] Furthermore, feeling becomes unified in one's advance

toward moral self-transcendence and at the summit, where God's love

consolidates one's interiority, there is found an affectivity of a

single piece, a psychic totality or wholeness.[84]

---

[81]
Ibid., p. 33.

[82]
Ibid., p. 34.

[83]
Ibid., p. 77.

[84]
It is important that we do not identify this unified affectivity with a state of complete harmony with the rhythms of the
psyche. As we shall see, the psyche is ambiguous; its structure is
dialectical. The psychic self-appropriation of the existential subject is an ongoing, never-ending task of integrating psychic energy
into the dynamism of intentionality toward self-transcendence. The
psyche cannot be given the upper hand in this process. The failure
of Jung adequately to distinguish psychic energy and intentionality
is, I fear, the basis of a potential psychic totalitarianism on the
part of his followers.

Now, the same objects may invoke different feelings in different individuals. One of the ways of ascertaining individual uniqueness in affective response is through the symbolic images evoked by or evoking a feeling. A symbol for Lonergan is precisely "an image of a real or imaginary object that evokes a feeling or is evoked by a feeling."[85] Affective development or aberration, then, is a process that may be ascertained or certified symbolically. It involves "a transvaluation and transformation of symbols. What before was moving no longer moves; what before did not move now is moving. So the symbols themselves change to express the new affective capacities and dispositions. . . . Inversely, symbols that do not submit to transvaluation and transformation seem to point to a block in development."[86]

The proper meaning of symbols is that they fulfill a need for internal communication on the part of the existential subject, a need which cannot be satisfied by logic, dialectic, or (we might add) cognitional analysis.

> Organic and psychic vitality have to reveal themselves to intentional consciousness and, inversely, intentional consciousness has to secure the collaboration of organism and psyche. Again, our apprehensions of value occur in intentional responses, in feelings: here too it is necessary for feelings to reveal their objects and, inversely, for objects to awaken feelings. It is through symbols that mind and body, mind and heart, heart and body communicate.[87]

85
Bernard Lonergan, Method in Theology, p. 64.

86
Ibid., p. 66.

87
Ibid., pp. 66f.

Thus the understanding or explanation or interpretation of the symbol is effected by appealing to the context of this internal communication with its associated images and feelings, memories and tendencies. There are many different interpretative contexts displayed in the various psychotherapeutic techniques, and Lonergan judges that this multiplicity reflects the different ways in which development and deviation can occur.

I find Lonergan's treatment of these matters illuminating and quite precise, and I believe he provides better than many psychotherapists a key for the integration of feeling into the sweep of the self-appropriation of interiority through a conscious--attentive, intelligent, reasonable, and responsible--negotiation of the symbolic function. From what has already been exposed of Lonergan's treatment, it is not difficult to argue for the construction of a new psychotherapeutic model which would view affective immediacy as imaginally constructed, the aim of psychotherapy as the integration of this immediacy into the dynamism of conscious intentionality to self-transcendence, and the significance of psychotherapy within the horizon of the subject as subject as facilitating the sublation of intellectual by moral conversion through the symbolically charged transformation of the feelings in which values are apprehended. Psychic wholeness and the self-transcendence of authentic subjectivity can be correlative and mutually reinforcing. This is implicit in Lonergan's qualifications of the summit of moral self-transcendence in the love of God, where "values are whatever one loves, and evils are whatever one hates" and where affectivity is of a single piece; in his discussion of psychotherapy within the context of authenticity;

and in his qualification of affective development and aberration as symbolically certifiable. I conclude: if psychotherapy is a matter of the differentiation and appropriation of feelings through the attentive, intelligent, reasonable, and responsible negotiation of the symbolic function; if this negotiation heals a rift between differentiated consciousness and the psyche at the root of contemporary individual and social ethical crises; if the feelings discovered and negotiated in psychotherapy are the locus of the apprehension of value; if our apprehension of value is crippled by the rift between differentiated consciousness and the symbolic function constitutive of feeling; and if psychotherapy, by healing this rift and promoting psychic wholeness in the interest of self-transcending subjectivity, reinstitutes on a new level of conscious awareness the ethically necessary commerce of the existential subject with symbolically charged feeling: then psychotherapy can function in strengthening something bearing remarkable resemblances to what Lonergan describes as moral conversion.

Religious Conversion

The nature of the higher integration of human living acknowledged as a necessity at the end of Chapter 18 of Insight is by now probably apparent from our references to religious values as the highest level of value in Lonergan's ascending scale of values, and from Lonergan's references in Method in Theology to the consolidating power of the gift of God's love. The higher integration of human living beyond that provided by man's intelligence, reasonableness, and responsibility, beyond one's intelligent, reasonable, and responsible efforts to integrate feelings and symbolic process into the dynamism of conscious intentionality toward the authenticity of self-transcendence, is the integration provided by the authentic religion that is the fruit of the gift of God's love. There is a further vector to the self-transcendence which constitutes human authenticity, a vector beyond the cognitional self-transcendence of the knowing subject faithful to the exigencies of the desire to know and the real self-transcendence of the moral subject faithful to the orientation to value as the criterion of his decisions, choices, and actions. This further vector we might call vertical self-transcendence.

The Question of God

Between the acknowledgement of the need for a higher integration of human living at the end of Chapter 18 of Insight and the specification of that higher integration in Chapter 20, there occurs a demonstration of the existence of God in Chapter 19. Lonergan has since pointed to an incongruity, not in the very notion of the kind of philosophy of God he presents in this chapter, but in the context of the chapter as a whole. "While my cognitional theory was based on a long and methodical appeal to experience, in contrast my account of God's existence and attributes made no appeal to religious experience."[88] Moreover, "if Method in Theology may be taken as the direction in which Insight was moving, then that direction implies not only intellectual conversion but also moral and religious

---

[88] Bernard Lonergan, Philosophy of God, and Theology, p. 12.

conversion. One might claim that Insight leaves room for moral and religious conversion, but one is less likely to assert that the room is very well furnished."[89]

The problem is not with the idea of a proof of God's existence but with the horizon presupposed by the system within which such a proof would occur. A horizon is "a differentiation of consciousness that has unfolded under the conditions and circumstances of a particular culture and a particular historical development."[90] Chapter 19 of Insight "made no effort to deal with the subject's religious horizon. It failed to acknowledge that the traditional viewpoint made sense only if one accepted first principles on the ground that they were intrinsically necessary and if one added the assumption that there is one right culture so that differences in subjectivity are irrelevant."[91] If objectivity is the fruit of authentic subjectivity, a philosophy of God must take into account not only intellectual conversion, but also moral and religious conversion as well.

The origin of a philosophy of God lies, then, in religious conversion. "Religious experience at its root is experience of an unconditioned and unrestricted being in love. But what we are in love with, remains something that we have to find out. When we find

---

[89]
  Ibid.

[90]
  Ibid.

[91]
  Ibid., p. 13.

it out in the context of a philosophy, there results a philosophy of God."[92] This philosophy deals with a series of questions on different levels. Lonergan distinguishes four forms of the question of God.

The basic form of the question of God consists in the questioning of our own questioning. A first form of this questioning relates to our questions for intelligence: what? why? how? what for?

> Answers to such questions are reached when the desire to understand expressed in the question is met by the satisfaction of actually understanding. Still the desire to understand is not simply a desire for a subjective satisfaction. It wants more. It wants to understand the persons and things that make up one's milieu and environment. How is it, then, that the subjective satisfaction of an act of understanding can be the revelation of the nature of the persons and things in one's milieu and environment? Obviously, if intelligence can reveal them, they must be intelligible. But how can they be intelligible? Does not the intelligibility of the object presuppose an intelligent ground? Does not an intelligent ground for everything in the universe presuppose the existence of God?[93]

Besides questions for intelligence, there are questions for reflection. Is it so? These questions are answered when we reach a

---

92
  Ibid., p. 51.

93
  Ibid., p. 53. "The possibility of inquiry on the side of the subject lies in his intelligence, in his drive to know what, why, how, and in his ability to reach intellectually satisfying answers. But why should the answers that satisfy the intelligence of the subject yield anything more than a subjective satisfaction? Why should they be supposed to possess any relevance to knowledge of the universe? Of course, we assume that they do. We can point to the fact that our assumption is confirmed by its fruits. So implicitly we grant that the universe is intelligible and, once that is granted, there arises the question whether the universe could be intelligible without having an intelligent ground. But that is the question of God." Bernard Lonergan, Method in Theology, p. 101.

virtually unconditioned, a conditioned whose conditions happen to be fulfilled. No objects in the sensible universe can be known in any other way. "Their existence is not necessary but conditioned. They are contingent beings and so they can be known to exist only when their existence has been verified. But can everything be contingent? Must there not exist necessary being, whose existence is unconditioned, to account for the existence of the beings whose existence is conditioned?"[94] Thus there arises a second form of the question of God.

The forms of the question of God arising from questioning our questions for intelligence and our questions for reflection are metaphysical. But besides questions for intelligence and questions for reflection, there are questions for deliberation. Questioning these questions results in a third form of the question of God.

> To deliberate is to ask whether this or that course of action is worthwhile. To deliberate about one's deliberating is to ask whether it is worthwhile ever to stop and ask whether one's course of action is worthwhile. No doubt, we are moral beings. No doubt, we are forever praising X and blaming Y. But the fundamental question is whether or not morality begins with the human race. If it does, then basically the universe is amoral;

94
Bernard Lonergan, Philosophy of God, and Theology, pp. 53f. "If we are to speak of a virtually unconditioned, we must first speak of an unconditioned. The virtually unconditioned has no unfulfilled conditions. The strictly unconditioned has no conditions whatever. In traditional terms, the former is a contingent being, and the latter is a necessary being. In more contemporary terms the former pertains to this world, to the world of possible experience, while the latter transcends this world in the sense that its reality is of a totally different order. But in either case we come to the question of God. Does a necessary being exist? Does there exist a reality that transcends the reality of this world?" Bernard Lonergan, Method in Theology, p. 102.

and if basically the universe is amoral, then are not man's
aspirations to be moral doomed to failure? But if man is not
the first instance of moral aspiration, if basically the universe is moral, then once more there arises the question of
God. One asks whether the necessarily existing and intelligent ground of the universe also is a highly moral being.[95]

Finally, the question of God arises when we question reli-

gious experience. Despite its many forms due to the variety of

human culture and its many aberrations resulting from the precarious-

ness of authenticity, "underneath the many forms and prior to the

many aberrations some have found that there exists an unrestricted

being in love, a mystery of love and awe, a being grasped by ulti-

mate concern, a happiness that has a determinate content but no

intellectually apprehended object. Such people will ask, With whom

are we in love? So in the fourth and final manner there arises the

question of God."[96]

---

[95]
      Bernard Lonergan, _Philosophy of God, and Theology_, p. 54.
"To deliberate about 'x' is to ask whether 'x' is worth while. To
deliberate about deliberating is to ask whether any deliberating is
worth while. Has 'worth while' any ultimate meaning? Is moral enterprise consonant with this world? We praise the developing subject
ever more capable of attention, insight, reasonableness, responsibility. We praise progress and denounce every manifestation of decline.
But is the universe on our side, or are we just gamblers and, if we
are gamblers, are we not perhaps fools, individually struggling for
authenticity and collectively endeavoring to snatch progress from the
ever mounting welter of decline? The questions arise and, clearly,
our attitudes and our resoluteness may be profoundly affected by the
answers. Does there or does there not necessarily exist a transcendent, intelligent ground of the universe? Is that ground or are we
the primary instance of moral consciousness? Are cosmogenesis, biological evolution, historical process basically cognate to us as
moral beings or are they indifferent and so alien to us?" Bernard
Lonergan, _Method in Theology_, pp. 102f.

[96]
      Bernard Lonergan, _Philosophy of God, and Theology_, p. 54.
"To our apprehension of vital, social, cultural, and personal values,
there is added an apprehension of transcendent value. This apprehension

In each instance, the question of God "rises out of our conscious intentionality, out of the a priori structured drive that promotes us from experiencing to the effort to understand, from understanding to the effort to judge truly, from judging to the effort to choose rightly."[97] It arises by questioning the pure question that the subject-as-subject is. This pure question, as one, unifies the four levels on which the question of God arises and renders the four forms of the question of God cumulative. "The question of God is epistemological, when we ask how the universe can be intelligible. It is philosophic when we ask why we should bow to the principle of sufficient reason, when there is no sufficient reason for the existence of contingent things. It is moral when we ask whether the universe has a moral ground and so a moral goal. It finally is religious when we ask whether there is anyone for us to love with all our heart and all our soul and all our mind and all our

---

consists in the experienced fulfilment of our unrestricted thrust to self-transcendence, in our actuated orientation towards the mystery of love and awe. Since that thrust is of intelligence to the intelligible, of reasonableness to the true and the real, of freedom and responsibility to the truly good, the experienced fulfilment of that thrust in its unrestrictedness may be objectified as a clouded revelation of absolute intelligence and intelligibility, absolute truth and reality, absolute goodness and holiness. With that objectification there recurs the question of God in a new form. For now it is primarily a question of decision. Will I love him in return, or will I refuse? Will I live out the gift of his love, or will I hold back, turn away, withdraw? Only secondarily do there arise the questions of God's existence and nature, and they are the questions of the lover seeking to know him or of the unbeliever seeking to escape him. Such is the basic option of the existential subject once called by God." Bernard Lonergan, Method in Theology, pp. 115f.

[97] Ibid., p. 103.

strength."[98]

Furthermore, while the basic form of the question of God is discovered by questioning our questioning, the basic question itself of God is the religious question. "The vast majority of mankind have been religious. One cannot claim that this religion has been based on some philosophy of God. One can easily argue that their religious concern arose out of their religious experience. In that case the basic question of God is the fourth question that arises out of religious experience. It is only in the climate of a philosophically differentiated culture that there occurs reflection on our questions for intelligence, our questions for reflection, and our questions for deliberation."[99]

Religious Experience

What is this experience which gives rise to the basic question of God? Lonergan employs various phrases, some borrowed from other authors, to describe religious conversion. With Paul Tillich, he speaks of "being grasped by ultimate concern."[100] With St. Paul, he speaks of "God's love flooding our hearts through the Holy Spirit given to us."[101] In terms of the theoretical stage of meaning

---

[98]
Bernard Lonergan, The Philosophy of God, and Theology, pp. 54f.

[99]
Ibid., p. 55.

[100]
Bernard Lonergan, Method in Theology, p. 240.

[101]
Ibid., p. 241.

represented by Augustine and Aquinas, religious conversion is operative grace as distinct from cooperative grace. But these are now described in scriptural imagery. "Operative grace is the replacement of the heart of stone by a heart of flesh, a replacement beyond the horizon of the heart of stone. Cooperative grace is the heart of flesh becoming effective in good works through human freedom."[102] In his own terminology, suited more to the stage of meaning when the world of interiority becomes the ground of theory, religious conversion is "other-worldly falling in love. It is total and permanent self-surrender without conditions, qualifications, reservations."[103] As such it is "being in love with God," which is "the basic fulfilment of our conscious intentionality. That fulfilment brings a radical peace, the peace that the world cannot give. That fulfilment bears fruit in a love of one's neighbor that strives mightily to bring about the kingdom of God on this earth."[104]

The experience of this love is that of "being in love in an unrestricted fashion" and as such is the proper fulfilment of the capacity for self-transcendence revealed in our unrestricted questioning. But it is not the product of our knowledge and choice. "On the contrary, it dismantles and abolishes the horizon in which our knowing and choosing went on and it sets up a new horizon in which

---

102
   Ibid.

103
   Ibid., p. 240.

104
   Ibid., p. 105.

the love of God will transvalue our values and the eyes of that
love will transform our knowing."[105] As conscious but not known,
the experience of this love is an experience of mystery, of the
holy. It belongs to the level of consciousness where deliberation,
judgment of value, decision, and free and responsible activity
take place.

> But it is this consciousness as brought to a fulfilment, as
> having undergone a conversion, as possessing a basis that may
> be broadened and deepened and heightened and enriched but not
> superseded, as ready to deliberate and judge and decide and
> act with the easy freedom of those that do all good because
> they are in love. So the gift of God's love occupies the
> ground and root of the fourth and highest level of man's in-
> tentional consciousness. It takes over the peak of the soul,
> the apex animae.[106]

There is a twofold expression of religious conversion.
Spontaneously it is manifested in changed attitudes, for which
Galatians 5.22f. provides something of a descriptive enumeration:
"The fruit of the Spirit is love, joy, peace, patience, kindness,
goodness, faithfulness, gentleness, self-control." But another kind
of expression is concerned with the base and focus of this experience,
the mysterium tremendum et fascinans itself. There is an enormous
variation to be discovered in the investigation of such expression
and Lonergan correlates this variety with the predominant stages of
meaning operative in one's self-understanding and in one's spontaneously assumed stance toward reality--i.e., with the manner in which
one's world is mediated by meaning. He constructs a series of stages

---

105
  Ibid., p. 106.

106
  Ibid., p. 117.

of meaning based on a cumulative differentiation of consciousness. These stages correspond to the three epochs of historical Western mind of which we spoke early in this chapter. In the Western tradition there have been three stages of meaning, and they can be ontogenetically reproduced in the life-history of a contemporary individual.

The first stage of meaning is governed by a common sense differentiation of consciousness, or, what amounts to the same thing, by a consciousness which is undifferentiated with respect to theory and interiority. The second stage of meaning is familiar also with theory, system, logic, and science, but is troubled because the difference of this from common sense is not adequately grasped. The third stage is prepared by all those modern philosophies governed by the turn to the subject, which thus take their stand on human interiority. Here consciousness is adequately differentiated into the various realms of meaning--common sense, theory, interiority, transcendence, scholarship, and art--and these realms are consciously related to one another. One consciously moves from one to the other by consciously changing his procedures.

In all three stages, meaning fulfills four functions. First, it is cognitive in that it mediates the real world in which we live out our lives. Secondly, it is efficient in that it governs our intention of what we do. Thirdly, it is constitutive in that it is an intrinsic component of human cultures and social institutions. And fourthly, it is communicative in that, through its various carriers--spontaneous intersubjectivity, art, symbol, language, and incarnation in the lives and deeds of persons--individual meaning

becomes common meaning, and, through the transmission of training
and education, generates history. But in the first stage these
functions are not clearly recognized and accurately articulated. So
the blend of the cognitive and constitutive functions, for example,
brings about the constitution not only of cultures and institutions
but also the story of the world's origins in myth. And just as the
constitutive function of meaning pretends to speculative capacities
beyond its genuine range, so the efficient function of meaning pretends to practical powers which a more differentiated consciousness
denominates as magic. Religious expression at this stage is a result
of the projective association or identification of religious experience with its outward occasion. The focus is on what we would call
the spatial, the specific, the external, the human, as contrasted
with the temporal, the generic, the internal, the divine. What is
indeed temporal, generic, internal, divine is associated with or
projected upon what is spatial, specific, external, human, and so
there result the gods of the moment, the god of this or that place,
of this or that person, of Abraham or Laban, of this or that group,
of the Canaanites, the Philistines, the Israelites.

A primitive language has little difficulty in expressing all
that can be pointed out or directly perceived or directly represented. But the generic cannot be directly pointed out or perceived or represented. So in Homer there were words for such
specific activities as glancing, peering, staring, but no
generic word for seeing. Again, in various American languages
of the aborigines one cannot simply say that the man is sick;
one also has to retail whether he is near or far, whether he can
or cannot be seen; and often the form of the sentence will also
reveal his place, position, and posture. Again, the temporal
cannot be pointed out or directly perceived or represented.
Time involves a synthesis of all events in a single continuum
of earlier and later. So an early language may have an abundance
of tenses but they are found to mean, not a synthesis of temporal
relationships, but different kinds of action. Thirdly, the

subject and his inner experience lie not on the side of the perceived but on the side of the perceiving. One can point to the whole man or to some part of him, but one cannot point out the pointer. So possessive pronouns develop before personal pronouns, for what one possesses can be pointed out, but oneself as a subject is another story. Again, inner processes of thinking or deliberating are represented in Homer, not as inner processes, but as personalized interchanges. The Homeric heroes do not think or deliberate; they converse with a god or goddess, with their horse or with a river, with some part of themselves such as their heart or their temper. Finally, the divine is the objective of questioning our questioning. It cannot be perceived or imagined. But it can be associated with the object or event, the ritual or the recitation that occasion religious experience, and so there arise the hierophanies.[107]

The key to the movement from the first stage of meaning to the second and to the religious development consequent upon this movement is to be located, however, not in the shift from exteriority, space, the specific, and the human, to interiority, time, the generic, and the divine, but in the differentiation of the functions of meaning. The advance of technique will enable the association of the efficient function with poiesis and praxis and reveal the inefficacy of magic. But far more important in its implications will be the differentiation of the cognitive function of meaning from the other three functions. As the key to the religious expression of an undifferentiated consciousness lies in insight into sensible presentations and representations, so the limitations of such consciousness to the spatial, the specific, the external, and the human will recede to the extent that the sensible presentations and representations are provided by language itself.[108] This does not mean, however, that a self-conscious

---

107
   Bernard Lonergan, Philosophy of God, and Theology, p. 2.

108
   Bernard Lonergan, Method in Theology, p. 92.

transposition to interiority, time, the generic, and the divine occurs. This must await the emergence of the third stage of meaning.

The second stage of meaning, then, is characterized by a twofold mediation of the world by meaning: in the realm of common sense and in that of theory. This split is troubling. It was interpreted by Plato in such a way that, at a certain stage in his thought, there seem to be two really distinct worlds, the transcendent world of eternal Forms and the transient world of appearance. In Aristotle, as we have seen, it led to the distinction, not between theory and common sense, but between necessity and contingence. The basic concepts of science--i.e., universal and necessary knowledge--were metaphysical, and so the sciences were conceived as continuous with philosophy.

The introduction of the theoretical capacity into religious living is represented in the dogmas, theology, and juridical structures of Western religion. But just as the two tables of Eddington--"the bulky, solid, colored desk at which he worked, and the manifold of colorless 'wavicles' so minute that the desk was mostly empty space"[109]--reveal the presence of a conflict between common sense and science, so in the realm of religion, "the God of Abraham, Isaac, and Jacob is set against the God of the philosphers and theologians. Honoring the Trinity and feeling compunction are set against learned discourse on the Trinity and against defining compunction. Nor can

---

[109]
   Ibid., p. 84.

this contrast be understood or the tension removed within the realms of common sense and of theory."[110] So there is demanded a movement to a third stage of meaning, the stage of the differentiation of consciousness through the appropriation of human interiority.

The sciences then come to be regarded, not as prolongations of philosophy, but as autonomous, ongoing processes; not as the demonstration of universal and necessary truths but as hypothetical and ever better approximations to truth through an ever more exact and comprehensive understanding of data. Philosophy is no longer a theory in the manner of science but the self-appropriation of intentional consciousness and the consequent distinguishing, relating, and grounding of the various realms of meaning, the grounding of the methods of the sciences, and the ongoing promotion of their unification. Theology then becomes, in large part, the understanding of the diversity of religious utterance on the basis of the differentiation and interrelation of the realms of common sense, theory, interiority, and transcendence. Religious experience is understood as correlated with this fourth realm of meaning, the realm of transcendence.

> What I have referred to as the gift of God's love, spontaneously reveals itself in love, joy, peace, patience, kindness, goodness, fidelity, gentleness, and self-control. In undifferentiated consciousness it will express its reference to the transcendent both through sacred objects, places, times and actions, and through the sacred offices of the shaman, the prophet, the lawgiver, the apostle, the priest, the preacher, the monk, the teacher. As consciousness differentiates into

---

110
  Ibid., p. 115.

the two realms of common sense and theory, it will give rise
to special theoretical questions concerning divinity, the
order of the universe, the destiny of mankind, and the lot of
each individual. When these three realms of common sense,
theory, and interiority are differentiated, the self-appropriation of the subject leads not only to the objectification
of experiencing, understanding, judging, and deciding, but
also of religious experience.

Quite distinct from these objectifications of the gift of
God's love in the realms of common sense and of theory and from
the realm of interiority, is the emergence of the gift as itself a differentiated realm. It is this emergence that is
cultivated by a life of prayer and self-denial and, when it
occurs, it has the twofold effect, first, of withdrawing the
subject from the realm of common sense, theory, and other interiority into a "cloud of unknowing" and then of intensifying,
purifying, clarifying, the objectifications referring to the
transcendent whether in the realm of common sense, or of
theory, or of other interiority.[111]

Religion as Higher Integration

In *Philosophy of God, and Theology*, religion is called "the

major factor in the integration and development of the person."[112]

Parallel to this claim is the analysis of authentic religion, in

the last chapter of *Insight*, as the higher integration of human living

acknowledged as necessary at the end of the chapter on ethics. This

higher integration is demanded because of the existence of a problem

of evil rooted in man's inherent incapacity for sustained development,

in a moral impotence which is part and parcel of the dynamic struc-

ture of human intelligence, reflection, and deliberation. For the

sake of completeness, it seems important that we present a summary

account of Lonergan's treatment of authentic religion in *Insight*.

111
   Ibid., p. 266.

112
   Bernard Lonergan, *Philosophy of God, and Theology*, p. 59.

Within the context of religious experience, the problem of evil becomes a question of what God is or has been doing about the fact of evil. Within this same context, the evil rooted in the moral impotence of man's incapacity for sustained development becomes sin. "The hopeless tangle of the social surd, of the impotence of common sense, of the endlessly multiplied philosophies, is not merely a cul-de-sac for human progress; it is also a reign of sin, a despotism of darkness; and men are its slaves."[113] The reign of sin is a twofold expectation of sin.

> On a primary level, it is the priority of living to learning how to live, to acquiring that willingness to live rightly, to developing the adaptation that makes right living habitual. On a second level, it is man's awareness of his plight and his self-surrender to it; on each occasion, he could reflect and through reflection avoid sinning; but he cannot bear the burden of perpetual reflection; and long before that burden has mounted to the limit of physical impossibility, he chooses the easy way out. On both the primary and the second levels, there is the transposition of the inner issue into the outer social milieu; concrete situations become infected with the social surd; they are intractable without dialectical analysis; and the intractability is taken as evidence that only in an increasingly limited fashion can intelligence and reasonableness and good will have any real bearing upon the conduct of human affairs. Finally, dialectical analysis can transpose the issue, but it cannot do so effectively. It goes beyond common sense to a critical human science that supposes a correct and accepted philosophy; but a correct philosophy will be but one of many philosophies and, precisely because it is correct, it will be too complicated to be commonly accessible and too alien to sinful man to be widely accepted.[114]

If the answers to the various forms of the question of God which arise from questioning our questioning lead to the affirmation

---

113
    Bernard Lonergan, Insight, p. 692.

114
    Ibid., p. 693.

of the existence of an omniscient, omnipotent, completely good God,
then this affirmation provides a further intelligibility to be
grasped beyond the intelligibility of the possibilities of intelligent, reasonable, and good courses of action on the part of man,
beyond the statistical intelligibility of their frequency, beyond
the direct intelligibility of actual good choices and the inverse
intelligibility that grasps that unintelligent, unreasonable, and
sinful courses of action are unintelligible. "Because God is omniscient, he knows man's plight. Because he is omnipotent, he can
remedy it. Because he is good, he wills to do so. The fact of evil
is not the whole story."[115]

The divine solution to the problem of evil will be one, universally accessible and permanent, a harmonious continuation of the
actual order of this universe.[116] Since the problem of evil is man's
problem, the solution will be a solution for man, and it will involve
the introduction of new habits in man's intelligence, willing, and
sensitivity.[117] These habits will reverse the priority of man's
living to man's intellect, will, and sensitivity, by being operative
throughout man's living.[118] According to a later formulation,

> . . . it used to be said, Nihil amatum nisi praecognitum,
> Knowledge precedes love. The truth of this tag is the fact

115
  Ibid., p. 694.

116
  Ibid., p. 696.

117
  Ibid., p. 696f.

118
  Ibid., p. 697.

that ordinarily operations on the fourth level of intentional
consciousness presuppose and complement corresponding
operations on the other three. There is a minor exception to
this rule inasmuch as people do fall in love, and that falling
in love is something disproportionate to its causes, conditions,
occasions, antecedents. For falling in love is a new beginning,
an exercise of vertical liberty in which one's world undergoes
a new organization. But the major exception to the Latin tag
is God's gift of his love flooding our hearts. Then we are in
the dynamic state of being in love. But who it is we love, is
neither given nor as yet understood. Our capacity for moral
self-transcendence has found a fulfilment that brings deep joy
and profound peace. Our love reveals to us values we had not
appreciated, values of prayer and worship, or repentance and
belief. But if we would know what is going on within us, if we
would learn to integrate it with the rest of our living, we have
to inquire, investigate, seek counsel. So it is that in religious matters love precedes knowledge and, as that love is God's
gift, the very beginning of faith is due to God's grace.[119]

So it is that the new habits introduced are in some sense trans-

cendent or supernatural. "They are not the result of accumulated in-

sights, for such accumulation takes time, and the problem arises

because man has to live during the interval in which insights are being

accumulated."[120]

The new habits, nonetheless, are a harmonious continuation of

a universe so ordered that successive higher integrations emerge to

systematize otherwise coincidental manifolds on lower levels. In this

way, the new habits constitute a new and higher integration of human

living, unifying and consolidating otherwise coincidental elements.[121]

The universe into which these habits are introduced develops from the

---

119
　　Bernard Lonergan, Method in Theology, pp. 122f.

120
　　Bernard Lonergan, Insight, p. 697.

121
　　Ibid.

lower static systems known by physics and chemistry to the higher dynamic systems known in biology, sensitive psychology, and cognitional theory or intentionality analysis, and so these new habits pertain not to static system but to system on the move. They "have to meet a problem that varies as man develops and declines, and so they too must be capable of some development and adaptation."[122]

All higher integrations within the actual order of the universe leave intact the laws of the underlying manifolds which they integrate. Consequently, the new habits or forms introduced into human subjectivity to meet the problem of evil "will come to men through their apprehension and with their consent."[123] The intelligibility of the emergence of the solution to the problem of evil and the intelligibility of its propagation, furthermore, will be statistical intelligibility, and the relevant probabilities to be understood are those "that regard the occurrence of man's intelligent and rational apprehension of the solution and his free and responsible consent to it."[124] Thus a distinction must be drawn between "the realization of the full solution and, on the other hand, the emergent trend in which the full solution becomes effectively probable."[125]

122
    Ibid.

123
    Ibid.

124
    Ibid., p. 698.

125
    Ibid.

According to the formulation of Insight, with which
Lonergan's later appeal to Romans 5.5 is in complete continuity,
the solution to the problem is further determined by stating that
"the appropriate willingness will be some type or species of
charity;"[126] a "love of God that is prompted not by a hope of one's
own advantage but simply by God's goodness;"[127] a love of God that
reaches for harmony with the order of the universe which, apart from
the surd of sin, is in love with God;[128] a love that wills every other
good because of the order of the universe, the order of the universe
because of the love of God,[129] and the good of all persons in the
universe because of the love of God;[130] a love that adopts the dialectical attitude of meeting evil with good, of loving one's enemies,
of praying for those who persecute and calumniate one, and so makes
of the social surd a potential good through a self-sacrificing love
that matches the dialectical method of intelligence grasping the
absurdity of evil and refusing to systematize and perpetuate it by
treating it as intelligible;[131] a love that repents of former blindness

---

126
  Ibid.
127
  Ibid.
128
  Ibid., pp. 698f.
129
  Ibid., p. 699.
130
  Ibid.
131
  Ibid.

and involvement in individual, group, and general bias, of past
flights from self-knowledge, rationalizations of wrong, surrender
to evil and commitment to error, and that repents not by feelings
of guilt but by acts of will informed by understanding and reasonableness;[132] a love whose repentance, then, takes the form of sorrow
flowing from a personal relation to the one with whom one is in love;[133]
a love, finally, which, while repentant over the past and self-sacrificing as it looks to the future, is at one with the universe in its
love of God and so joyfully shares a "dynamic resilience and expectancy" which rises above past achievement, urges generic potential
forward to specific perfection, meets evil with good, wills with the
dynamic joy and zeal of the order of the universe.[134]

Besides this love which makes one's willing good, the solution
to the problem of evil will involve the introduction of a hope through
which one's willing makes one's intelligence good by a deliberate
decision to overrule the competition of attached and interested sensitive and intersubjective desire with the intention of being and truth
which is the pure desire to know. The objective of the desire to know
is the knowledge of God, and the deliberate decision to take issue
with conflicting tendencies will be a decision against both "the
hopelessness that allows man's spirit to surrender the legitimate

---

132
    Ibid., p. 700.

133
    Ibid.

134
    Ibid.

aspirations of the unrestricted desire and to seek comfort in the
all too human ambitions of the Kantian and the positivist,"[135]
and the presumption which would locate the conditions for the
achievement of the objective of the pure desire to know, not in God
but in man. The hope introduced by being in love with God is confident that "God will bring man's intellect to a knowledge, participation, possession of the unrestricted act of understanding."[136]

Nonetheless, hope's assurance and love's motivation rest
also on present knowledge. The solution to the problem of evil calls,
then, for a present, "universally accessible and permanently effective manner of pulling men's minds out of the counter-positions, of
fixing them in the positions, of securing for them certitude that
God exists and that he has provided a solution which they are to
acknowledge and accept."[137] This knowledge, though, has no probability of being immanently generated because the root of the problem
of evil lies in the very structure of human intentionality. But
there may be an attainment of truth both possible and probable
through the communication of reliable knowledge and its reception in
belief.[138]

135
   Ibid., p. 701.

136
   Ibid., p. 702.

137
   Ibid.

138
   Ibid., pp. 702f.

What, then, is believing? Belief is the reception of reliably communicated knowledge. The general context of belief is "the collaboration of mankind in the advancement and dissemination of knowledge,"[139] a collaboration in which men contribute to a common fund of knowledge in virtue of their own experience, understanding, and judgment, but also receive from this fund in a manner other than that which informs their contribution. Collaboration in the advancement and dissemination of knowledge is inevitable.

> Our senses are limited to an extremely narrow strip of space-time and, unless we are ready to rely on the senses of others, we must leave blank all other places and times or, as is more likely, fill them with our conjectures and then explain our conjectures with myths. Again, the personal contribution of any individual to the advance of human understanding is never large. We may be astounded by men of genius; but the way for their discoveries was prepared by many others in a long succession; and if they took enormous strides, commonly it was because the logic of their circumstances left them no opportunity to take shorter ones. But without collaboration each successive generation, instead of beginning where its predecessor left off, would have to begin at the very beginning and so could never advance beyond the most rudimentary of primitive levels.[140]

Collaboration, moreover, is not only inevitable but also cumulative. As a result, "the mentality of any individual becomes a composite product in which it is impossible to separate immanently generated knowledge and belief."[141] In fact there are not many items of immanently generated knowledge totally independent of beliefs. "One does not simply know that England is an island. Neither does one

---

[139] *Ibid.*, p. 703.

[140] *Ibid.*, p. 704.

[141] *Ibid.*, p. 706.

merely believe it. Perhaps no one has immanently generated knowledge that general relativity is more accurate than Newtonian
theory on the perihelion of Mercury. But it does not follow that
for everyone it is purely a matter of belief."[142] While the consequence of collaboration in the pursuit of truth is a symbiosis of
knowledge and belief, its alternative is a necessarily primitive
ignorance.

> The development of the human mind is by the self-correcting
> process of learning, and in that process personal knowledge
> and belief practise an unrelenting symbiosis. The broadening
> of individual experience includes hearing the opinions and
> convictions of others. The deepening of individual under-
> standing includes the exploration of many viewpoints. The
> formation of individual judgment is a process of differentiation,
> clarification, and revision, in which the shock of contradictory
> judgments is as relevant as one's own observation and memory,
> one's own intelligent inquiry and critical reflection. So each
> of us advances from the nescience of infancy to the fixed men-
> tality of old age and however large and indeterminate the con-
> tributions of belief to the shaping of our minds, still every
> belief and all its implications have been submitted to the
> endlessly repeated, if unnoticed, test of fresh experiences, of
> further questions and new insights, of clarifying and quali-
> fying revisions of judgment.[143]

There are five stages to the typical process of true belief:

(1) preliminary judgments on the value of belief in general,
on the reliability of the source for this belief, and on
the accuracy of the communication from the source,

(2) a reflective act of understanding that, in virtue of the
preliminary judgments, grasps as virtually unconditioned
the value of deciding to believe some particular propo-
sition,

(3) the consequent judgment of value,

(4) the consequent decision of the will, and

142
   Ibid.

143.
   Ibid.

(5)   the assent that is the act of believing.[144]

Nonetheless, any belief is only as intelligent and reasonable as is the collaboration of men in the advancement and dissemination of knowledge.   There are not only intelligent and reasonable beliefs, but also mistaken beliefs, and they are rooted in "the
scotosis of the dramatic subject, in the individual, group and
general bias of the practical subject, in the counter-positions of
philosophy, and in their ethical implications and consequences."[145]
They are conditioned by the proximity of their relevant fields of
data to the very stuff of human living.

> In belief as in personal thought and judgment, men go wrong
> when they have to understand and to judge either themselves
> or other things in relation to themselves.   The serenity and
> sure-footedness of the mathematician, the physicist, the
> chemist, are not independent of the remoteness of these
> fields from human living. . . .   On the other hand, when it
> comes to the study of life, of the psychological depths, of
> human institutions, of the history of nations, cultures, and
> religions, then diversity multiplies, differences become ir-
> reconcilable, and the name of science can be invoked with
> plausibility only by introducing methodological conventions
> that exclude from scientific consideration the heart of the
> matter.   The life of man on earth lies under the shadow of a
> problem of evil; the evil invades his mind; and as it diverts
> his immanently generated knowledge, so also it distorts his
> beliefs.[146]

As important, then, as an analysis of the process of belief is an
understanding of what is involved in a critique of mistaken beliefs.

Learning one's errors is but a particular case of learning.
It takes as its starting-point and clue the discovery of some

---

144
   Ibid., p. 708.

145
   Ibid., p. 714.

146
   Ibid.

precise issue on which undoubtedly one was mistaken. It
advances by inquiring into the sources that may have contributed to that error and, perhaps, contributed to other
errors as well. It asks about the motives and the suppor-
ting judgments that, as they once confirmed one in that
error, may still be holding one in others. It investigates
the consequences of the view one now rejects and it seeks
to determine whether or not they too are to be rejected.
The process is cumulative. The discovery of one error is
exploited to lead to the discovery of others; and the discovery of the others provides a still larger base to proceed to the discovery of still more. Moreover, this cumulative process not only takes advantage of the mind's native
processes of learning, in which one insight leads on to
other insights, but it also exploits the insistence of
rational consciousness on consistency; for just as our love
of consistency, once we have made one mistake, leads us to
make others, so the same love of consistency leads us to
reject other mistakes, when one is rejected and, at the
same time, it provides us with abundant clues for finding
the others that are to be rejected.147

There is nothing unintelligent or unreasonable or irrespon-

sible, then, about believing, nor is the correction of mistaken

beliefs to be regarded as either impossible or as evidence for the

futility of all belief. There is, then, no contradiction with the

actual order of the universe implied in affirming that the knowledge

underlying hope's assurance and love's motivation in the divine

solution to the problem of evil will be some kind of belief. Fur-

thermore, the solution as cognitively informed by belief will involve

"a new and higher collaboration of men in the pursuit of truth . . .

Because the solution is a harmonious continuation of the actual order,

it too will be a collaboration that involves belief, truthfulness,

accuracy, and immanently generated knowledge. Again, because the

solution is a higher integration, it will be a new and higher

---

147
    Ibid., pp. 714f.

collaboration. Finally, because the solution meets a problem of
error and sin, the new and higher collaboration in the pursuit of
truth will provide an antidote to the errors to which man is
inclined."[148]

This new and higher collaboration will not simply be one of
men with one another but fundamentally a collaboration of man with
God in working out the solution to man's problem of evil. One's
entrance into this higher collaboration and one's participation in
its fruits will be through faith, through a transcendent belief
which "makes a man a participant in the new and higher collaboration
in which God is the initiator and the principal agent."[149] This
faith will be "an assent of intellect to truths transmitted through
the collaboration and it will be motivated by man's reliance on the
truthfulness of God."[150] It will include "an affirmation of man's
spiritual nature, of his freedom, responsibility, and sinfulness,
of God's existence and nature, and of the transcendent solution God
provides for man's problem of evil."[151] Intelligent and reasonable
participation in the new and higher collaboration will entail an
acknowledgment of the problem of evil; of man's inability to cope
with this problem; of God's ability to provide a solution and God's

---

148
    Ibid., p. 719

149
    Ibid., p. 720.

150
    Ibid.

151
    Ibid., p. 721.

goodness in exercising that ability; of an emergent trend and a
full realization in human history of a solution to the problem of
evil; of the value of assenting to the new and higher collaboration;
and of the wisdom of deciding to join that collaboration, by making
known to others the good news of the solution, by seeing that it is
transmitted from one generation to the next, perhaps by helping to
recast the expression of the solution so that it can be understood
by people of different places, times, classes, and cultures, or by
attempting to conceive and express the solution in terms of the transcendental infrastructure of human subjectivity, or by announcing in
concrete and successive situations of individuals, classes, nations,
and the world the relevance and effectiveness of the divinely
initiated solution to the problem of evil.[152]

As the divinely originated solution to man's problem of
evil leaves man's freedom intact, even man's collaboration in its
execution will be marked by deficiencies and failures of human origin.
But these aberrations will not eliminate the solution, for the solution
is the work not of man but of God.[153]

As the humanity for which evil is a problem is not only capable of intelligence and willing but also endowed with a consciousness which, in the main, flows in dramatic and practical patterns of
experience, the solution to the problem of evil will involve not

---

152
   Ibid., pp. 721f.

153
   Ibid., pp. 722f.

only the introduction of faith and hope and love into man's intelligence, reasonableness, and willing, but must also penetrate to human sensitivity and intersubjectivity through images and symbols.

> Inasmuch as intelligence and reasonableness and will issue into human words matched with deeds, they need at their disposal images so charged with affects that they succeed both in guiding and in propelling action. Again, besides the image that is a sign of intelligible and rational contents and the image that is a psychic force, there is the image that symbolizes man's orientation into the known unknown; and since faith gives more truth than understanding comprehends, since hope reinforces the detached, disinterested, unrestricted desire to know, man's sensitivity needs symbols that unlock its transforming dynamism and bring it into harmony with the vast but impalpable pressures of the pure desire, of hope, and of self-sacrificing charity.[154]

The newness of God's solution to the problem of evil will thus be that of "a mystery that is at once symbol of the uncomprehended and sign of what is grasped and psychic force that sweeps living human bodies, linked in charity, to the joyful, courageous, whole-hearted, yet intelligently controlled performance of the tasks set by a world order in which the problem of evil is not suppressed but transcended."[155] The mystery that is demanded must be a matter, not of fiction but of fact, not of story but of history, for the problem of evil is a fact to be found in man's living within the actual order of the universe. But it will also have a nature and content and meaning and power of its own, for it will introduce a new level on which human living develops and rejoices.[156] While every solution which introduces a new

---

[154] Ibid., p. 723.

[155] Ibid., pp. 723f.

[156] Ibid., p. 724.

and higher integration into human living may be called transcendent, while every solution which is constituted by faith and hope and love that look primarily to God will be religious, to the extent that the solution goes beyong these minimal demands, it will reveal to faith "truths that man never could discover for himself nor, even when he assented to them, could he understand them in an adequate fashion."[157] If the solution to the problem of evil is one, finally, whose sole ground and measure is God himself, if consequently faith includes objects inaccessible to any finite understanding, if hope is for a vision of God that exhausts our unrestricted desire to know, if love is "the transport, the ecstasy, and unbounded intimacy that result from the communication of the absolute love that is God himself and alone can respond to the vision of God,"[158] then the divinely originated solution to man's problem of evil is to be understood not simply as in some sense transcendent, but as absolutely supernatural, as absolutely disproportionate to the capacities of human nature, human reason, human good will, human esteem. If that is the case, the tension which always accompanies the integration of otherwise coincidental manifolds by some higher order will be in this instance significantly heightened.

> The supernatural solution involves a transcendence of humanism, and the imperfect realization of the supernatural solution is apt to oscillate between an emphasis on the supernatural and an emphasis on the solution. Imperfect faith can insist on believing

---

157
 Ibid., p. 725.

158
 Ibid., p. 726.

to the neglect of the understanding that makes faith an effective
factor in human living and human history; and an even less perfect faith can endanger the general collaboration in its hurry to
show forth its social and cultural fruits. Imperfect hope can so
expect the New Jerusalem as to oppose any foretaste of intellectual bliss and union in this life; and an even less perfect hope
can forget that a supernatural solution involves a real displacement of the centre of human concerns. Imperfect charity lacks the
resources needed to combine both true loving and the true transformation of loving. It can be absorbed in the union of the
family, in the intersubjectivity of comrades in work and in adventure, in the common cause of fellows in nationality and in citi-
zenship, in the common aspiration of associates in scientific,
cultural, and humanitarian pursuits. On the other hand, it can
withdraw from home and country, from human cares and human ambitions, from the clamour of the senses and the entanglement of the
social surd, to fix its gaze upon the unseen ultimate, to respond
to an impalpable presence, to grow inwardly to the stature of
eternity. But imperfect charity, inasmuch as it is imperfect,
will not realize at once the opposed facets of its perfection; if
it is in the world, it ever risks being of the world; and if it
withdraws from the world, the human basis of its ascent to God
risks a contraction and an atrophy.[159]

This heightened tension will find its objectification in the dialecti-

cal succession of human situations:

There will be a humanism in revolt against the proffered supernatural solution. It will ignore the problem of evil; it will con-
test the fact of a solution; it will condemn mystery as myth; it
will demand reason and exclude faith; it will repudiate hope and
labour passionately to build the city of man with the hands of man;
it will be ready to love God in song and dance, in human feasting
and human sorrow, with human intelligence and human good will, but
only so. For a time, it may base its case upon the shortcomings
of those that profess the solution but live it imperfectly or in-
termittently or not at all. But this incidental argument sooner
or later will give place to its real basis. For it rests on man's
proud content to be just a man, and its tragedy is that, on the
present supposition of a supernatural solution, to be just a man
is what man cannot be. If he would be truly a man, he would submit to the unrestricted desire and discover the problem of evil
and affirm the existence of a solution and accept the solution
that exists. But if he would be only a man, he has to be less.
He has to forsake the openness of the pure desire; he has to take
refuge in the counter-positions; he has to develop what counter-

---

159
    Ibid., pp. 727f.

philosophies he can to save his dwindling humanism from further losses; and there will not be lacking men clear-sighted enough to grasp that the issue is between God and man, logical enough to grant that intelligence and reason are orientated towards God, ruthless enough to summon to their aid the dark forces of passion and of violence.[160]

The Existential Subject as Psychic

I have already called attention to a significant transposition in Lonergan's location of the psyche within the transcendental infrastructure of human subjectivity. In Insight, the psyche "reaches the wealth and fullness of its apprehensions and responses under the higher integration of human intelligence."[161] In Method in Theology, both human intelligence and psyche are sublated and unified by the deliberations of the authentic existential subject. The key to this change, as I have emphasized, is the emergence of the good as a distinct notion from the intelligent and reasonable. Mediating between judgments of fact and judgments concerning what is good and worth while, is the apprehension of potential values and satisfactions in feelings. And feelings are said to be symbolically certifiable. The psyche, then, is a constituent feature of the deciding, deliberating, evaluating existential subject. The wealth and fullness of its apprehensions and responses is reached, not under the higher integration of human intelligence, but in the free and responsible decisions of the authentic existential subject.

160
   Ibid., pp. 728f.

161
   Ibid., p. 726.

The stage has been set, then, for arguing that the self-appropriation of intentional consciousness in method can be complemented by and include psychic self-appropriation, and that this psychic self-appropriation is a further refinement of the self-knowledge of the existential subject. In addition to the mediation of immediacy by meaning which occurs when one objectifies cognitional process, there is that which occurs when one discovers, identifies, accepts one's submerged feelings in psychotherapy.[162] Self-appropriation and the mediation of immediacy or of the transcendental infrastructure of human subjectivity are one and the same process. Cognitional self-appropriation satisfies a critical-methodological exigence awakened by the scientific revolution and by the anthropological turn in modern philosophy. Psychic self-appropriation satisfies a further and complementary exigence, a therapeutic exigence, awakened by the crises of personal and political living that are reflected in psychoanalysis, Marxism, and existentialism. Furthermore, as Lonergan has developed the structure of method based on the mediation of intentionality, so I wish to begin to detail the potential methodological complement afforded by the mediation of psyche within the context provided by Lonergan. It will be my contention that intentionality analysis, as articulated in a pattern of judgments concerning cognitional fact, moral being, and religious experience, can be complemented by a psychic conversion which can critically ground one's moral and religious living in an expanding concrete pattern of judgments of value and one's

---

162
    Bernard Lonergan, Method in Theology, p. 77.

sublation of an intellectually converted critical consciousness by
moral and religious consciousness. Through this greater concreteness
on the side of the subject, theology can come closer to accepting the
possibilities which now, perhaps for the first time in its history as
a systematic discipline, are available to it. For in our age not
only are we confronted with the relativity of systematic conceptual
schemes of all kinds, in every area, but also, precisely because of
this seemingly very uncertain and ambivalent state of affairs, the
individual is given

> . . . the (often desperate, yet maximally human) opportunity to
> interpret life and experiencing directly. The historical cross-
> roads of such a time is: either the reimposition of certain set
> values and schemes, or a task never before attempted: to learn
> how, in a rational way, to relate concepts to direct experiencing;
> to investigate the way in which symbolizing affects and is affec-
> ted by felt experiencing; to devise a social and scientific voca-
> bulary that can interact with experiencing, so that communication
> about it becomes possible, so that schemes can be considered in
> relation to experiential meanings, and so that an objective
> science can be related to and guided by experiencing.163

What Eugene Gendlin here envisions for "objective science" and particularly for the science of man can also be the goal of theology and is,
in fact, the impetus to all contemporary creative theological endeavor,
culminating in the revolution in theological foundations proposed by
Lonergan. For, according to the dynamic operative in Lonergan's articulation of theological foundations, as we shall see, the foundational
reality of all theological endeavor is the subjectivity of the theologian himself. Lonergan has articulated foundational reality in
terms of religious, moral, and intellectual conversion. Our

163
    Eugene Gendlin, Experiencing and the Creation of Meaning
(Toronto: Free Press of Glencoe, 1962), p. 4.

articulation would develop and refine still further this formulation:
the foundations of theology lie in the objectification of cognitive,
psychic, moral, and religious subjectivity in a patterned set of
judgments of cognitional fact and of value cumulatively heading
toward the full position on the human subject.

It is my contention that our age marks the beginning of a
qualitative mutation in the evolution of human consciousness, one sign
of which is that we can now, for the first time in history, speak of
such an evolution in more than purely descriptive terms. More specifically, I would say we are moving into the third major epoch in the
Western history of human consciousness. We have already seen that
Lonergan presents us with a very illuminating understanding of this
evolution in terms of stages of meaning. A complementary understanding
of psychic evolution in terms of the relations between intentionality
and the psyche can also be developed, and, while reserving a detailed
account for a future work, I shall present some few of its features
in the present volume. I will find these two accounts parallel and
complementary. Each is an explanation and at the same time a self-
conscious foundation of the understanding of further human development.
It is in terms of this evolution that the emerging relations between
philosophy, depth psychology, and theology are to be understood. I
fully accept Lonergan's statement that, "once philosophy becomes existential and historical, once it asks about man, not in the abstract,
not as he would be in some state of pure nature, but as in fact he is
here and now in all the concreteness of his living and dying, the very
possibility of the old distinction between philosophy and theology

vanishes."[164] This distinction was characteristic of the second
stage in human conscious evolution, that of the emergence of logos
from mythos, and will vanish from the scene as we move more and more
into the third, that of the emergence of method from logic. In
addition, however, this same movement to a third stage of meaning,
founded as it is in the self-appropriation of human interiority,
calls for a self-conscious return to mytho-poetic imagination through
depth psychology. For the self-appropriation of human interiority
is not coincident with the self-appropriation of cognitional process.
This is especially obvious from the primacy of the existential in the
writings of the "later Lonergan." Method itself, then, in the person
of the self-appropriating subject, can participate in the depth-
psychological effort at disengaging the symbolic constitutive structure-in-process of human experience. The objectification of the movement of human interiority in a patterned set of judgments of cognitional fact and of value will provide the foundations of theology
and of the science of man in the third epoch of human conscious evolution. These foundations will serve not only for systematic theology but also for a more all-embracing dialectically informed discipline which we might call an evaluative cultural hermeneutic. This
discipline would derive its data from everything that enters or has
entered into the consciousness or the life of man. Aside from this,
there are no data. This unified, though variegated, field of data,
insofar as it serves as the material for the objectification of the

---

164
    Bernard Lonergan, "Dimensions of Meaning," p. 266.

self-appropriation of human interiority, is what leads me to
encourage and perhaps to try to hasten a bit the emerging unity-
in-differentiation of philosophy, depth psychology, and theology.
A methodically exigent consciousness can now engage in the differentiation and appropriation of the psychic bases of human experience.
It is from such a perspective that the present work is undertaken.
What happens when self-appropriating subjectivity, carefully tutored
by Lonergan's intentionality analysis, becomes psychically self-
appropriating subjectivity? What effect does it have for theology
and for the science of man when one thus self-consciously--that is,
attentively, intelligently, reasonably, and responsibly--extends the
self-appropriation of human interiority and thus of the unified field
of data for thoughtful reflection? These questions are primary in
the pages which follow. At this point, I am able to treat them only
methodologically. I am not yet prepared to write a phenomenology of
the psyche. Nonetheless, by pointing to the emerging unity-in-differentiation of philosophy, depth psychology, and theology through
the objectification of the transcendental infrastructure of human
subjectivity, I wish also to signal the future sublation into method
of the psychotherapeutic phenomenon in a new constitution and control
of meaning through a self-conscious and critically retrieved transcendental aesthetic. Psychotherapy as we have known it is clearly
a transitional stage, not only in the lives of individuals but also
in the evolution of Western culture. It must be relativized, not only
by method, but also by the "soul beyond psychology," the soul in
dialogue and concert with the Lord and Victim of human history, the
soul that is the life to which both method in its entirety and

psychotherapy in particular point and which both method and psychotherapy mediate in a new way. Depth psychology leads beyond itself.
It is an intermediary between the ages; it can lead to a creative
life that can only be lived beyond itself; it initiates a process
of self-knowledge which will continue to feed this life, but the
life itself will turn from the "treadmill of self-conscious analysis"[165] to the arenas of love and strife that are the habitat of man.
It achieves its fulfilment only beyond itself in the existential
subjectivity of self-transcending men and women in love with the
earth and with its origin and destiny.

The theologian Ernst Fuchs has said that what the essential
word or authentic language does is to announce what it is time for.
It cannot give a direct guarantee of itself, that it is essential or
authentic. It can only determine the situation anew by calling a
new world into being, the world waiting to be born.[166] From such a
perspective, nobody has contributed to the essential word for our age
with greater precision and finality than Lonergan. I find the poetic
description of Heidegger applicable: "The thought of being guards
the Word and fulfills its function in such guardianship, namely care
for the use of language. Out of long guarded speechlessness and the
careful clarification of the field thus cleared, comes the utterance

---

165
    Ira Progoff, The Death and Rebirth of Psychology, p. 258.

166
    Robert W. Funk, Language, Hermeneutic, and Word of God
(New York: Harper and Row, 1966), p. 55.

of the thinker."[167] In announcing the exigence of our time as the
exigence for the differentiation and appropriation of human interiority, Lonergan has announced what it is time for. The only guarantee of the authenticity of his word has come from heeding his invitation. Such acceptance has slowly, so slowly, made his essential
word public, a ground of unity for a gradually growing community.

Only against this background can I speak of the potential
complementary effect of depth psychology with respect to intentionality analysis. John Dunne speaks of climbing a mountain in order
to discover a vantage point, a fastness of autonomy. The most complete autonomy comes, he says, from the knowledge, not of external
things, but of knowledge itself.

> A knowing of knowing would be like a view from a mountain-
> top. By knowing all about knowing itself one would know in
> some manner everything there is to know. It would be like
> seeing everything from a great height. One would see every-
> thing near and far, all the way to the horizon, but there would
> be some loss of detail on account of the distances. The knowing
> of knowing would mean being in possession of all the various
> methods of knowing. It would mean knowing how an artist thinks,
> putting a thing together; knowing how a scientist thinks, taking
> a thing apart; knowing how a practical man thinks, sizing up a
> situation; knowing how a man of understanding thinks, grasping
> the principle of a thing; knowing how a man of wisdom thinks,
> reflecting upon human experience. . . .
> At the top of the mountain, as we have been describing it,
> there is a kind of madness--not the madness that consists in
> having lost one's reason, but a madness that consists in having
> lost everything except one's reason. The knowing of knowing, to
> be sure, seems worthy of God and worthy of man. The only thing
> wrong is that man at the top of the mountain, by escaping from
> love and war, will have lost everything else. He will have with-
> drawn into that element of his nature which is most characteris-
> tic of him and sets him apart from other animals. It is the
> thing in him which is most human. Perhaps he will never realize

---

167
    Ibid., p. 41, quoting from Heidegger's "What is Meta-
physics?"

what it is to be human unless he does attempt this withdrawal.
Even so, the realization that he has lost everything except
his reason, that he has found pure humanity but not full
humanity, changes his wisdom from a knowledge of knowledge
into a knowledge of ignorance. He realizes that he has something yet to learn, something that he cannot learn at the top
of the mountain but only at the bottom of the valley.[168]

While Dunne's description would seem far more applicable to

Hegel than to Lonergan, nonetheless nobody can read these words, if

he is familiar with Lonergan, without thinking of one of the most

daring claims any thinker has ever offered for his own work, true

as it is: "Thoroughly understand what it is to understand, and not

only will you understand the broad lines of all there is to be

understood but also you will possess a fixed base, an invariant

pattern, opening upon all further developments of understanding."[169]

There is too, however, a difference, in that the understanding of

understanding is not the same thing as the knowing of knowing.

Understanding is much more tied to imagination than knowing. One

can understand without knowing, without understanding correctly,

without achieving cognitional self-transcendence. While the true

understanding of understanding would be a knowing of knowing, the

thorough understanding of understanding would not entail the kind of

"madness" of which Dunne speaks, for it would also include an under-

standing of the essential dynamics of the flight from understanding,

of the desire not to know, of life at the bottom of the valley.

168
John S. Dunne, The Way of All the Earth (New York:
Macmillan, 1972), pp. 17-19.

169
Bernard Lonergan, Insight, p. xxviii.

Still, to allow one's knowledge of knowledge to be changed into a knowledge of ignorance may well involve the realization that there are many things in heaven and on earth that are not dreamed of in one's philosophy. It may then lead to the grasp that much of this life in the valley enters into one's life without being consciously objectified and appropriated, without providing data for one's knowing of knowing, without formally coming to light in even the most thoroughgoing intentionality analysis. One may discover a dark yet potentially creative and beneficial power at work in the valley and expend his efforts by means of a different kind of withdrawal or introversion--into a forest or desert, in imitation of Gotama or Jesus, rather than up to a mountaintop--at appropriating, befriending, and to a certain extent transforming this dark power of nature so that it is not only creative of life but originative of value. If he succeeds in this very risky adventure, he will have undergone a profound conversion.

The relocation of the psychic in Lonergan's recent explorations of value marks, if you will, a return from the mountaintop of cognitional analysis to the valley in which the existential subject decides for himself what he is to make of himself. And our task is that of articulating the integration of psychic energy into the thrust of conscious intentionality toward the love of God. There is a psychic energy manifested in the pure question of the transcendental infrastructure of the subject-as-subject. The articulation of its integration into the thrust of intentionality toward authentic religious living is a problem of mammoth proportions. That the articulation is possible is suggested by the many references of

Jung to the God-archetype or God-image in the psyche. That Jung achieved a successful articulation of the relationship between psyche and intentionality is questionable. The problem lay, not in his knowledge of the psyche but in his understanding of intentionality. It is that problem alone which I hope to rectify in the present work, by presenting what I believe is a more adequate methodological framework for such depth psychological articulation. The actual articulation of the integration of psyche into method must be done in another work.

The principal methodological contribution I intend in this work speaks of psychic conversion. Conversion is the central theme in Lonergan's recasting of the foundations of theology. While Lonergan speaks of intellectual, moral, and religious conversion, what I will propose is something different from these. Essentially it is the gaining of a critically and methodically mediated capacity attentively, intelligently, reasonably, and responsibly to disengage the symbolic constitution of the feelings in which values are apprehended and to live from that disengagement. As I shall argue in Chapter 6, it figures in the foundations of theology as facilitating the sublation of intellectual conversion by moral and religious conversion.

I share the conviction of Dunne that something like a new religion is coming, must come, into being, and with Dunne I think of its genesis as largely a process of imaginative "passing over" from one's own culture to others, from one's own way of life to others, from one's own religion to others, and as a matter of coming back to one's own culture, one's own way of life, one's own religion,

with new insight and creativity.[170] It seems to me that this
adventure is happening by reason of something like a psychic law.
But I believe that the contemporary age is in need of criteria for
evaluating these experiments with truth, and that the criteria are
to be discovered in method as the mediation of the transcendental
infrastructure of human subjectivity. The conversion I call psychic,
when integrated into intentionality analysis, might further enable
the subject to venture forth on other adventures and to articulate
the truth he discovers. It might free the subject, in a phrase
Dunne appropriates from Goethe, to turn poetry into truth and truth
into poetry. The latter poetry would feature in the theology appropriate to our age. The symbolic consciousness mediated by the
psychic self-appropriation of the existential subject will render
possible the critical use of poetic categories in systematic theology. Though poetic, these categories would be--perhaps contrary to
the expectations of method untempered by the psychic journey--expla-
natory, because generated by heeding the exigence for the appropriation of interiority.

I have been convinced for quite some time that practically
all of the criticism levelled at Lonergan's work, at least as reflected in Insight, results from a failure to realize and accept
what Lonergan himself articulated concerning Insight at the 1970
International Congress on his work: "My purpose was not a study of

---

170
    John S. Dunne, op. cit., p. ix.

human life but a study of human understanding."[171] More recently,
however, I have wondered whether some of the enthusiasm inspired by
this philosophical monument may not suffer from the same oversight.
As the prolific and provocative Jungian analyst, James Hillman, has
said in a completely different context and with no reference to
Lonergan: "The discrimination of spirit is not at all of the same
order as the cultivation of soul. If the first is active mind in its
broadest sense, the second is the realm of the imaginal, equally
embracing, but very different."[172] This distinction escapes too much
of the current comment on Lonergan, I fear, whether this comment be
favorable or adverse.

If the appropriation of cognitional process is not coextensive
with the mediation of the transcendental infrastructure of human subjectivity in method, new vistas are opened for those who have already
accepted Lonergan's invitation and found it rewarding. The reward is
not without its price, but it is important that this price not be one
exacted by an oversight of the cultivation of the imaginal, especially
if this latter cultivation can be brought to figure in the self-
appropriation of the existential subject.

We may, I believe, characterize the intellectual journey
guided by Lonergan as an appropriation of the logos principle. We
might perhaps understand it archetypally in Jungian terms as an appropriation of animus, thus correcting what I believe to be a mistaken

---

171
   See Philip McShane, ed., Language, Truth, and Meaning, p. 310.

172
   James Hillman, "Anima," Spring: An Annual of Archetypal
Psychology and Jungian Thought, 1973, p. 116.

assumption that animus is to be thought of only in contrasexual terms. If some Jungians are now abandoning the notion of anima as exclusively contrasexual,[173] the same revision of a mistaken assumption will probably follow in due time with respect to animus. Archetypally, animus is masculine, anima feminine: from this it by no means follows that they are to be understood only contrasexually. Hillman already seems to suggest as much: "Animus refers to spirit, to logos, word, idea, intellect, principle, abstraction, meaning, ratio, nous."[174] If this is the case, Lonergan's invitation is clearly to the discrimination and appropriation of animus.

On the other hand, Hillman redefines anima as "archetype of psyche."[175] Then it would be the case that those who have gone the route of intentionality analysis might be able to demonstrate that the appropriation of animus is a very good beginning of the appropriation of interiority. Like any beginning, it must at the right moment give way to the next steps, while not repudiating the beginning. It is from this perspective that I offer my suggestion that the appropriation of psyche will aid the emergence of the authentic existential subject in Lonergan's sense. The eventual outcome would be something like a unity of opposites, of animus and anima, a coniunctio of the basic principles of being human, of the archetypal masculine and the

---

173
    This is one of the most illuminating of Hillman's many proposals in the article cited in the above footnote.

174
    Ibid.

175
    Ibid., p. 120.

archetypal feminine, of logos and psyche or mythos. As animus
needs anima, so intentionality analysis needs psychic analysis.
The discrimination of spirit must be complemented by the cultivation
of soul and finally by the surrender of both spirit and soul in
authentic religion. In the final moment of surrender, too little
understood in psychotherapeutic circles, one finds the soul beyond
psychology in the return to life from the treadmill of self-conscious
analysis.

Gilbert Durand has stated that at some fateful moment
Western man made a radical option not to remain feminine.[176] Archetypally, this was an option for animus rather than for anima, for
spirit, logos, word, idea, intellect, principle, abstraction,
meaning, ratio, nous, rather than for psyche, mythos, image, symbol,
atmosphere, feeling, relation, earth, nature, rhythm. This option
has given rise to what we have come to know as Western civilization.
The archetypal significance of Lonergan's achievement, then, would
be that, for the first time in the history of the unfolding of this
radical option, the very structure of the option itself is laid bare
and rendered capable of appropriation by those who have succeeded
its makers. But today there would seem to be a cultural exigence,
manifested throughout the Western world, to retrieve the option not
taken at our origins. In most instances, this exigence is being
responded to blindly, on the basis of a repudiation of the option
that is our heritage. The cultural significance of Lonergan's

---

[176] Gilbert Durand, "Exploration of the Imaginal," Spring,
1971, p. 94.

achievement, then, at least from this archetypal point of view, is that the appropriation to which he invites us also renders possible a heeding of this new cultural exigence for the retrieval of anima, a heeding that is not blind, that does not involve a repudiation of our archetypally masculine heritage, that is attentive, intelligent, reasonable, and responsibly discriminating. Might it not be that this is the meaning of the recent shift in the writings of Lonergan to an atmosphere more permeated by an acknowledgment of feeling, symbol, love, the heart? And then, furthermore, the meaning of Lonergan's achievement for psychotherapy becomes clear. For the psychotherapeutic movement has been in the vanguard of this retrieval of psyche, but without, in many instances, an adequate appropriation of animus, without a satisfactory appreciation of intentionality, without a correct cognitional theory, and thus without a consistent account of the relationship between psychotherapy and man's knowledge, morality, and religion. Psychic exploration without method can lead to the romantic agony; but method needs to be complemented by psyche. The twofold appropriation of intentionality and psyche is what can enable the coming-to-pass of a fully awake naïveté of the twice-born adult which Paul Ricoeur calls a second, post-critical immediacy.[177] The articulate utterance of such an adult would constitute, in part, a transcendental aesthetic, a poetics of the will, a "transformation of intentionality into kerygma,

---

[177] Paul Ricoeur, Freud and Philosophy, p. 496.

manifestation, proclamation."[178]

What follows, then, is a methodological argument for re-establishing what Gilbert Durand has called "the scandal of spiritual concretism."[179] To the present, our most reliable source of data and locus of verification for the argument is depth psychology, and, with qualifications, in particular that inspired by Jung. But this psychology becomes a source of data and locus of verification, not when it is merely studied as another theory, but only when it is heeded as a personal invitation to travel paths just as labyrinthine as those along which Lonergan guides us, as an invitation into the forest or desert after the ascent of the mountain but on the way back to the homeland of one's own life. With specific reference to theology, we might say that, just as Lonergan could frame his new context for theology only after having come to understand what it is to understand, so the significance of depth psychology for theology is progressively discovered only as one learns to cultivate soul with its aid and to surrender both spirit and soul in an embrace of the earth which is simultaneously the prayerful acknowledgment of one's creaturehood and the agreement to return to the homeland and live among one's fellows once again.

178
   Ibid., p. 30.

179
   Gilbert Durand, op. cit., p. 87.

CHAPTER II

SECOND IMMEDIACY

In the following four chapters, I wish to articulate appropriate methodological categories for understanding the process of
psychic self-appropriation within the context of Lonergan's analysis
of the existential subject. I begin, then, with a discussion of
immediacy.

Primordial Immediacy and Second Immediacy

The key to method is the subject-as-subject. Method, as we
have seen, calls for "a release from all logics, all closed systems
or language games, all concepts, all symbolic constructs to allow an
abiding at the level of the presence of the subject to himself."[1]
Method is the objectification of the transcendental infrastructure
of the subject-as-subject. Let us call this infrastructure the
primordial immediacy of the human subject.

The fact that an adult's world is mediated by meaning renders
that world different from the infant's world of immediacy. But the
adult for all that is not deprived of an immediacy to this world
mediated by meaning. If he were, the statement of Lonergan's which
I have chosen as crucial to my present analysis would lose all significance: "Besides the immediate world of the infant and the adult's

---

[1]
Frederick Lawrence, "Self-Knowledge in History in Gadamer
and Lonergan," p. 203.

world mediated by meaning, there is the mediation of immediacy by
meaning when one objectifies cognitional process in transcendental
method and when one discovers, identifies, accepts one's submerged
feelings in psychotherapy."[2] Surely neither the immediacy mediated
by cognitional theory nor that brought to articulate utterance in
psychotherapy is that of the infant. In either case we are dealing
with the immediacy of one for whom the world is mediated by acts of
understanding, affirmation or denial, and evaluation, with the primordial immediacy of a human subject, with the infrastructure of
human subjectivity. This primordial immediacy is coextensive with
the experience which underlies all understanding, judging, deciding
and acting. The basic structure of this primordial immediacy is
disengaged in Lonergan's intentionality analysis, in his articulation of the dynamic structure of conscious intentionality. This
articulation is method. Method, then, is more than the objectification of cognitional process, for the subject is not only a knowing
subject but also an existential subject.

The emergence of a distinct notion of the good in Method in
Theology locates for us the point of insertion of the second
mediation of immediacy--that which occurs in psychotherapy--within
the total context provided by method.[3] For the primordial apprehension of the good occurs in feelings, and feelings are symbolically

---

2
Bernard Lonergan, Method in Theology, p. 77.

3
This is not to assert that all in search of psychotherapy
are methodologists! Rather, method is what enables us to understand
what psychotherapy is all about.

certifiable. Thus we may understand the process of psychic self-appropriation as facilitating the emergence of a capacity on the part of the existential subject to disengage the symbolic constitution of the feelings in which both values and satisfactions are apprehended, and from this disengagement to gauge the measure of self-transcendence operative in his affective orientation as Being-in-the-world. Method thus includes psychic self-appropriation; it provides room for a critically mediated symbolic consciousness. To borrow a metaphor from Lonergan, in his own writings, the room may not yet be very well furnished. But it is there, and it is my intention to phrase a methodological understanding of the process of furnishing it. The details of the arrangement of the furniture and the appointments of the room can be provided only in a phenomenology of the psyche. But the understanding of the process as a constituent feature of method is possible without going into the business of interior decorating.

The subject-as-subject is one. His unity is a function of the transcendental infrastructure of human subjectivity which I have called primordial immediacy. It is the unity that in the eleventh chapter of _Insight_ is called "the unity of consciousness" and that there is dealt with in relation to knowing.

> Conscious acts are not so many isolated, random atoms of knowing, but many acts coalesce into a single knowing. Not only is there a similarity between my seeing and your hearing, inasmuch as both acts are conscious; there also is an identity involved when my seeing and my hearing or your seeing and your hearing are compared. Moreover, this identity extends all along the line. Not only is the percept inquired about, understood, formulated, reflected on, grasped as unconditioned, and affirmed, but also there is an identity involved in perceiving, inquiring, understanding, formulating, reflecting, grasping the unconditioned,

and affirming. Indeed, consciousness is much more obviously of this unity in diverse acts than of the diverse acts, for it is within the unity that the acts are found and distinguished, and it is to the unity that we appeal when we talk about a single field of consciousness and draw a distinction between conscious acts occurring within the field and unconscious acts occurring outside it.[4]

This unity is not a postulate but a given.[5] With the emergence of a distinct notion of the good, it is made a more embracing unity, the unity of "a single transcendental intending of plural, interchangeable objectives"[6] including the intelligible, the true, and the good. The unity is provided by a process of sublation which retains lower levels but completes them by higher levels in a relationship of functional interdependence. Primordial immediacy, as identical with the transcendental infrastructure of the subject-as-subject, is thus unified, and this unity not only is what enables Lonergan to speak of distinct but related levels of consciousness, but is also what will shortly enable us to ground a differentiation of primordial immediacy into its cognitive and dispositional aspects without separating these dimensions from one another. That both knowing and feeling are sublated in the intention of value indicates that they join in a functional unity-in-differentiation.

In addition to this primordial immediacy, I wish to speak of second immediacy. I borrow the term from Paul Ricoeur's study of

---

4
Bernard Lonergan, Insight, p. 325.

5
Ibid., pp. 326-328.

6
Bernard Lonergan, The Subject, p. 22.

Sigmund Freud, but its meaning in my thought, while inclusive of
Ricoeur's meaning, is, I believe, more far-reaching. Second immediacy is the result of method's objectification of primordial immediacy. It is the self-possession of the subject-as-subject achieved
in the mediation of the transcendental infrastructure of human subjectivity, in the objectification of the single transcendental
intending of the intelligible, the true, and the good, in the self-
appropriation of the cognitional and existential subject which is
the fulfilment of the anthropologische Wendung of modern philosophy.[7]
Second immediacy is the probably always asymptotic recovery of primordial immediacy through method.

Ricoeur's notion of second immediacy, however, is not alien
to my own. In Ricoeur's philosophy, second immediacy is a particular
quality of awareness and speech, a second naiveté intended in
Ricoeur's entire philosophical project, a hoped-for conclusion of the
quest for wisdom, a desired unity of intentionality and psychic
energy in kerygmatic listening and speaking. Thus it has to do with
what I am calling a transcendental aesthetic, with Ricoeur's poetics
of the will, with a "transformation of intentionality into kerygma,
manifestation, proclamation."[8] Ricoeur's notion of second immediacy

---

7
"Philosophy finds its proper data in intentional consciousness. Its primary function is to promote the self-appropriation
that cuts to the root of philosophic differences and incomprehensions.
It has further, secondary functions in distinguishing, relating,
grounding the several realms of meaning and, no less, in grounding
the methods of the sciences and so promoting their unification."
Bernard Lonergan, Method in Theology, p. 95.

8
Paul Ricoeur, Freud and Philosophy, p. 30.

is directly relevant to the psychic complement to the self-appropriation of the existential subject which I am here proposing. But the second immediacy of critical (or post-critical) symbolic consciousness is a portion of the second immediacy that is the fruit of the mediation of primordial immediacy in transcendental method, and it is the latter that provides us with a correct apprehension of the point of insertion of the former in the self-appropriation of the existential subject. We shall devote considerable space to Ricoeur in the next chapter. For the moment, I wish simply to indicate that I have no quarrel whatsoever with his notion of second immediacy, but that I understand it within the context of a more inclusive notion of second immediacy.

I have a suspicion, moreover, that what I am calling primordial immediacy is what Martin Heidegger calls Dasein. I cannot verify this suspicion at this point through a textual analysis of Heidegger's many and difficult writings. Let it suffice, then, to indicate that in Being and Time, Heidegger speaks of two interlocking and equiprimordial constitutive ways of being the "there:" Verstehen and Befindlichkeit.[9] Let us link this assertion with Lonergan's statement that "there is the mediation of immediacy by meaning when one objectifies cognitional process in transcendental method and when one discovers, identifies, accepts one's submerged

---

[9]
Martin Heidegger, Being and Time, translated by John Macquarrie and Edward Robinson (New York: Harper and Row, 1962), pp. 171f.

feelings in psychotherapy."[10] From the suspicion, the link, and the understanding of Lonergan articulated in my first chapter, I am led to claim that the primordial immediacy that is _Dasein_ is mediated in two manners: through intentionality analysis and through psychic analysis. The result of the full mediation would be a second immediacy, achieved in self-appropriation, through which the interlocking constitutive features of primordial immediacy are mediated to the subject in search of authenticity in his knowing, his doing, and his religion. Intentionality analysis or method provides the overall context for it is concerned with the totality of the subject as knowing and doing. The subject as knowing is mediated, to my satisfaction at least, by Lonergan. The mediation of the subject as doing, as existential subject, however, could profit from further refinement. I do not question the structure already provided by Lonergan. But to a large extent, psychic self-appropriation is what will furnish the room, through the emergence of a consciousness familiar with the symbols and images which constitute the feelings in which the existential subject experiences the primordial apprehension of values. Method as intentionality analysis articulates the overall dynamic: the appropriation or recovery of primordial immediacy. Psychotherapy, then, will be one of the ways of appropriating the dispositional aspect of primordial immediacy. It can aid the emergence of the existential subject by mediating a capacity to disengage the symbolic or imaginal

---

10
Bernard Lonergan, _Method in Theology_, p. 77.

constitution of the feelings in which values are apprehended. Primordial immediacy is the pure question which is the transcendental infrastructure of the subject-as-subject. This pure question is variously differentiated, and one of these variants, the one granted primacy in Lonergan's later writings, is the question which makes the subject an existential subject. The primordial apprehensions which generate the emergence of the question-as-existential occur in feelings. Feelings are symbolically certifiable. The psychic, then, is a constitutive feature of the subject as existential, as moral and religious. Perhaps the finality of the psychotherapeutic movement, then, will some day come to be understood as the fuller emergence of the subject as originative value, as free and responsible constitutive agent of the human world.

Dispositional Immediacy

Lonergan's statement about the two mediations of immediacy and Heidegger's assertion of two equiprimordial constitutive ways of being the "there," Verstehen and Befindlichkeit, lead me to suggest that primordial immediacy can be differentiated into cognitional and dispositional aspects. I focus on its dispositional aspect, for it is primarily this that is brought to objectification in the psychic moment of method which is my concern.

Eugene Gendlin, in his very clearly written book, Experiencing and the Creation of Meaning, refers to this dispositional aspect of immediacy as "experiencing," and describes it as follows:

> It is something so simple, so easily available to every person, that at first its very simplicity makes it hard to point to.

Another term for it is "felt meaning," or "feeling." However, "feeling" is a word usually used for specific contents--for this or that feeling, emotion, or tone, for feeling good, or bad, or blue, or pretty fair. But regardless of the many changes in what we feel--that is to say, really, how we feel-- there always is the concretely present flow of feeling. At any moment we can individually and privately direct our attention inward, and when we do that, there it is. Of course we have this or that specific idea, wish, emotion, perception, word, or thought, but we always have concrete feeling, an in- ward sensing whose nature is broader. It is a concrete mass in the sense that it is "there" for us. It is not at all vague in its being there. It may be vague only in that we may not know what it is. We can put only a few aspects of it into words. The mass itself is always something there, no matter what we say it "is." Our definitions, our knowing "what it is," are symbols that specify aspects of it, "parts" of it, as we say. Whether we name it, divide it, or not, there it is.11

Its importance is further highlighted in a manner more appro-

priate to a discussion of the existential subject:

For the sake of (this or that aspect of) experiencing mankind can do all they do in a lifespan. Within experiencing lie the mysteries of all that we are. For the sake of our experi- ential sense of what we observe, we react as we do. From out of it we create what we create. And, because of its puzzles, and for the desperation of some of its puzzles, we overthrow good sense, obviousness, and reality, if need be. . . . If our direct touch with our own personally important experien- cing becomes too clouded, narrowed, or lost, we go to any length to regain it; we go to a friend, to a therapist, or to the desert. For nothing is as debilitating as a confused or distant functioning of experiencing. And the chief malaise of our society is perhaps that it allows so little pause and gives so little specifying response and interpersonal com- munion to our experiencing, so that we must much of the time pretend that we are only what we seem externally, and that our meanings are only the objective references and the logical meanings of our words.12

We are concerned, then, with this ever-present flow of mood,

now quiet, now turbulent, now easily designated, now undifferentiated,

---

11
    Eugene Gendlin, Experiencing and the Creation of Meaning, p. 11.

12
    Ibid., pp. 15f.

which accompanies every act of attending, seeing, tasting,
hearing, conversing, questioning, understanding, reflecting, affirming, denying, deliberating, deciding, being attracted or repelled,
meditating, praying, fleeing meditation, seeking distraction,
drifting creatively, drifting in dissipation, falling in love,
falling out of love, being active, being passive. If we attend sufficiently to the function of this flow of feeling, however, we shall
discover that it not only accompanies these acts, but qualifies
them, gives them a style, renders them aesthetically meaningful or
gross, and even determines whether they take place or not. Thus, for
example, the various biases discussed by Lonergan,[13] which interfere
with intelligent and reasonable inquiry and shortcircuit it, are not
simply a matter of a deficiency of understanding, but are radically
associated with the dynamics of the flow of mood. Moreover, the
inner flow of feeling accompanies, qualifies, and organizes in a
specific way not only our perception and dealings with the outer data
of sense, but also and more radically our awareness of ourselves, our
presence to the data of consciousness, and especially our constitution
of ourselves as subjects through whose capacity for meaning and language the world is both mediated and constituted.

Psychotherapeutic investigations have sharpened our sensitivity to the centrality of the flow of feeling in the constitution of
human life. What psychotherapists have all too frequently declined to
admit, however, is that the domain of their discovery has also been

---

[13]
Bernard Lonergan, Insight, Chapter 7.

dealt with and addressed profoundly and with deep respect and awe since time immemorial by such figures as Lao-Tzu, Gotama, and Jesus. Psychotherapy needs humbly to admit the continuity of its concern with the scriptures of the great world religions, or the resources discovered by psychological investigations will not be integrated into the spiritual quest for wisdom and truth which is, I believe, the genuine finality of psychotherapeutic insight. The propriety and worth of this integration pertain also to what I am here proposing and to what I wish to study in depth in a work on Jung and the phenomenology of the psyche. Not only were the original discoveries of Freudian analysis accompanied by a number of questionable theories, but the potential spiritual finality of these discoveries has yet to be consistently defended against the temptations of an egalitarian professionalism perhaps best understood in terms of group bias.[14] I believe one very plausible

---

14
        The refusal to deal with the possibility of such an integration is the most serious shortcoming in James Hillman's otherwise very good book, The Myth of Analysis. The book is probably the most consistent and honest endeavor at professional self-relativization to date within the Jungian circle. Hillman's concern is to articulate the appropriate myth according to which psychoanalysts, at least of the Jungian variety, can understand themselves. The myth of Psyche and Amor, a myth of "soul-making," is found by Hillman to be appropriate. With all of this, I have no quarrel; far from it, I believe the profession of analytic work needs this sort of relativizing treatment. Where I would differ from Hillman is over his insistence that soul-making and spiritual direction are two quite separate processes. Thus he finds the images of both healing and enlightenment unsatisfactory as articulations of the analyst's self-understanding. ". . . our tradition is only partly represented by the medical pattern of our forebears--Galen, Mesmer, Pinel, Charcot. . . . So, too, the spiritual-director models of guru, rabbi, of Ignatius or Fenelon, of Zen master, are only substitutions on which we lean for want of surety about the true model

dialectical interpretation of the career of Carl Jung, for example, could be delivered by viewing his cumulative researches and reflections as a kind of reparation for the extravagances of the initial enthusiasm which limited the horizon within which he viewed the human significance of the psychoanalytic revolution--even as a kind of sustained reaching, ever ambivalent, for the religious significance of the breakthrough. This significance might be stated very succinctly by postulating that the unappropriated functioning of the ever-present flow of mood is the root, not only of the neurotic guilt and neurotic anxiety which render so difficult even the first steps in psychic self-appropriation, but also of the less neurotic but thus also perhaps more necessary fears and desires,-- e.g., the fear of living and the fear of dying--which prevent the emergence into spiritual freedom counseled by Lao-Tzu, Gotama,

---

for psychology. Because the psyche is hidden in illness or in ignorance, it must be healed or taught. So one is played by these other roles, based on other models. But one is played by the opus itself into these other roles for the purpose of reaching that fundamental aim, which is neither healing nor teaching but the awakening or engendering of soul." Ibid., p. 21.

Surely I do not wish to propose an undifferentiated unity of role for the analyst and the spiritual director. But I do maintain that method enables a unity-in-differentiation. Both psychotherapy and spiritual direction have to do with the appropriation of dispositional immediacy and with the advance to second immediacy. While I have long been convinced that spiritual direction ought to profit from the best insights of depth psychology, my experience at the C. G. Jung Institute in Zürich has convinced me also that Jungian analysis not informed by and related to the insights of the spiritual traditions of the various world religions is proceeding blindly and headlong for the romantic agony. We may understand the romantic agony, I believe, as a capitulation of intentionality to the rhythms and processes of the psyche. Its clearest expression is in the attempt to integrate evil psychically in a manner analogous to Hegel's attempt to integrate it speculatively. Some current variants of Jungian analysis are not immune to this charge.

Confucius, and Jesus.

I choose to speak of dispositional immediacy or, with Heidegger, of Befindlichkeit, as a way of referring to that which is recovered in the second mediation of immediacy by meaning. In the remainder of this work, I shall use this term, rather than "feeling," as my central referent. My main reason for this choice is that the principal psychologist whose work I am interested in is Jung, and Jung has a very definite meaning for the word "feeling," a meaning which by no means covers all that is dealt with in this mediation, but refers rather to a particular function of personality, dominant in some people, recessive in others.[15] But I believe it is fair to say that Jungian psychotherapy, as all psychotherapy, is concerned primarily with the mediation of the dispositional aspect of primordial immediacy.

In itself, then, dispositional immediacy is something very easy to designate. It is a matter of one's mood. It is what we inquire about when we sincerely ask another, "How are you?" This heuristic definition is, I believe, quite clear. In such a question we are not usually inquiring about another's latest ideas or insights, the progress or hesitation of his ongoing project, or even about the state of his physical health. Any or all of these may be somehow connected with his answer, but the question intends something else, a peculiar quality of being, of being here and now, of being the person one is. "How do you find yourself?"

---

[15] See C. G. Jung, Psychological Types, Collected Works, Vol. 6 (Princeton: Bollingen Series XX, 1971).

Now, no matter what type of personality one is--and typo-
logies are legion and, Jung's included, purely descriptive and not
explanatory--, no matter whether one is, in Jung's scheme, a sensation type, an intuitive type, a feeling type, a thinking type, an
extravert or an introvert, this question, when one finds oneself
addressed by it, may be the most baffling of all questions. One may
indeed find or suspect that he or she is completely incapable of
answering it. Generally, anything but this puzzlement is what is
reflected in one's answer, which is apt to be something as banal as
"Fine." If one has adverted to the puzzlement, however, one is a
step ahead of an unknowingly banal answer. Such advertence can be
the first step in leading one to seek help. It is the awareness
that one is, in one's self-conscious being, out of touch with something rather important and, for all its seeming simplicity, very
deep and mysterious. For reasons I will explain later, I prefer to
describe this with Lonergan as an incommensurability of objectified
and differentiated consciousness with the undifferentiated or nonobjectified, of the self as objectified with the self as conscious,
rather than as a split between consciousness and the "unconscious."[16]
The latter term has been used in very misleading ways. At any rate,
what one is out of touch with is the dispositional aspect of one's
primordial immediacy. One does not know how one is, but has at
least begun to advert to the fact of one's unknowing and secretly
to admit it to oneself. The process of the mediation of

---

[16]
Bernard Lonergan, Method in Theology, p. 34.

dispositional immediacy by meaning in psychotherapy begins with this secret admission of confusion, of being out of touch, of not knowing how one is, who one is.

The notion of an appropriated dispositional immediacy, on the other hand--a notion central to Ricoeur's study and critique of Freud--defines in a rather precise manner the achievement of the mediation of the dispositional aspect of immediacy by meaning which is our present concern. We shall later have to examine in some detail Ricoeur's understanding of this appropriation. At the moment, I wish only to indicate that I share Ricoeur's problematic of attempting to pave the way for an intelligent mediation of dispositional immediacy on the part of the man of modernity, of the man who has concerned himself with the modes of the mediation of immediacy and with their interrelations, but perhaps at the expense of a certain fullness of immediacy. The critical mentality of post-Kantian philosophy, the introduction of various critical techniques into every area of sustained inquiry, have rendered us "sicklied o'er with the pale cast of thought." Is there a way for us to return, not simply in spite of, but through the instruction of, the critique of naive consciousness, to the fullness of speech simply heard and understood? This is Ricoeur's question and it is also mine.[17] What would be the structure of such a recovery, of such a restoration?

---

[17]
Ricoeur shares a concern with the "new hermeneutic" of Gerhard Ebeling and Ernst Fuchs, in that he confronts the question of hermeneutic from the standpoint, first, of hearing the language anew in which meaning was first expressed. But he has significantly

Our first chapter has, I trust, made clear that I regard the crucial critique of naive consciousness to be that of Lonergan. This critique can be employed in understanding the mediation of dispositional immediacy which occurs in psychotherapy. It can also be used to help us sublate this mediation into the movement of method. Appropriated dispositional immediacy is not dependent on an appropriated cognitional immediacy, on the affirmation of the correct positions on knowing, being, and objectivity, for successful psychotherapy obviously occurs independently of whether the analysand or the analyst have read Insight! But the appropriation of dispositional immediacy also can figure as a part of method, as a feature in the existential subject's self-appropriation as heeding the methodical exigence. It is not achieved by attaining the correct positions on knowing, being, and objectivity, nor even, it would seem, by remaining consistently faithful to these positions. But these positions are indispensable in understanding it correctly. Intentionality analysis can even aid its effectiveness, in that the appropriation of dispositional immediacy stands the best chance of being successful if it is self-consciously attentive, intelligent,

---

advanced the hermeneutic discussion, I believe, by correlating interpretation with symbolic or double-meaning linguistic expressions, with language which is overdetermined. For such a correlation, coupled with the internal variance within the hermeneutic field between the hermeneutic of recovery and that of suspicion, is explanatory of the contemporary failure of the language of faith bemoaned by the adherents of the new hermeneutic. Precisely because of this correlation, hermeneutic has become dialectical. The restoration of post-critical man to a fullness of immediacy occurs only through a resolution of this dialectic. We shall in the next chapter present a more detailed analysis of Ricoeur's notions of symbol and hermeneutic, while introducing our own qualifications on the therapeutic nature of the dialectic involved in the process Ricoeur proposes.

reasonable, and responsible. While the appropriation is of the hitherto undifferentiated, its agent is consciousness, and the better differentiated the agent, the more accurate and complete is its agency.

Perhaps we may say, then, that a mediation of primordial immediacy in its fullness involves appropriating oneself as a question for intelligibility and truth by raising and answering what we may call the critical questions: What am I doing when I am knowing? Why is that knowing? What do I know when I do that?; appropriating oneself as a question for value by attending to one's constitutive responsibility for the human world; and appropriating the playground of one's desires and fears which is one's own imagination. There is obviously successful psychotherapy within a less comprehensive context. There is also authentic moral and religious subjectivity without psychotherapy. Authentic religion, moreover, surely has something to do with an exhortation of Jesus to men and women who were far from post-critical: "Therefore do not be anxious about tomorrow, for tomorrow will be anxious for itself. Let the day's own evil be sufficient for the day" (Matt. 6.34). But the mediation of primordial immediacy in its fullness involves the discrimination of spirit or intentionality, the cultivation of soul or psyche, and the surrender of both spirit and soul to the action of God's love in the world. Second immediacy would be enjoyed by one who has labored to achieve a self-conscious integration of intentionality and psyche or who has learned to live attentively, intelligently, reasonably, responsibly, lovingly, with their customary duality and tension. For perhaps their full integration occurs only in the "mediated return to immediacy in the mating of lovers and in the prayerful mystic's cloud of unknowing."[18]

---

[18] Bernard Lonergan, _Method in Theology_, p. 77.

CHAPTER III

SYMBOLS

Any human subject whose world is mediated and constituted
by meaning is primordially in a condition of cognitional and dispositional immediacy to that world. Second immediacy is the recovery
of this infrastructure in method. One way of recovering the dispositional aspect of primordial immediacy is through psychotherapy.
This dimension of immediacy is accessible to conscious intentionality
by the latter's focusing on the ever-present flow of mood which is
constitutive of one's concomitant awareness of himself in all of
his intentional operations. "In every case Dasein always has some
mood."[1] Primordial immediacy is immediacy to one's mediated world.
Its dispositional mode is an immediacy of feeling, of mood, of "how
one is," of how one finds oneself. It is what we intend when we ask
another, "How are you?" "The mood has already disclosed, in every
case, Being-in-the-world as a whole, and makes it possible first of
all to direct oneself towards something."[2] We are concerned, then,
with a state of immediacy of feeling or of mood, and with its mediation.
The mediation occurs in the objectification which takes place in

_____

[1]
Martin Heidegger, Being and Time, p. 173.

[2]
Ibid., p. 176.

132

psychotherapy.

Disposition and Symbol

In Chapter One, we saw the connection established by Lonergan between dispositional immediacy and the symbol. To repeat, a symbol is "an image of a real or imaginary object that evokes a feeling or is evoked by a feeling."[3] These symbolic images provide one of the ways of ascertaining both individual uniqueness in dispositional response to objects and individual affective development or aberration and deviation. Symbols function in aid of internal communication on the part of the existential subject; they provide a disclosure of organic and psychic vitality to intentional consciousness and an instrument whereby the latter can secure the collaboration of organism and psyche in the existential subject's participation in the constitution of the human world.

In dependence on Lonergan's analysis, then, I wish to suggest that the dispositional aspect of immediacy is imaginally constructed, symbolically constituted. Our dispositional immediacy to the world mediated and constituted by meaning is structured by imagination, by the playground of our desires and fears. Thus the subject in his immediacy can be understood archetypally.

But this imaginal constitution or archetypal determination is often not accessible to conscious intentionality in the same way as is the disposition itself. It often cannot be discovered simply by a heightened attentiveness to the ever-present flow of mood, but

---

3

Bernard Lonergan, Method in Theology, p. 64.

must be disengaged by specific techniques of psychological analysis.
When one is out of touch with dispositional immediacy, these techniques of symbolic disengagement may be needed to enable one's dispositional immediacy to be objectified, appropriated, known. When
so disengaged, symbols not only reveal "how it stands" between the
explicit articulate self-understanding of the existential subject
and a larger totality, between the self as objectified and the self
as conscious, but also enable one's self-understanding to approximate one's reality. If one is out of touch with how one is, with
who one is, one needs to disengage the imaginal constitution of
this larger totality. One cannot tell the story of one's own being
as existential subject, but the story inevitably goes forward all
the same. Psychic self-appropriation is a matter of gaining the
capacity to articulate this story correctly and to guide it responsibly. It frequently involves a reversal of a cumulative misinterpre-
tation of experience. Everyone tells his own story, but not all can
tell it as it is.

I hazard that the most effective techniques yet developed
for disengaging the story of felt meaning are the Jungian procedures
of dream interpretation and active imagination and an associated
process developed by Ira Progoff known as "twilight imaging."[4] In
this chapter, though, rather than detailing these techniques, I wish
to call attention to the realm or dimension of human subjectivity whose

---

4
   On twilight imaging, see Ira Progoff, The Symbolic and the
Real (New York: McGraw-Hill Paperbacks, 1973); on active imagi-
nation, see Rix Weaver, The Old Wise Woman (New York: C. G. Jung
Foundation, 1973).

articulation and appropriation constitutes in large part the mediation of dispositional immediacy. This dimension is referred to by Paul Ricoeur as the "mytho-poetic core of imagination,"[5] which gives rise to the spontaneous elemental symbols which in fact constitute and reflect for each individual the structure of <u>Befindlichkeit</u>.

While I believe that the finest philosophical study of symbolism to date is probably that of Ricoeur,[6] I have serious reservations as to whether philosophical reflection as understood by Ricoeur can sufficiently penetrate to the creative spontaneity which renders possible individual uniqueness in symbolic response, and thus as to whether Ricoeur does not overvalue the capacity of reflective philosophy to achieve, on the basis of its own resources, an appropriation of the symbolic dimension. Ricoeur is quite insistent that philosophy, in the interests of the self-appropriation of the depths of the reflective subject, must become a hermeneutic of the symbolic contingencies of cultures. More radically, I will maintain that there is an individual core of spontaneous elemental imagination which is to be recovered by intelligent, reasonable, existential subjectivity in the interests of self-appropriation, and that this recovery is not achieved in a philosophical hermeneutic of cultural objectifications

---

[5] Paul Ricoeur, <u>Freud and Philosophy</u>, p. 35.

[6] I have yet to do a detailed study of Ernst Cassirer's philosophy of symbol. For Ricoeur, Cassirer makes the notion of symbol too extensive, so much so that it includes expressions which are not overdetermined, whose meaning is both obvious and univocal. This is certainly what would be expected in one whose inspiration is a Kantian-based conceptualism.

but in an existential, evaluative, dialectical hermeneutic of one's dreams, of one's own most radical individual spontaneity. It is this recovery which both moves psyche into the thrust of intentionality and provides one with the symbolic foundations for engaging in a hermeneutic of culture and religion.

Nonetheless, for four reasons I feel justified in detailing at some length Ricoeur's achievement in his study of Freud. First, Ricoeur has displayed the need of self-appropriation to have recourse to the interpretation of concrete symbols. Secondly, I find myself ever more impressed with the suggestiveness of his analysis of the dialectical structure of symbolic process. Thirdly, through Ricoeur's analysis we are introduced in superb fashion to Freud, whose work must figure in our understanding of the psychic self-appropriation of the existential subject. Fourthly, I can most expeditiously present my own philosophy of the symbol by indicating where I agree with Ricoeur and where I wish greater precision.

The Tension of the Symbol

The Hermeneutic Conflict

Ricoeur's philosophical project is surely among the most ambitious and sophisticated intellectual endeavors of our century. His treatment of cultural and religious symbolism figures as a part of a vast philosophical undertaking concerned with delineating the essential structures, limits, and possibilities of human existence. Ricoeur has moved from the structural phenomenological analysis of his earlier works[7] to a concrete hermeneutic phenomenology of symbols[8] because of a conviction that the self which it is philosophy's task to recover is not a datum for naive immediacy but can be retrieved only by a detour through the non-self. The _Sum_ of the _Cogito_ "has to be 'mediated' by the ideas, actions, works, institutions, and monuments that objectify it."[9] "I must recover something which has first been lost; I make 'proper to me' what has ceased being mine. I make 'mine' what I am separated from by space or time, by distraction or 'diversion,' or because of some culpable forgetfulness. . . . I do not at

---

7
        Paul Ricoeur, _Freedom and Nature: The Voluntary and the Involuntary_, translated by Erazim Kohak (Evanston: Northwestern University Press, 1966) and _Fallible Man_, translated by Charles Kelbley (Chicago: Henry Regnery, 1965).

8
        The beginnings of this turn are reflected in Ricoeur, _The Symbolism of Evil_, translated by Emerson Buchanan (Boston: The Beacon Press, 1969). _Freedom and Nature_ is the first volume of a projected three-volume philosophy of the will. The second volume is to contain three parts, the first two of which are _Fallible Man_ and _The Symbolism of Evil_. _Freedom and Nature_ is referred to by Ricoeur as an eidetics of the will, employing the method of pure description in order to reveal in the abstract man's fundamental possibilities. Two important factors are omitted from the eidetics, fault and transcendence. _Fallible Man_ and _The Symbolism of Evil_ consider the domain of fault, the first from the standpoint of investigating that in man which permits fault to arise, the second by investigating hermeneutically the "language of avowal," in which man confesses his fault. The projected third part of this second volume would deal with transcendence, and the third volume is a projected poetics of the will. _Freud and Philosophy_, while not part of the philosophy of the will volumes, sharpens the hermeneutic tools first employed in _The Symbolism of Evil_. See Kelbley's "Translator's Introduction," _Fallible Man_, pp. ix-xv, and Don Ihde, _Hermeneutic Phenomenology: The Philosophy of Paul Ricoeur_ (Evanston: Northwestern, 1971), p. 181.

9
        Paul Ricoeur, _Freud and Philosophy_, p. 43.

first possess what I am."[10] Philosophical reflection is to recover
the I am through reflection on the works of man. The I am as such
is not given as an immediate datum of experience. Knowledge of it
occurs only through a displacement of the home of meaning away from
immediate consciousness, a displacement which for Ricoeur means an
understanding of man's objectifications in knowledge, action, and
culture. Phenomenology becomes hermeneutic when it becomes a matter
of understanding man's experience by understanding his expressions.

The meaning of these objectifications or works, however, is
neither immediately evident nor univocal. Man's self-expressions
are capable of being variously interpreted. A privileged instance
of this susceptibility to different interpretations is found in
man's language. Ricoeur designates the realm of equivocal or
plurivocal linguistic expressions as the domain of symbolism and
correlates its exploration with the task of hermeneutic or interpretation. "I have decided to define, i.e., limit, the notions of
symbol and interpretation through one another. Thus a symbol is a
double-meaning linguistic expression that requires an interpretation,
and interpretation is a work of understanding that aims at
deciphering symbols."[11]

10
   Ibid., p. 45.

11
   Ibid., p. 9.

The symbolic function consists in the designation of something other than what is said, through what is said.[12] "Symbols occur when language produces signs of composite degree in which the meaning, not satisfied with designating some one thing, designates another meaning attainable only in and through the first intentionality."[13] Symbolism is peculiar to and dependent upon man's language. Its power may be rooted in the expressiveness of the cosmos, in the _vouloir-dire_ of human desire, and in man's imagination, yet, for Ricoeur, it appears as such in language. "There is no symbolism prior to man who speaks."[14] It is the perhaps interminable task of interpretation to reveal the richness and over-determination of symbols and to demonstrate that symbols have a role to play in human discourse.

The manifest meaning of a symbol, according to one style of interpretation, points beyond itself to a second, latent meaning or to a series of such meanings, by a type of analogy which cannot be dominated intellectually. The symbol is rather a movement which we can follow, a movement of the primary meaning intentionally assimilating us to the symbolized.[15]

---

[12] "To mean something other than what is said--this is the symbolic function." _Ibid._, p. 12.

[13] _Ibid._, p. 16.

[14] _Ibid._

[15] _Ibid._, p. 17.

Such is the operative notion of symbol in the phenomenology
of religion. The symbols of any of the great religions of the world
enable the historian to be drawn toward that religion's conception of
the sacred and its relation to man. Much of the work of a scholar
such as Mircea Eliade is a matter of moving with the symbols and
being drawn by them to a universe structured in a particular way and
to a god or gods relating in a certain manner to man's world as he
experiences it. Thus, for example, the predominance of certain symbolic indications enables Eliade to distinguish religions of the
"eternal return" from religions of historically oriented faith.[16]
The process of assimilation by which the primary meaning moves us,
draws us on, to a latent, symbolized meaning, is identified by
Ricoeur as "intentional analogy." Symbols are "the manifestation in
the sensible--in imagination, gestures, and feelings--of a further
reality, the expression of a depth which both shows and hides
itself."[17]

But such intentional analogy is not the only kind of relationship that can exist between manifest and latent meaning. The manifest
meaning may indeed be a pointer toward an analogous second meaning,
but it may also be a cunning distortion of latent meaning. In either
case, however, ". . . a symbol exists . . . where linguistic expression
lends itself by its double or multiple meanings to a work of

---

[16]
Mircea Eliade, Cosmos and History: The Myth of the Eternal
Return, translated by William R. Trask (New York: Harper and Row,
1959), Chapter 4.

[17]
Paul Ricoeur, Freud and Philosophy, p. 7.

interpretation." There are no symbols without the beginnings of interpretation. "Where one man dreams, prophecies, or poetizes, another rises up to interpret. Interpretation organically belongs to symbolic thought and its double meaning."[18]

The opposition of these two relationships between manifest and latent meaning gives rise to the problem of conflicting hermeneutical styles. Ricoeur dramatizes the conflict by highlighting the differences between the phenomenology of religion and the psychoanalysis of Sigmund Freud. For the latter, dreams, works of art, linguistic expressions, and cultural objectifications are the dissimulation of basic desire rather than manifestations of a further reality beyond themselves. They conceal an unsurpassable instinct and thus their interpretation takes the form of the reduction of the illusion effected in consciousness by their manifest meaning. These two different styles of interpretation, the hermeneutic of recovery and the hermeneutic of suspicion, while not constituting a complete enumeration of hermeneutical styles, represent the polar extremes in contemporary hermeneutic, and point to the key difficulty of hermeneutic, the absence of a universal canon of interpretation. The hermeneutic field is "internally at variance with itself."[19] For the suspicious pole, hermeneutic is a demystification, a reduction of illusion. For the hermeneutic of recovery, the task is a restoration

---

18
    Ibid., pp. 18f.

19
    Ibid., p. 27.

of meaning addressed to me as a message, a proclamation, a kerygma. We oscillate for the most part between demystification and recovery because we are the victims of a crisis of language peculiar to our age. Is the conflict of suspicion and recovery definitive, or is it provisional? Can we achieve a standpoint beyond it? The crisis gives rise to dialectic.

In The Symbolism of Evil, where Ricoeur begins his attempt to read man's experience by interpreting his symbolic expressions, the task is still phenomenological. The hermeneutic war is not yet the problem. But hermeneutic phenomenology is nonetheless a departure from what we might call structural phenomenology in that it involves a wager which shatters the descriptive neutrality of most phenomenological work. "I wager that I shall have a better understanding of man and the bond between the being of man and the being of all beings if I follow the indication of symbolic thought."[20] In Freud and Philosophy, the same wager is seen to qualify the phenomenology of religion, which is animated by an intention, a series of philosophical decisions which lie hidden even within its apparent neutrality, a rational faith which employs a phenomenological hermeneutic as an instrument of achieving the restoration of meaning. The implicit intention of hermeneutic phenomenology is "an expectancy of a new Word, of a new tidings of the Word."[21] Such interpretation, then, does not attempt to reach behind the symbols for underlying

---

[20] Paul Ricoeur, The Symbolism of Evil, p. 355.

[21] Paul Ricoeur, Freud and Philosophy, p. 31.

instinctual determinants but rather attempts to follow them forward, to follow their indications. "Symbols alone give what they say."[22]

Nevertheless hermeneutic phenomenology is not a matter of naive immediacy. To interpret symbols phenomenologically is to re-enact them in sympathetic imagination, not through an immediate belief but through the recovery of implicit intentionality. One would reenact a myth through an immediate belief if one were to accept it, with its original adherents, as explanatory or etiological. To reenact it by sympathetically immersing oneself in its intention-ality and following its indications, however, is to accept it as exploratory of man, his place in the cosmos, his destiny. The cos-mic significance which the symbol intends is not actually given in the symbol. If it were, the latter would cease to be a symbol. Symbols are intentions without fulfillments.

The phenomenology of religion may proceed either by analyzing the inherent structures of symbols and myths, or by relating them to one another in an evolutionary perspective or by relations of trans-position, of opposition and identity of intentionality. In either case, says Ricoeur, three philosophical decisions are featured.

First, the decision is made to accent the object of the phenomenological investigation. A hermeneutic of recovery is a rational faith characterized by care for the object. This care is inherited from a more neutral phenomenology, which wishes to describe and not to reduce. Thus the phenomenology of religion intends to

---

22
Ibid.

disengage the implicit object in myth, ritual, and belief rather than
to focus upon subjective or sociological motivations and determinants
of behavior. The task of the phenomenology of religion is "to dis-
implicate (the sacred) from the various intentions of behavior, discourse, and emotion."[23] Behind such concern, as we shall see, is the
expectation of being addressed by the sacred and the placing of an intrinsic confidence in human discourse, "the belief that language, which
bears symbols, is not so much spoken by men as spoken to men, that men
are born into language, into the light of the logos 'who enlightens
every man who comes into the world.'"[24]

Second, the hermeneutic of recovery is pervaded by a concern
for the truth or fullness of symbols. In symbols we meet the fullness
of language in the overdetermination of meaning. Here again the supposed neutrality of phenomenological research is broken, for one is
placed within a kind of hermeneutic circle of faith and understanding.

> I admit that what deeply motivates the interest in full language,
> in bound language, is this inversion of the movement of thought
> which now addresses itself to me and makes me a subject spoken
> to. And this inversion is produced in analogy. How? How does
> that which binds meaning to meaning bind me? The movement that
> draws me toward the second meaning assimilates me to what is said,
> makes me participate in what is announced to me. The similitude
> in which the force of symbols resides and from which they draw
> their revealing power is not an objective likeness, which I may
> look upon like a relation laid out before me; it is an existential
> assimilation, according to the movement of analogy, of my being
> to being.[25]

23
  Ibid., p. 29.

24
  Ibid., pp. 29f.

25
  Ibid., p. 31.

Thirdly, then, the intention of such phenomenology is that
one may "finally greet the revealing power of the primal word."[26]
The hermeneutic of recovery is characterized by something like the
Platonic theme of participation and reminiscence. "After the silence
and forgetfulness made widespread by the manipulation of empty signs
and the construction of formalized languages, the modern concern for
symbols expresses a new desire to be addressed."[27] The phenomenology
of religion functions as a propadeutic to the revelation of meaning.[28]

The opposed character of the hermeneutic of suspicion can be
understood in terms of these three decisions. This conflicting style
of interpretation reverses the three decisions made by the phenomeno-
logist of religion. The hermeneutic task, moreover, cannot remain at
a phenomenological level because of the mighty invasion of the hermeneutic of suspicion into modern thought. First, then, the focus of
concern is not the object of investigation itself, the expression,
but the underlying determinants of such expression. Secondly, the
latent meaning of symbolic expression is not to be discovered by
trusting in the fullness of language and thus following it forward,
but by moving back to the realm of unsurpassable instinctual desire
lying behind and determining the mendacious deliverances of consciousness. Thirdly, the intention of the phenomenology of religion to be

---

26
   Ibid., p. 32.

27
   Ibid., p. 31

28
   Ibid., p. 32.

spoken to anew by the primal Word is reversed when religion is described with Freud as the universal obsessional neurosis of mankind.
While this description is Freud's and Freud is but one representative
of the hermeneutic of suspicion, Ricoeur finds a common intention in
all of its representatives, "the decision to look upon the whole of
consciousness primarily as 'false' consciousness. They thereby take
up again . . . the problem of the Cartesian doubt, to carry it to
the very heart of the Cartesian stronghold. . . . After the doubt
about things, we have started to doubt consciousness."[29] This doubt
is the core of the hermeneutic of suspicion, the essence of the stamp
it has imprinted, perhaps indelibly, on modernity.

The Dialectic of the Symbol

In psychology, such doubt of naive consciousness is reflected
not only in the psychoanalysis of Freud but also in the very different
analytical psychology of Jung. And in philosophy not only does it
animate the thought of a Nietzsche but it is also central to Ricoeur's
notion of philosophical reflection. Thus perhaps, despite its radical
contrariety to any phenomenology of the sacred or to any hermeneutic
understood nondialectically as the recollection of meaning, its ultimate significance may be quite other, even with regard to religion,
than would appear from Freud or Nietzsche. The doubt of naive consciousness is carried to quite different religious conclusions by Jung
and Ricoeur. And the same doubt permeates Lonergan's clearing of a
previously undifferentiated structure of intentional consciousness in

---

[29]
Ibid., p. 33.

direct opposition to the philosophy he calls naive realism. So perhaps the philosopher's task is that of the dialectical resolution of the hermeneutic conflict. This is the task attempted by Ricoeur. In the course of executing it, he uncovers a notion of the symbol which should be operative in the mediation of psyche which we are here proposing and which was in fact operative in Jung's writings, though-- as unfortunately is the case with most of Jung--it was never articulated with sufficient philosophic rigor.

Ricoeur judges that a long-term dialectical view of this radical doubt of immediate consciousness would find it salvific for authentic religious belief. It has cleared the horizon for a more authentic word, "a new reign of Truth,"[30] the deidolization of religion. The way is open, too, for a mediate science of meaning, irreducible to the immediate consciousness of meaning.[31] Thus the hermeneutic of suspicion is, in the last analysis, no more a detractor of consciousness than is Ricoeur himself, or, we might add, Jung or Lonergan. Rather it aims at extending consciousness. Freud, for example, aims "to substitute for an immediate and dissimulating consciousness a mediate consciousness taught by the reality principle."[32] Nonetheless--as is dramatically evident in the differences between Freud and Jung--the controversy itself involves the fate of the

---

30
 Ibid.

31
 Ibid., pp. 33f.

32
 Ibid., p. 35.

"mytho-poetic core of imagination," the very condition of possibility for "the upsurge of the possible," for newness and creativity, and thus for the revelation of the primal Word. "Does not this discipline of the real, this ascesis of the necessary, lack the grace of imagination? . . . And does not the grace of imagination have something to do with the Word as Revelation?"[33]

Thus the importance of the conflict cannot be minimized. If, in fact, the hermeneutic war cannot be mediated, the thinker--be he philosopher, theologian, or psychologist--is left with a seemingly arbitrary option between these two styles, an option in its arbitrariness perhaps itself determined not by the exigencies of evidence and disinterested inquiry but by the instinctual determinants of one's own psychic makeup. If the war cannot be mediated, the odds would seem to lie with the hermeneutic of suspicion, since either option in itself would appear arbitrary and thus itself an expression of unsurpassable instinct. The thinker's task would then be iconoclastic, purely and simply. He would proceed to "purify discourse of its excrescences, liquidate the idols, go from drunkenness to sobriety, realize our state of poverty once and for all."[34]

If the conflict can be mediated, though, the hermeneutic of suspicion would remain, but this iconoclastic form of interpretation would be taken up into the task of recovery, which would then become, not a parallel task, exclusive of and opposed to that of demystification,

---

33
   Ibid., pp. 35f.

34
   Ibid., p. 27.

but inclusive of the latter. The thinker would then "use the most
'nihilistic,' destructive, iconoclastic movement so as to let speak
what once, what each time, was said, when meaning appeared anew, when
meaning was at its fullest."[35] The recovery of meaning would occur,
not through a mere phenomenology of symbol, as in the phenomenology
of religion, but by philosophical reflection in its fullest sense
and in reliance upon a process of rigorous dialectic which would
include extreme iconoclasm as a moment in the restoration of meaning.

Ricoeur favors the possibility of such a philosophic resolution of the hermeneutic conflict. The conflict can and must be
moved onto the level of philosophical reflection, which Ricoeur understands as "the appropriation of our effort to exist and of our desire
to be, through the works which bear witness to that effort and desire."[36]
As against Descartes, the Cogito ergo sum "remains as abstract and
empty as it is invincible,"[37] and as against Kant, epistemology is
only a part of the foundational concern of philosophy to recover the
act of existing, the Sum of the Cogito, in all the density of its
works. Philosophical reflection thus becomes the task of making my
concrete experience equal to the positing of the 'I am.'"[38] The
emergence of our effort to exist or our desire to be--the Sum of the

---

35
   Ibid.

36
   Ibid., p. 46.

37
   Ibid., p. 43.

38
   Ibid., p. 45. This task is identical to what we have called
the mediation of primordial immediacy through method.

Cogito--is, then, delivered to reflection only through works whose meaning remains doubtful and revocable, and through symbolic utterance in particular. Symbols and myths, while prephilosophical, are instructive and nourishing for philosophical reflection. They can be treated by a philosophical exegesis which regards them as exploratory pointers opening upon a world of meaning. Symbols call for philosophical reflection because through them attempts are made "to generalize human experience on the level of a universal concept or paradigm in which we can read our condition and history."[39] It is their paradigmatic quality which invites philosophical reflection. In myths, symbols confer "universality, temporality, and ontological import upon our self-understanding,"[40] for the myth is a second-order symbol which adds to primary symbols the temporal characteristics of narrative.[41] But, because the issue is one of conflict, of the concrete, the dynamic, and the contradictory, the reflection adequate to meeting it is neither phenomenological nor hermeneutical but dialectical. And as such it must resolve not only differences in standpoint and correlative content but also differences in underlying decisions in which one chooses one's standpoint, and it must prepare the subject for a further decision in which he chooses a more

---

39
 Ibid., pp. 38f.

40
 Ibid., p. 39.

41
 Paul Ricoeur, The Symbolism of Evil, p. 18.

inclusive standpoint.[42]   Whereas reflection must have recourse to
hermeneutic, the hermeneutic conflict must be arbitrated by a return
to an expanded, dialectical, reflective critique of interpretations,
which, although expanded, is also more concrete, penetrating as it
does more profoundly into the effort to exist and the desire to be
which reflection must appropriate through the expressions of man.
"To destroy the idols, to listen to symbols--are not these . . .
one and the same enterprise? Indeed, the profound unity of the demystifying and remythicizing of discourse can be seen only at the end
of an ascesis of reflection," in which "the dispossession of consciousness to the profit of another home of meaning" is "the first gesture
of reappropriation."[43]

And so Ricoeur moves to the task of integrating the discourse
of Freudian psychoanalysis, a leading instance of demystifying hermeneutic, into philosophical reflection, into the reappropriation of
the Sum of the Cogito. Freudian psychoanalysis provides Ricoeur with
an archeology of the subject. Thus the level on which Ricoeur proceeds
with his investigation is the same level as that on which we are encouraging the appropriation of psyche as a complement to the appropriation of logos effected by Lonergan in method. My insistence that
intentionality analysis sublate psychic analysis is parallel to Ricoeur's
insistence that philosophical reflection must become in part a

---

42
    This articulation of the dynamic of dialectic is Lonergan's,
but it surely expresses what Ricoeur is driving at. See Bernard
Lonergan, Method in Theology, pp. 128-30.

43
    Paul Ricoeur, Freud and Philosophy, pp. 54f.

hermeneutic and dialectic of symbols. The basic level for both
Ricoeur and myself is the level of transcendental reflection, of
the "movement of self-appropriation by self which constitutes reflective activity."[44] Ricoeur has correctly argued, I believe, that this
movement is not exhausted by its cognitional moment, which for Ricoeur
is represented by Kant, and for me by Lonergan. Symbols play an a
priori role in this movement of self-appropriation because of the
connection between reflection on the Sum of the Cogito and "the
signs scattered in the various cultures by that act of existing."[45]
Ricoeur goes so far as to say that this connection "opens up a new
field of experience, objectivity, and reality"[46]--the field I shall
later qualify as a genuine sphere of being and call the imaginal.
To this field a transcendental logic of double meaning is said to
pertain; this logic is disengaged by Ricoeur, at least in part, and
it will be operative in the appropriation of psyche to which the psychotherapeutic movement gives rise and must give way.

The Archeology of the Subject

On Ricoeur's analysis, then, Freudian psychology is motivated
by an intention to provide a critique of immediate consciousness, a

---

44
  Ibid., p. 52.

45
  Ibid.

46
  Ibid.

decentering of the home of significations, a displacement of the birth of meaning. Freud's psychological topography and economics make me completely homeless, forcing me to admit the inadequacy of immediate consciousness despite the apodictic and irrefutable character of the Cogito ergo sum. A twofold movement permeates Freudian discourse: a displacement of meaning away from consciousness toward unconscious process and a recapturing of meaning in interpretation. Even the apodictic, though empty, character of the Cogito ergo sum never figures as such in Freud's systematization; the ego functions only as an economic variable. Nevertheless, the movement of interpretation is a first step toward becoming conscious, in the sense of becoming equal to the authentic Cogito. This movement of interpretation is possible only because instincts, however unknowable and unapproachable, are designated in the psyche by ideas and affects that represent them. Thus there is a certain homogeneity between unconscious process and consciousness. The reality of the psychical representatives of instinct exists only for interpretation. "The reality of the unconscious . . . is relative to the operations that give it meaning."[47]

Philosophical reflection as self-appropriation, then, can speak of the emergence of desire, of the Sum at the heart of the Cogito, as giving rise to an archeology of the subject. To do so, it examines the Freudian economics, which becomes for philosophical interpretation not simply a model but a total view of things and of man in the world of things, a revelation of the archaic, a manifestation of

---

47
Ibid., p. 436.

the ever prior.

Thus, dreams and neuroses reveal "the unconscious" to be timeless in character and desire to be "unsurpassable." Such an archeology climaxes in the theory of narcissism, "the original form of desire to which one always returns."[48] Since ideals and illusions are the analogues of dreams and neuroses, the psychoanalytic inter-pretation of culture is also archeological. This archeology culmi-nates in Freud's critique of religion, "the universal obsessional neurosis of mankind."[49] The ethical world, too, and the superego which accounts for it, are seen to have distinctively archaic fea-tures, and the death instinct is the archaic index of all the instincts and of the pleasure principle itself. Man is drawn back-ward, by a detemporalizing agency, to a destiny in reverse.

Can such an archeology be understood within a philosophy of the subject? To answer this question, says Ricoeur, we must first ask about the ultimate meaning of Freud's economic point of view. There is a point within the economic perspective where the fate of the affective representatives of instinct no longer coincides with that of the ideational representatives. At this point, psychoanalysis becomes the borderline knowledge of that which, in representation, does not pass into ideas--i.e., desire *qua* desire, "the mute, the nonspoken and non-speaking, the unnameable at the origin of speech."[50]

---

[48] *Ibid.*, p. 445.

[49] *Ibid.*, p. 447.

[50] *Ibid.*, p. 454.

Only the energy metaphors of the economics can speak this muteness.
This regressive movement of psychoanalysis designates, from the
border, the Sum of the Cogito. "Just as the 'relinquishing' of
consciousness in a topography is intelligible only because of a 're-
capture' in the act of becoming conscious, so too a pure economics
of desire is intelligible only as the possibility of recognizing the
emergence of desire in the series of its derivatives, in the density
and at the borderline of the signifying."[51] Thus, drawing upon
Leibniz, Ricoeur states: " . . . as standing for objects or things,
representation is pretension to truth; but it is also the expression
of life, expression of effort or appetite."[52] "Desire is both the
nonspoken and the wish-to-speak, the unnameable and the potency to
speak."[53]

What does such an archeology tell us, then, about human
existence? Our representations must be studied, not only by an epistemology which views them as intentional relations ruled by objects,
but also by an exegesis of the desires that lie hidden in that intentionality. Thus human knowledge is not autonomous but rooted in
existence, desire, and effort. Epistemology is but one part of
reflective philosophy. Life and desire, which alone are unsurpassable,
tend to interfere with the intentionality which is the concern of

---

51
Ibid.

52
Ibid., p. 456.

53
Ibid., p. 457.

epistemology. Truth becomes, in such an analysis, not a given, but
a task. The movement of reflective philosophy to the sublation of
the psyche makes of that philosophy a semantics of human desire.

The dependence of the knowing subject on the emergence of
desire cannot be grasped in immediate experience. It can only be
interpreted, deciphered through dreams, fantasies, and myths, "the
indirect discourse of [the] mute darkness" of desire.[54] Reflective
consciousness must move with Ricoeur beyond structural phenomenology
and the phenomenology of perception to hermeneutic phenomenology,
for only hermeneutic can understand this rootedness of knowledge in
life. The hermeneutic turn proves to be justified in terms of the
very interest and project of philosophical reflection.

Archeology and Teleology

For the sake of concreteness, says Ricoeur, an archeology
of the subject must be placed in a relationship of dialectical
tension with a teleology of the subject. Only through such a
relationship can self-appropriation become concrete. A second dispossession of immediate consciousness is required, precisely for the
sake of becoming conscious, i.e., of attaining to the true being of
the subject. This process of appropriating the meaning of one's
existence is mediated through figures which give a goal to the process.
The goal is expanded or heightened consciousness. The figures which
mediate the process serially constitute what Hegel calls Geist. They
determine a new decentering of meaning away from immediate consciousness.

54
Ibid., p. 458.

Heuristically, we may say that, for Ricoeur, to understand the
relation between these two dispossessions of consciousness is to
understand that the hermeneutic conflict can be resolved. The dialectic of archeology and teleology is "the true philosophical basis
for understanding the complementarity of opposed hermeneutics in
relation to the mytho-poetic formations of culture."[55]

Freudianism itself is far more dialectical in nature than
Freud admitted. It may be an explicit and thematized archeology, but
it relates in and of itself to an implicit and unthematized teleology,
much as Hegel's Phenomenology is an explicit teleological account of
the achieving of consciousness, but emerging out of the substrate of
life and desire, and thus an implicit archeology.[56]

Hegel presents a phenomenology of figures, categories, and
symbols which guide the developmental process along the lines of a
progressive synthesis. Man becomes adult by assuming the new forms
of master-slave, stoic thought, skepticism, the unhappy consciousness,
service of the devoted mind, etc., which serially constitute Geist.
A given consciousness must encounter and appropriate those spheres
of meaning if it is to reflect itself as a self, a human, adult,
conscious self. Consciousness is the internalization of this movement,

---

55
   Ibid., p. 460.

56
   "I do not confuse Hegel with Freud, but I seek to find in
Freud an inverted image of Hegel, in order to discern, with the help
of this schema, certain dialectical features which, though obviously
operative in analytic practice, have not found in the theory a complete systematic elaboration." Ibid., pp. 461f.

which must be captured in the objective structures of institutions, monuments, works of art and culture. Consciousness becomes self-consciousness only through this mediation, thus only by allowing a shift of the center of meaning away from itself just as much as in psychoanalysis.

Ricoeur takes two facets of Hegelian phenomenology[57] as guides in the development of a Freudian dialectic: its form and its content. The form of Hegelian dialectic is that of a progressive synthesis in which each figure receives its meaning from the <u>subsequent</u> one. As regards content, what is at stake in the progressive synthesis is the production of the self of self-consciousness. The form contrasts with the analytic and regressive character of psycho-analysis. The self that is at stake cannot figure in a topography or an economics. The "education" of the self is not understood economically as a return to narcissism from object-libido. The self <u>in itself</u> will only know itself in reflection, where the self is finally <u>for itself</u>. The way is open for creativity, since each moment includes in its certainty an element of the not-known that all the later moments mediate and make explicit. In contrast, Freudianism appears to be a strange and profound philosophy of fate. Whereas <u>Geist</u> has its meaning in later forms or figures, "the unconscious" in psychoanalysis means that intelligibility always proceeds from earlier figures. "Spirit [<u>Geist</u>] is history and the unconscious is fate."[58]

57
On the growing importance of Hegel for Ricoeur, see Ihde, <u>op</u>. <u>cit</u>., p. 15.

58
Paul Ricoeur, <u>Freud and Philosophy</u>, p. 468.

Nevertheless, the Freudian problematic also appears within Hegelian phenomenology. The emergence of desire is central to the spiritual process of the reduplication of consciousness; the satisfaction of desire is inherent in the self-recognition of achieved self-consciousness. The education of the self proceeds on and arises from the substrate of life and desire, which has a teleological dimension to its dynamism. Life is the obscure density which self-consciousness, in its advance, reveals behind itself as the source of the synthetic movement. Life and desire are both surpassed, in the sense of being progressively mediated, and unsurpassable, in the sense of being originary.

Conversely, the Hegelian problematic is within Freudianism. Ricoeur finds that three areas of Freudianism reveal an implicit teleology: the theory's operative concepts, the notion of identification, and the question of sublimation.

By "operative concepts," Ricoeur means concepts that Freud uses but does not thematize. Principal among these is the intersubjective nature of the analytic situation, which contrasts with the solipsism of the topography of the psyche. Because of this intersubjectivity, the analytic relation between patient and analyst can be understood as "a dialectic of consciousness, rising from life to self-consciousness, from the satisfaction of desire to the recognition of the other consciousness."[59] By the attainment of the equality of the two consciousnesses, the patient is no longer

---

59
Ibid., p. 474.

alienated, no longer primarily another; he has become a self. Even
more important, the therapeutic relation serves as a "mirror image
in reviving a whole series of situations all of which were already
intersubjective. . . . All the dramas psychoanalysis discovers are
located on the path that leads from 'satisfaction' to 'recognition.'"[60]

The genesis of the superego in Freudian theory also relates
to an unthematized teleological dialectic by reason of the concept
of identification. Because of the external nature of authority, an
acquired differentiation of desire takes place, along with a semantics
of ideals. Again, this differentiation is homologous to the Hegelian
reduplication of consciousness. The desire in question here, one
which precedes the Oedipus complex and is strengthened by its dissolution, is the desire to be like. This process of consciousness-to-
consciousness can be understood only by an interpretation other than
the Freudian metapsychology. It is a process which founds affec-
tionate trends of feeling and cultural objectifications. As such, it
eludes the economics. Freud's writings can thus be reread from the
standpoint of the emergence of self-consciousness.[61]

Finally, there is the question of sublimation, which is only
a question in Freud's theory. The more Freud distinguishes sublimation
from other mechanisms, and in particular from repression and reaction-
formation, the more its own mechanism remains unexplained. Sublimation is a displacement of energy, but not a repression of it. It

---

60
  Ibid.

61
  See ibid., pp. 477-483.

precedes and embraces all of the formations derived by way of aesthetic transfer of sensual pleasure from erotogenic zones or by way of desexualization of the libido during the dissolution of the Oedipus complex. Ultimately, the task of becoming I, the finality of analysis, a task set within the economics of desire, is in principle irreducible to the economics.[62]

The Concrete Symbol

For Ricoeur, the dialectic of archeology and teleology is the first step leading from abstract reflection to concrete reflection. To understand that symbols are the area of identity between progression and regression, though, is fully to enter into concrete reflection and to demonstrate most dramatically that self-appropriation needs to have recourse to symbols. The dialectic of opposed hermeneutics is rooted in a dialectic within the symbol itself. While the key to the solution of the hermeneutic conflict lies in the dialectic between archeology and teleology, these are found together in the concrete mixed texture of the symbol. These two lines of interpretation find their point of intersection in the meaningful texture of symbols. Symbols are thus the concrete, though not immediate, moment of the dialectic. After thought, after the ascesis of reflection, after the decentering of the origin of meaning away from naive consciousness--and only after--may one return to the simple attitude of listening to symbols, the "second naivete." "In order to think in accord with symbols one must subject them to a dialectic;

---

[62]
See ibid., pp. 483-493.

only then is it possible to set the dialectic within interpretation itself and come back to living speech."[63] This is the transition to concrete reflection. "In returning to the attitude of listening to language, reflection passes into the fullness of speech simply heard and understood."[64]

Let us not be mistaken about the meaning of this last stage: this return to the immediate is not a return to silence, but rather to the spoken word, to the fullness of language. Nor is it a return to the dense enigma of initial, immediate speech, but to speech that has been instructed by the whole process of meaning. Hence this concrete reflection does not imply any concession to irrationality or effusiveness. In its return to the spoken word, reflection continues to be reflection, that is, the understanding of meaning; reflection becomes hermeneutic; this is the only way in which it can become concrete and still remain reflection. The second naiveté is not the first naiveté; it is postcritical and not precritical; it is an informed naiveté.[65]

Ricoeur's thesis is formulated as follows:

. . . what psychoanalysis calls overdetermination cannot be understood apart from a dialectic between two functions which are thought to be opposed to one another but which symbols coordinate in a concrete unity. Thus the ambiguity of symbolism is not a lack of univocity but is rather the possibility of carrying and engendering opposed interpretations, each of which is self-consistent.[66]

Symbols carry two vectors--repetition of our childhood (individually, culturally, racially, and species-wise) and exploration of our adult life. But these two functions are not external to one another; they

---

63
  Ibid., p. 495.

64
  Ibid., p. 496.

65
  Ibid.

66
  Ibid.

constitute the overdetermination of authentic symbols. Authentic
symbols are truly regressive-progressive; remembrance gives rise to
anticipation, archaism to prophecy.

The intentional structure of symbols may be described in
terms of the unity of concealing and showing. At this point,
Ricoeur becomes, I believe, very similar to Heidegger in the latter's
notions of truth and language. True symbols both disguise and reveal.
While they conceal the aims of our instincts, they disclose the process of self-consciousness. "Disguise, reveal; conceal, show; these
two functions are no longer external to one another; they express the
two sides of a single symbolic function. . . . Advancement of
meaning occurs only in the sphere of the projections of desire, of
the derivatives of the unconscious, of the revivals of archaism. . . .
The opposed hermeneutics disjoin and decompose what concrete reflection recomposes through a return to speech simply heard and understood."[67]

Freud's inadequate theory of symbolism and language leads
Ricoeur to suggest that we distinguish various levels of creativity
within the symbolic realm. At the lowest level we come upon "sedimented symbolism," symbols so encrusted with age and worn with use
that they have nothing but a past. Such, says Ricoeur, are the symbols of dreams, fairy tales, and legends. At a higher level are
symbols that function, often without our knowing it, in ordinary human
commerce. Interestingly enough, Ricoeur states that these are the

---

[67]
Ibid., p. 497.

symbols appropriate for study by structural anthropology. Finally,
there is the level of prospective symbols, creations of meaning
which take up the traditional symbols with their multiple significations and serve as the vehicles of new meanings. The task of one
concerned with the future symbolic capabilities of man, says Ricoeur,
is to grasp symbols in this creative moment, not when they arrive at
the end of their course and are revived in dreams.[68]

A Further Radicalization

I accept from Ricoeur the archeological-teleological unity-
in-tension of the concrete symbol. But I differ from him on several
counts. My qualifications of his analysis are not in the interests
of returning to naive consciousness untutored by criticism. The
mediation of immediacy is a matter of the appropriation and articulation of what is otherwise undifferentiated and nonobjectified. In
both its cognitive and dispositional dimensions, it effects a displacement of the home of meaning away from naive consciousness. But I start
with the displacement effected, not by Kantian epistemology or
Husserlian phenomenology but by Lonergan's cognitional analysis. The
latter effects a mediation of cognitive immediacy or Verstehen by
enabling one to answer correctly three questions: what am I doing
when I am knowing? why is that knowing? what do I know when I do
that? The displacement of the home or core of meaning away from naive
awareness is achieved in the startling strangeness of the combination
of judgments which affirm that knowing is knowing being, but that being

---

68
Ibid., pp. 504ff.

is not a subdivision of the "already out there now," but is rather
whatever can be intelligently grasped and reasonably affirmed.[69]

First, then, I wish to radicalize the significance of the
dialectical overdetermination of symbols. While it is true that
reflective philosophy must move through a concrete hermeneutical
turn to the dialectic of the symbol, the issue is not so much one
of understanding man's experience by understanding man's expressions
as it is one of understanding man's expressions by a more radical
and concrete understanding of man's experience, by a mediation of
dispositional immediacy through the disengagement of its symbolic
constitution. The task of philosophy has become, with the work of
Lonergan, that of the mediation of immediacy through self-appropriation. This task is not fulfilled primarily by moving from an understanding of man's objectifications in language, culture, and action
to an understanding of experience, no matter how dialectical, even
no matter how accurate, the understanding of man's objectifications
may be. The essential movement is the other way around, and its
cognitive dimensions are expressed in Lonergan's programmatic invitation: "Thoroughly understand what it is to understand, and not
only will you understand the broad lines of all there is to be understood, but also you will possess a fixed base, an invariant pattern,
opening upon all further developments of understanding."[70] Something
similar may be said of the roots of desire and fear in human imagination:

69
  Bernard Lonergan, Insight, Ch. 12.

70
  Ibid., p. xxviii.

Come to know as existential subject the contingent figures, the structure, the process, and the archetypal spontaneity of your own psyche, and you will come into possession of an expanding base and an intelligible pattern illuminating the vouloir-dire of human desire as it is brought to expression in the cultural and religious objectifications of human history.

Secondly, and relatedly, as we shall discover in detail in the next chapter, a far more generous evaluation can be provided of the role of the dream than that accorded it by Ricoeur. The Jungian understanding of the dream is, I believe, far more accurate than the Freudian interpretation preserved by Ricoeur. Dreams are anything but the revival of sedimented symbols that have nothing but a past.

Finally, this more generous evaluation of the dream is bound up with a notion of the psyche itself which is explicitly teleological in part. Thus the dialectical counterpart to Freud in understanding the archeological-teleological unity-in-tension of even the most spontaneous dream symbols should be, not Hegel, but a philosophically criticized Jung. While I must severely criticize Jung's lack of serious philosophic underpinnings, I believe his notions of the structure and dynamics of the psyche, when coupled with Freud's, will provide us with a better understanding of the unity-in-tension that is the concrete symbol than can be afforded by placing Freud and Hegel in dialectical relationship to one another or by finding Freud's problematic in Hegel and Hegel's in Freud. The authentic symbol is a spontaneous psychic production. It is not a matter of Geist except insofar as the latter, reinterpreted as the existential subject, has influenced or failed to influence psyche. While the ultimate dialectic of the

existential subject is that between intentionality and psyche, the
ultimate dialectic of the symbol itself is located within psyche.

I am maintaining, then, that the appropriated dispositional
immediacy which is Ricoeur's second naiveté is not precisely the
result of the dialectic which Ricoeur elaborates, a dialectic of
opposed hermeneutics, but of another dialectic, a specifically
therapeutic dialectic, a dialectic within the psyche. Philosophy
as we have known it cannot bring one to appropriated immediacy in
the dispositional realm, but only point the way, open possibilities,
and discuss eventualities. This, of course, Ricoeur has done, and
he has done so in masterful fashion. But the process of moving
forward to an existential appropriation of dispositional immediacy
is a different kind of process. It is, indeed, dialectical and
hermeneutic and it is also reflective in Ricoeur's sense of this
word. But it is not philosophy as we have known philosophy, or even
as Ricoeur understands philosophy. It is a different kind of mediation. With Lonergan philosophy has become method. But method can
sublate psychic analysis and psychic synthesis. Within the methodical exigence, as one of its constituent features, there is the
therapeutic exigence.

The therapeutic dialectic of the psyche may be understood,
then, as a principal dimension in the achievement of self-transcending
existential subjectivity. It may be placed into the more inclusive
context of the dialectic of intentionality and psyche. But the fact
that an archeological-teleological unity-in-tension pertains to the
most elemental spontaneous symbolic productions of the psyche of the
dreaming subject indicates a dialectical suspension or tension within

psyche itself. There is the potential, suggested and almost
sufficiently disengaged by Jung (whose psychology collapses on the
final psychic complex of the negotiation of evil through the Father),
that psyche may be brought to join in the dynamism of intentionality
toward value, indeed toward the upper reaches of an ascending scale
of values. And there is the opposed possibility that psyche may
drift in the direction of the loss of the existential subject as
the potential for self-transcending authenticity, that the subject
may simply come to drift in the direction of the now harsh and now
seductive rhythms of psyche and nature and thus fail to achieve
genuine humanity. I do not believe Ricoeur highlights strongly
enough the fact that the tension within symbolism points to a
tension within the mytho-poetic core of imagination itself. There
seems to be in psyche itself a teleological orientation toward
joining the dynamism of intentionality toward being, truth, and
value, as well as an archeological regressive tendency toward the
inertness of non-living matter. Psyche, it is true, cannot resolve
the tension. That is the formidable task of the existential subject
finding out for himself that it is up to him to decide what he is to
make of himself, asking himself the most crucial of all questions,
What do I want to make of myself? The conscious mind, or better, the
ego is all too often "reluctant to see or admit the polarity of its
own background" so that incompatible contents remain nonobjectified
or are habitually and assiduously overlooked. "The more this is so,
the more the [psyche] will build up its counterposition."[71] But the

_____

71
    C. G. Jung, Mysterium Coniunctionis, Collected Works, vol.

conscious mind can also take stock of psychic polarity, and then there can occur a progressive articulation and differentiation of the inner space of psyche and a progressive though dialectical conscription of psyche into the thrust of intentionality to the freedom of originating value.

Thus, within what Jung calls "the unconscious" itself, there are tendencies which are opposites. The two most inclusive of these we may call the tendency to matter and the tendency to spirit. Because of the dialectic present in a psyche which is human, both are to be consciously realized, and not on an intermittent ad hoc basis--now matter, now spirit--, a basis which could only be specified by a process of deduction from so-called principles. Rather, their realization is to be consistent and permanent, through a psychic reconciliation of one with the other, a process which individuates both of these tendencies. This is the therapeutic dialectic. While it is effected by the existential subject's engaging the symbolic manifestations of dreams, which are intentions without fulfillments, in a continual process of coming to terms, this dialectic of intentionality and psyche is conditioned by a dialectic within the psyche itself. The symbolic manifestations of dreams undergo a story of development or aberration according as they are dealt with by the consciousness of the existential subject, and they take on a particular flavor from the individual existential subject whose dispositional immediacy they represent, whose story they narrate. Since they are relatively autonomous, however, they cannot be integrated into

---

14 (Princeton: Bollingen Series XX, 1963), p. xviii.

conscious life through philosophy, but only by a different kind of dialectical procedure which often takes the form of a dialogue. "Usually the process runs a dramatic course, with many ups and downs. It expresses itself in, or is accompanied by, dream symbols that are related to the 'representations collectives,' which in the form of mythological motifs have portrayed psychic processes of transformation since the earliest times."[72]

As a way of expressing the therapeutic exigence as a part of the new movement of historical Western mind of which I spoke in the first chapter, we might say that for Hegel the unity of opposites is conceptual and its comprehension is speculative knowledge, whereas in concrete method, when the latter is extended to the psyche, the unity of opposites is psychic, the progressive result of a dialectical process that is lived while and according as it is comprehended.

Mystery and Myth

I accept from Ricoeur, then, both the possibility of a second naiveté and the characterization of this naiveté as involving the ambiguity of symbolism, though I place the latter more radically in the realm of the pre-verbal and spontaneous elemental psyche. From Ricoeur I accept also one further qualification of the symbolic realm of which one becomes more aware as the therapeutic dialectic goes forward: symbols are exploratory rather than etiological or explanatory. Such a distinction is entailed in Ricoeur's well-known phrase,

---

72
C. G. Jung, "Archetypes of the Collective Unconscious," in The Archetypes and the Collective Unconscious, Collected Works, vol. 9a (Princeton: Bollingen Series XX, 1969), p. 41, par. 85.

171

"the symbol gives rise to thought."[73] To interpret symbols as
exploratory is, on Ricoeur's analysis, to reenact them in sympathetic imagination, not through an immediate belief but through
the dialectical recovery of their intentionality. In this way
the elemental symbol is found to be an interpretation of oneself
as existential subject, of one's background, potential future, and
present status. Such a relation to symbols I designate as _mystery_.
To reenact a symbol through immediate belief, on the other hand,
would be to accept it as explanatory. This relation to symbol is
myth, in the pejorative sense of this plurivocal word. I accept
from Ricoeur the notion of symbols as intentions without fulfillments, and would add that this unfulfilled nature of the symbol as
such is itself expressive of its archeological-teleological unity-
in-tension, of its concrete, dynamic, and dialectically contradictory possibilities. Only the existential subject can resolve the
dialectic. What do I want to make of myself?

Jung speaks of a tendency which leads us either to regard
symbols as explanatory or to neglect them in favor of concepts:

> We all have an understandable desire for crystal clarity, but
> we are apt to forget that in psychic matters we are dealing
> with processes of experience, that is, with transformations
> which should never be given hard and fast names if their
> living movement is not to petrify into something static. The
> protean mythologem and the shimmering symbol express the pro-
> cesses of the psyche far more trenchantly and, in the end,
> far more clearly than the clearest concept; for the symbol not
> only conveys a visualization of the process but--and this is
> perhaps just as important--it also brings a re-experiencing of

73
   Paul Ricoeur, The Symbolism of Evil, p. 374; Freud and
Philosophy, p. 38.

it, of that twilight which we can learn to understand only
through inoffensive empathy, but which too much clarity only
dispels.[74]

Of what is the symbol exploratory? Can we be more precise
on this point without falling into the conceptualism indicted by
Jung? I find helpful some distinctions offered by Lonergan in
Method in Theology and already discussed in our first chapter.[75]
If we insist that the symbol is to be accepted as exploratory rather
than explanatory, then we may say that a post-critical symbolic
consciousness would understand the elemental symbol as a manifestation of what is interior rather than exterior, as referring to the
temporal before the spatial, the generic before the specific, and as
related to the divine and the anti-divine, to grace and sin, and not
simply to the human. The concrete symbol is exploratory of the
affective interiority of man, of the dispositional aspect of primordial immediacy. It is exploratory of his journey through time and,
when produced spontaneously by the psyche of an individual, indicative
of his present stance in time. To say that it refers to the generic
before the specific would be to indicate that spontaneously produced
symbols function rather as barometer than thermometer.[76] That is,
they are indicative of the atmosphere, of its pressures and potentialities,

---

74
    C. G. Jung, "Paracelsus as a Spiritual Phenomenon," in
Alchemical Studies, pp. 162f., par. 199.

75
    Bernard Lonergan, Method in Theology, pp. 96 and 108.

76
    I am indebted for this formulation to Rev. Charles Goldsmith,
Ph.D., clinical psychologist and chaplain, Deaconness Hospital,
Milwaukee.

rather than explicative of the precise temperature and of its causes. Finally, to say that symbols are related to the realm of transcendence is to indicate that they are ciphers of the existential subject's relation to the upper levels of the scale of values, where the authenticity of self-transcendence is the fruit of the gift of God's love. Thus the symbols spontaneously produced in the dreams and fantasies of the existential subject are to be regarded in the first instance as opening up for appropriation some element of the psychic constitution of their author, of the temporal relations in terms of which he or she is this concrete man or woman at this point in his or her personal history, and of the stance that he or she is adopting or can adopt to the movement of intentionality toward self-transcendence. The attentive presence to this complex congeries beckons thoughtful reflection, hermeneutic reflection, dialectical reflection, but also therapeutic reflection.

Finally, I must relate my distinction between mystery and myth to Lonergan's.[77] Lonergan has recently rearticulated this distinction: "My contrast of mystery and myth was between symbolic expressions of positions and of counterpositions."[78] Mystery for me is a posture vis-a-vis symbols which searches for the intention of intelligibility, truth, and value in the symbolic revelations themselves. Myth is an opposite posture which regards the symbol itself as fulfillment, which does not intelligently, reasonably, and responsibly

---

77
Bernard Lonergan, _Insight_, pp. 531-549.

78
Bernard Lonergan, "_Insight_ Revisited," p. 14.

discriminate the dialectic of the symbol, and which thus runs the risk of the capitulation of intentionality to psyche that is the romantic agony. While the former attitude is the condition of possibility of the symbolic expression of positions, the latter is the inevitability of the symbolic expression of counterpositions.[79]

Individuation

Jungian psychology makes an acute and very important distinction between the first half of life and the second half of life. During the first half of life, which extends at least through one's early 30's, one seeks his natural self-expression in external life. Thus a conscious ego is developed, which, together with its "outward face," the persona, determines for better or for worse an individual's position in regard to what is exterior, spatial, specific, and human. In the second half of life, one seeks new channels and new sources of self-expression and meaning. On our analysis, one can then cultivate the world of interiority, and consequently can come to value time before space and what is generic as the condition of what is specific, and to discriminate the psyche in terms of what Christian spiritual tradition has called the discernment of spirits. The inner law of the second half of life manifests itself in the movement to what Jung calls individuation. The transition from the first half of life to the second half of life is a very difficult affair. It demands the

---

[79] The tension of the symbol is also dealt with by Matthew L. Lamb, "Myth and the Crisis of Historical Consciousness," paper prepared for discussion at the convention of the American Academy of Religion, November, 1974.

relativization of the outer-directed ego and thus of one's relations to what is exterior, spatial, specific, and human. It
demands that the ego surrender its position as the supposed center
of the total personality--a position it had to adopt during the
first half of life--and that it give way to a deeper center, a more
mysterious center, a center which can never be completely circum-
scribed and grasped but which can, at best, be circumambulated.
This deeper center Jung refers to as the Self. I find no reason for
not identifying it with what Ricoeur calls the Sum of the Cogito.
For Jung, it is symbolized--inadequately and abstractly, I believe--
by such figures as a mandala, a stone, or a steadily burning flame.
On the other hand, once the ego gives way to the Self as center,
there are further and seemingly more treacherous difficulties to be
negotiated, which only time and determination enable one to resolve.
For one can then identify one's ego-consciousness with the Self,
resulting in "an inflation which threatens consciousness with dissolution."[80] In these moments, as Erich Neumann warns, the "ecstatic
demolition" of the ego may occur, either through a negative intro-
version or, by projection, through an outward mysticism culminating
in a pantheistic seizure. In either case the ego would be overpowered
and one would be on the borders of psychosis. Tertium datur. There
is the possibility, achieved only by ever greater approximation, of
being attached to the numinous and at home in oneself, at rest and
in creative motion, in the world and outside it at the same time, and

---

80
    C. G. Jung, "Concerning Rebirth," in The Archetypes and
the Collective Unconscious, p. 145, par. 254.

of being thus self-consciously, through individuation.[81]

The individuating aspects of such a task are difficult. "The self is the hero, threatened already at birth by envious collective forces; the jewel that is coveted by all and arouses jealous strife; and finally the god who is dismembered by the old, evil power of darkness. In its psychological meaning, individuation is an opus contra naturam, which creates a horror vacui in the collective layer and is only too likely to collapse under the impact of the collective forces of the psyche."[82] These collective forces could be those to which the persona responds, in which case the movement into the second half of life would not occur psychically at all; or they may be what Jung has called the collective unconscious, in which case the psychoses referred to by Neumann are imminent.

The notion of the Self is a permanently heuristic notion which is appropriately described only in symbolic language. Jung speaks of the Self as "psychic totality and at the same time a centre, neither of which coincides with the ego but includes it, just as a larger circle encloses a smaller one."[83] Insofar as it is the sum of conscious and unconscious processes, it is by definition beyond conceptual grasp.[84] The notion of the Self is the type of notion which

_____

[81]
See Erich Neumann's paper, "Mystical Man," Eranos-Jahrbuch XVI (1959), p. 44.

[82]
C. G. Jung, op. cit., pp. 146f., par. 256.

[83]
Ibid., p. 142, par. 148.

[84]
C. G. Jung, Mysterium Coniunctionis, p. 63.

James Hillman qualifies as indefinable.[85] I am convinced that
Sebastian Moore's discovery of the image of the Crucified at the far
end of the psyche[86] is a far more adequate identification of what
Jung was reaching for in his notion of the Self than any of the
suggestions offered by Jung, for I believe that the true Self emerges
out of one's negotiation of man's problem of evil and more specifically
out of one's progressive discovery of the meaning for oneself of the
divinely originated solution to man's problem of evil. How am I to
participate in this solution?

The Jungian notion of individuation, then, is quite susceptible
of reinterpretation within the context of the self-appropriation of the
existential subject. Individuation is the psychic complement of the
self-appropriation of intentionality aided by Lonergan. It is the movement of an individual to the appropriation of the dispositional aspect
of immediacy. The movement from the ego to the Self is a movement
toward the appropriation of dispositional primordial immediacy. Ironi-
cally enough, however, it would appear that this movement toward the
appropriation of immediacy is a movement away frcm naive consciousness.
For it is a movement toward centering oneself in what can only be
circumambulated and it takes place through a process of relativizing
naive consciousness. It is a movement from what is exterior, spatial,
specific, and human, to what is interior, temporal, generic, and in the

---

85
    James Hillman, The Myth of Analysis (Evanston: Northwestern,
1972), p. 79.

86
    Sebastian Moore, Journey into a Crucifix.

realm of the divine solution to man's problem of evil. It involves a withdrawal of those projections which enable one to find one's realization and meaning in the "already out there now real." This movement thus affects the heart of one's desire to be, of one's striving toward existence. It is a movement, if you wish, toward an autonomy not only of one's cognitional being, such that my knowledge is a matter of my raising and answering questions, but also of one's source of desire and conatus. The existential and psychic complement to the disinterestedness of the pure desire to know is a movement toward the second innocence of agape. It is Western man's way of moving toward what the Bhagavad Gita calls "acting while renouncing the fruits of one's actions," toward the innocence which the ancient Chinese scripture, the I Ching, describes in this way: "If one does not count on the harvest while plowing nor on the use of the field while clearing it, then it furthers one to undertake something." It is a movement toward the non-alienation of those who are free to seek only the kingdom of God and his righteousness, confident that everything they need for their life will be given them. This movement can be aided symbolically.

Failures to achieve individuation, on the other hand, are a matter radically of the "loss of the 'symbolical attitude,'" of "a break in the spontaneous relationship between the conscious mind and its matrix, the unconscious."[87] For Jung, " . . . the collective unconscious . . . does not understand the language of the conscious

---

[87]
Gerhard Adler, The Living Symbol: A Case Study of the Process of Individuation (Princeton: Bollingen, 1961), p. 9.

mind. Therefore it is necessary to have the magic of the symbol which contains those primitive analogies that speak to the unconscious. The unconscious can be reached and expressed only by symbols, and for this reason the process of individuation can never do without the symbol. The symbol is the primitive exponent of the unconscious, but at the same time an idea that corresponds to the highest intuitions of the conscious mind."[88]

Joseph Henderson contrasts the Jungian notion of the Self with the Hindu conception of Atman and shows the supreme importance of the symbol for the former.

> For the East the supreme ground of Being, Atman, is suprapersonal and completely transcendent, rendering its possessor capable of maintaining an attitude of selfless non-attachment to all wishes or compulsions of the ego. The Western Self, in contrast, is personal as well as impersonal. Through the ego it is attached to life in a meaningful and fateful way, while its transcendent aim relates it to the higher goal of individual differentiation from collective social patterns. In this sense individuation, therefore, involves the experience of conflict between the claims of the ego and the claims of the Self. Resolution occurs only at the nodal points of life where harmony can be established between these two claims by the creation of a reconciling symbol which performs its work by joining in a totally spontaneous or unexpected fashion the images of attachment with images of what is liberating for a transcendent experience. In these significant moments a man may become, as Wordsworth says, 'true to the kindred points of heaven and home.'[89]

From this perspective, appropriated dispositional immediacy involves a knowledge of one's own most spontaneous conditions and

---

88
    C. G. Jung, "The Secret of the Golden Flower," in Alchemical Studies, p. 28, par. 44. This passage from Jung highlights the dialectic within the psyche itself.

89
    Joseph L. Henderson, The Wisdom of the Serpent (New York: Braziller, 1963), p. 14.

roots through an appropriation of the archetypal symbolic determinants or qualifications of one's own inner order and meaning.
The symbolic revelations of dreams are for Gerhard Adler "'living
symbols' representing 'the inexpressible in an unsurpassable way.'"[90]
Adler quotes Ruth Monroe, Schools of Psychoanalytic Thought: "The
living symbol does not merely represent wider experience on the pars
pro toto principle. . . . Nor is it the agreed-upon sign for highly
abstract relationships as in mathematics and the natural sciences.
It is creative. . . . Jung's major point is that the symbols are
used creatively in dreams, in art, in psychosis, in many social phenomena."[91]

More important for Jung than the forgotten, the repressed,
the subliminally perceived, thought, and felt acquisitions of one's
personal existence, retrieved through a reduction to the original infantile situation, is the appropriation of the transpersonal source of
imaging itself, which he refers to variously as the collective unconscious and the objective psyche, and which I shall rename the archetypal function. James Hillman has identified it with Augustine's
memoria.[92] This transpersonal source of imaging is identical also, I

90
    Gerhard Adler, loc. cit.

91
    Ibid. In continuity with Ricoeur's analysis of the dialec-
tic of the symbol, may we suggest that the dream is both a wish and
an indication of a pathway to self-realization through what Gaston
Bachelard has called dialectical sublimation? See The Psychoanalysis
of Fire (New York: Beacon Press, 1964), pp. 99f.

92
    James Hillman, The Myth of Analysis, p. 171.

believe, with the transcendental imagination which lured Kant and captured Heidegger. Thus psychic self-appropriation is the differentiation and appropriation of the primordial time-structure of one's dispositional immediacy to the world mediated by meaning. This time-structure is not only the form of inner sense, as with Kant, but the very constitution of Befindlichkeit in its primordiality, unity, and totality, as with Heidegger. To say that the transcendental imagination captured Heidegger means that for him it constitutes not only Befindlichkeit but intentionality as a whole. This I deny, strongly and emphatically. But it is the condition of the possibility of the archeological-teleological unity-in-tension of the concrete symbol. The transcendental time-structure of imagination (Einbildungskraft--the word is important) and thus of man's primordial concern for "world," is fragile. When one is out of touch, it is because the imaginal constitution of dispositional immediacy has been fractured or distorted, so that one's future does not beckon one's "having been" into one's present. Genuine psychotherapy is the recovery of the primordial time-structure of Befindlichkeit through a release of the creative potentialities of the archetypal function which gives rise to primordial time. This recovery occurs in a progressive reconciliation of previously undifferentiated psychic opposites. In each case these opposites take the form of future and "having been," of teleology and archeology. Their reconciliation is in each instance a progressive emergence of the authentic, self-transcending existential subject. Only when the opposites are those of good and evil, grace and sin, is reconciliation impossible. This is the subtle point missed by Jung. The solution to the problem of

evil is not integration of evil into the psyche; it is not reconciliation or integration of evil with good. The assertion that it
is so may well have something to do with the blasphemy against the
Holy Spirit of which Jesus accused those who charged that he was
possessed by the devil.[93] The solution to the problem of evil _is_
embodied in a symbol of reconciliation, but it is the symbol of the
reconciliation of archeology and teleology, alpha and omega, origin
and destiny, creation and eschaton--the Crucified. The impossibility
of a reconciliation of good and evil psychically as well as speculatively is the best cipher of the moment calling for total surrender
to God's love, for the movement to the soul beyond psychology. God's
love deals with evil, not by reconciling it with good nor by integrating it psychically, but by transcending it in the Crucified and
in the collaboration set loose upon the world by that Figure, by the
historical incarnation both of God's Son and of the Self at those
farthest reaches of the human psyche where Psyche becomes Wisdom in
the act of surrender to the Father.

93
Mark 3.29.

CHAPTER IV

SUBLATIONS

Being is "what is to be known by the totality of true judgments."[1] There are various spheres of being. The true judgments of
mathematics comprise a sphere of being as do the true judgments intended in the various sciences and those made in cognitional analysis.
When true judgments are made concerning the symbolic constitution of
Befindlichkeit, they concern a sphere of being which I call the
imaginal.

The continuity of the psychic self-appropriation of the imaginal with the self-appropriation of intentionality in method must be
further specified. Thus, the differentiation and appropriation of
imaginally constituted dispositional immediacy are enabled to come to
pass by a sublation on the part of conscious intentionality that is
additional to the sublations explained by Lonergan. In addition to the
sublation of sensory experience by understanding, of experience and
understanding by reasonable judgment, and of experience, understanding,
and judgment by the moral responsibility and cooperative-intersubjective
consciousness of the existential subject, there is a sublation of the
imaginal, and principally of the symbolic revelations of dreams, on the
part of the whole of attentive, intelligent, reasonable, responsible,

_____

[1]
Bernard Lonergan, Insight, p. 350.

183

cooperative-intersubjective existential consciousness. Thus, in
addition to the attentive, intelligent, reasonable, and responsible
appropriation of one's rational self-consciousness, there is the
attentive, intelligent, reasonable, and responsible appropriation
and negotiation of one's psychic spontaneity and irrationality.

The Imaginal as Operator: A First Determination

The possibility of such a sublation is implicit in Lonergan's
reference to the approach of existential psychology, which "thinks of
the dream, not as the twilight of life, but as its dawn, the beginning
of the transition from impersonal existence to presence in the world,
to constitution of one's self in one's world."[2] My analysis extends
this reference to an explicit utterance, by speaking of an additional
sublation, through which the archetypal constitution of "how one is"
is mediated to the existential subject. The imaginal elucidation of
one's dispositions is released to consciousness in dreams. Second
immediacy includes the capacity to objectify the imaginal structure
of dispositional primordial immediacy through the interpretation of
dreams, through which the dispositional aspect of immediacy is released from muteness and confusion. The concrete symbols revealed
in dreams are to be taken as a kind of text or story whose meaning
can be delineated by interpretative understanding, reasonable judgment, and evaluative deliberation.

The term, the imaginal, I borrow from some recent articles

---

[2] Bernard Lonergan, Method in Theology, p. 69.

in Jungian publications,[3] but not without changing its meaning. For
the authors of these articles, the term is used in an overly Platonic sense, so that there is a _mundus imaginalis_ somewhere in suspension between the _mundus sensibilis_ and the _mundus intelligibilis_.
This world is highly archetypal and is experienced in dreams and
fantasy. I am using the term to refer instead to what becomes known
when one learns to relate disposition to elemental symbolization
through the interpretation of the symbols spontaneously produced by
the psyche in dreams and fantasies. As we shall see, these symbols,
far from constituting an independent world in themselves, are
operators effecting a sublation of neural and psychic process into
the realm of recognition and interpretation, and as such are the most
primordial signals of one's orientation as existential subject in the
world mediated and constituted by meaning. Again, far from constituting an independent world in themselves, they issue the existential
subject into an ever new world of his own, if he intelligently, reasonably, and responsibly appropriates their meaning and constitutes
his world on this basis. By using "imaginal" as a qualification of
immediacy, then, and by speaking of appropriation, I am, in fact,
speaking of a fuller entrance into appropriation of the feelings which
constitute the primordial apprehension of value. Primordial immediacy
is always dispositionally qualified, but this disposition is frequently inarticulate. It becomes articulate in dreams. Dreams are

---

[3]
    Gilbert Durand, "Exploration of the Imaginal," _Spring_, 1971,
pp. 84-100, and Henri Corbin, "Mundus Imaginalis, or the Imaginary and
the Imaginal," _Spring_, 1972, pp. 1-19.

the story of dispositional immediacy. The hermeneutic and dialectical interpretation of dreams is an appropriation of the dispositions which permeate one's immediacy to the world mediated by meaning. Such an appropriation gives access to the archetypal constitution and possibilities of existential subjectivity.

I have already referred to Eugene Gendlin's notion of "experiencing," which is his term for the dispositional immediacy available to everyone in all of one's conscious operations. It is "that partly unformed stream of feeling that we have at every moment, . . . the flow of feeling, concretely, to which you can every moment attend inwardly, if you wish."[4] Gendlin has, in effect, attempted to delineate other ways besides dream interpretation of symbolizing dispositional immediacy, by proposing techniques by which symbols can be reciprocally related to felt experiencing. When symbolic meanings occur in interaction with experiencing, they can change, and when one employs symbols to attend to a feeling, it can change. In fact, Gendlin proposes seven different kinds of functional relationships between feeling and symbols. In an effort to highlight what I mean by the symbolic structure of feeling, I shall summarize these relationships. Three of them are called parallel relationships and four creative relationships. My only caution regarding the employment of Gendlin's techniques is that dispositional immediacy is adequately symbolized only when the symbols issue from and reflect the same depth dimension from which dreams proceed. Gendlin's techniques, I believe, can be

---

4
    Eugene Gendlin, Experiencing and the Creation of Meaning,
p. 3.

quite effective if one has already learned the connection between
feelings and the elemental symbolization of the dream.

The first parallel functional relationship, the one least
relevant to our discussion, is called direct reference. It involves
directly referring to the felt meaning; it is an individual's
reference to a present felt meaning and not to any object, concept,
or anything else that may be related to the felt meaning. Verbal
articulations, such as "this feeling," refer but without naming the
felt meaning to which they refer. They depend for their meaning on
direct reference to the felt meaning, just as demonstratives depend
on present sense perception. Thus the felt meaning in direct reference is meaningful independently of representative conceptualization.
Without at least some kind of demonstrative reference, of course,
there cannot be "a" felt meaning; feeling would be permeated, but not
at all mediated, by meaning. But without felt meaning, such demonstrative reference would have no function to perform. Meaning in
direct reference is defined as that which is set off in some sense
as "one," "a" or "this" felt meaning.

The second parallel functional relationship is recognition.
Here, what Gendlin calls symbols adequately objectify and call
forth in us the felt meanings that constitute our recognizing the
meanings of the symbols. We hear or see or think a symbol, and in
that act feel its meaning. We recognize, not the having of the meaning,
but the felt meaning itself. Without such recognition, the symbol
would be meaningless. The relationship of feeling and symbol is the
reverse of that operative in direct reference, for the symbol means
and calls forth feeling. A meaning is a recognition feeling capable

of being called forth.

The third parallel functional relationship is _explication_.
Here felt meaning, once called forth, gives rise to symbols which
further explicate it. These symbols appear as a result of concentrating on the felt meaning itself. Part at least of the technique
which Jung calls active imagination, I believe, is based on this
process, for in active imagination a feeling or disposition gives
rise to an image, and imaginative dialogue with the image gives rise
to insight into the image and, if sufficiently pursued, may explicate and even modify both the disposition and the image. Thus the
disposition has the independent power to be meaningful and to select
the symbols. The latter are instruments of recognition, which in
turn have the power to call out and fill out the disposition which
gave rise to them.

In the creative functional relationships, symbols already
meaningful in parallel relationships enter into relation with dispositions or feelings which have as yet no parallel symbols. A creative functional relationship is one between a partly unsymbolized
felt meaning and a symbol that usually means something else.

The first of these creative functional relationships is
metaphor, a term used by Gendlin in a perhaps more general sense
than is usually employed by literary critics. Thus in metaphor a
new meaning is achieved by drawing on old experience and by using
the symbols for this familiar experience to refer to a new and otherwise unsymbolized experience. These symbols thus have two felt
meanings, the old and the new.

The second creative functional relationship is <u>comprehension</u>.
Here one concentrates on a felt meaning, as in explication, but,
finding no extant symbols to express it exactly, he <u>invents</u> a metaphor for its expression. The felt meaning is itself active, enabling
us to feel whether the invented expression succeeds in symbolizing it.
It changes in the process, since it becomes a meaning in a new sense
and in a new functional relationship with the symbol. Its implicit
content, however, remains but becomes explicit. Comprehension differs
from metaphor in that the novel creation of the relationship begins
with the felt meaning, not with the old, extant symbol.

The third creative functional relationship is <u>relevance</u>.
Here felt meanings are appealed to in order to make symbolizations
understandable, even though these may refer to only a few specific
felt meanings. It is an appeal to experience, to the context which
renders a given symbol understandable. The set of symbols may be
understood differently and to a different degree, given different
felt meanings in terms of which they can be understood.

The fourth creative functional relationship is <u>circumlocution</u>.
This is the creative modification and creative building up of the
felt meaning needed for understanding a symbol. Each of the symbols
employed already has an associated felt meaning. These interact
creatively to give rise to new felt meanings. Circumlocution is related to relevance, in that it creates a felt context out of which
other symbolizations will be understandable.

Two Clarifications

My interpretation of the term, the imaginal, as operator leads me to suggest two other alterations of familiar psychological terminology. I suggest that we replace the term, the unconscious, with the term, the undifferentiated, and the Jungian term, the collective unconscious, with the expression, the archetypal function. The first alteration is suggested for two reasons. First, as the term, the unconscious, has come to be used in both Freudian and Jungian literature, it obfuscates the matter by suggesting an "already down there now real" to be known by looking--but of course by looking down! It is reifying in a naively realistic and ultimately mystifying and mythic manner. Secondly, the replacement of this term with "the undifferentiated" highlights the fact that primordial affective immediacy, however nonobjectified, is directly pertinent to consciousness. It is, I believe, a more accurate English rendition of the German Unbewusstsein, which more literally means "not known," "not objectified," or undifferentiated. Consciousness is not knowledge. Moreover, it is partly differentiated and partly undifferentiated. The basic psychotherapeutic distinction is not that between consciousness and "the unconscious," but that between the self as objectified and the self as conscious. The self as conscious includes the self as differentiated and the self as undifferentiated. The psychotherapeutic intention is to render the self as differentiated approximate to the self as conscious.

The second alteration is suggested for much the same reasons. It is not a denial of the truth Jung was reaching for in his speaking

of the collective unconscious: namely, that there are certain
innate and inherited universal symbolic patterns determinative of
much that is human. But we must demystify the substantialist and
reifying associations too easily joined to the term, collective
unconscious. As Gendlin insists, our psychological categories
must reflect process if they are to refer to direct experience.[5]
The specific value of the term, the collective unconscious, is
that it emphasizes the potential social relevance of Jung's psychology, indeed its cross-cultural relevance. It points to the fact
that, through negotiation of archetypal images, the existential
subject is at the farthest possible remove from solipsism. But the
cognitional confusion attendant upon the terminology of "unconscious"
is nonetheless strong enough to warrant a change of vocabulary. The
confusion is reflected in the following passage from Jung:

> Empirically . . . [consciousness] always finds its limit when
> it comes up against the unknown. This consists of everything
> we do not know which, therefore, is not related to the ego as
> the centre of the field of consciousness. The unknown falls
> into two groups of objects: those which are outside and can
> be experienced by the senses, and those which are inside and
> are experienced immediately. The first group comprises the
> unknown in the outer world; the second, the unknown in the
> inner world. We call this latter territory the unconscious.[6]

It is true that Jung speaks of the inappropriateness of the term,
subconscious, because of its connotations of something "down there,"
but his suggested alternatives are still given in spatial terms.

_____

5
 Ibid., p. 32.

6
 C. G. Jung, Aion, Collected Works, vol. 9b (Princeton:
Bollingen Series XX, 1973), p. 3., par. 2.

" . . . how inept it is to designate [the unconscious] as the 'subconscious': it is not merely 'below' consciousness but also above it."[7] The truth is that "it" is not anywhere, is not some thing.

Thus I suggest that we speak of the undifferentiated to refer to everything included under what has been called the unconscious, whether personal or collective, and of the archetypal function to further designate what Jung calls the collective unconscious. The former we might also call the unknown psychic.[8] Jung includes under this notion: "everything of which I know, but of which I am not at the moment thinking; everything of which I was once conscious but have now forgotten; everything which, involuntarily and without paying attention to it, I feel, think, remember, want, and do; all the future things that are taking shape in me and will sometime come to consciousness; . . . the Freudian findings . . . [and] the psychoid functions that are not capable of consciousness and of whose existence we have only indirect knowledge."[9]

My suggested changes were confirmed in a personal experiment of reading Jung while substituting the undifferentiated for the unconscious, the archetypal function for the collective unconscious,

---

[7] C. G. Jung, "Phenomenology of the Spirit in Fairytales," in The Archetypes and the Collective Unconscious, p. 239, par. 433.

[8] C. G. Jung, "On the Nature of the Psyche," p. 185, par. 382.

[9] Ibid.

and differentiated consciousness or ego for Jung's "consciousness."
The latter term, then, is to be used exclusively in Lonergan's sense
of the subject's presence to himself, inclusive of what is differentiated and undifferentiated.

The Symbolic A Priori

My initial intention was to rename the collective unconscious
as the symbolic a priori. Properly understood this designation is
quite correct and acceptable. But a proper understanding of the a
priori elements of human subjectivity is hard to come by. Perhaps it
would be well, then, to examine the question of the a priori first in
terms of cognition. Giovanni Sala has studied the a priori of human
knowledge in Immanuel Kant's Critique of Pure Reason and Lonergan's
Insight.[10] I shall summarize his findings in order to aid me in discussing the notion of the symbolic a priori and in arriving at a notion
of it in continuity with Lonergan's notion of the a priori rather than,
as Jung does, with Kant's.

The Cognitional A Priori

Kant's Critique of Pure Reason is in quest of the a priori
component of human knowledge. Kant wished to ground the synthetic a
priori judgments in which scientific knowledge consists. Now, for

---

[10]
Giovanni Sala, Das Apriori in der menschlichen Erkenntnis:
Eine Studie über Kants Kritik der reinen Vernunft und Lonergans
Insight (Meisenheim am Glan: Verlag Anton Hain, 1971). My quotations
are from a summary of this work presented at the 1970 International
Lonergan Congress and scheduled for publication in the third volume of
papers from that Congress. The paper is entitled "The Notion of Apri-
ori in Kant's Critique of Pure Reason and Lonergan's Insight."

Kant, scientific knowledge is knowledge of the universal and necessary. Such knowledge cannot arise _a posteriori_ from experience and therefore must be _a priori_. "Experience" is given at least two meanings in the _Critique of Pure Reason_: pure sense knowledge (_Empfindung_) and human knowledge in the full sense, which is sensible and intellectual together. If experience is taken in the first sense, necessity and universality do not originate in experience.

Now, _a priori_ elements are necessary to give universality and necessity because the object of knowledge for Kant is given us through the senses and only through them. Thus the cognitive phases which follow upon experience as pure sensation cannot raise the representation of the sense object to a universal and necessary representation, because they do not contribute a partial object of their own to the constitution of the final and total object of knowledge. "To understand the sense object and to reflect on what has been understood is not to know a further, different object. The content of knowledge is simply repeated in going from the sense level over to the level of the _Verstand_."[11] Sala qualifies this statement in a footnote, where he notes an inconsistency, in that "the _a priori_ of Kant has its own objective content." This will be seen further in what follows. In general, for Kant, intuition, _Erfahrung_ taken as mere sense experience, tells _what_ _is_ but not that it must necessarily be so. For the latter we need the _a priori_.

---

[11] _Ibid._, p. 4.

Now, from Lonergan's perspective, knowledge of the universal and necessary represents the classical, not the modern, ideal of science. Also, the notion that the object of knowledge is given us through the senses and only through them, that the following phases of cognitive process do not contribute a partial object of their own to the constitution of the final and total object of knowledge, reflects an unacceptable intuitionist principle. "Experience itself is knowledge neither of the 'what' nor of the 'is'; it is purely and simply presentation. To know 'what' is represented and whether this 'what' really is, belong to the intelligent and rational phases which follow the sensible phase."[12] Universality and necessity, such as they are, are also seen to have a different origin from the Kantian a priori. "As formal determination is added to the object as a mere datum through understanding, and then existence is added through judgment, so the universality of the formal determination as well as the factual necessity of existence is added to the same sense object. We must consider the entire structure of knowledge in order to grasp how a process which is clearly also empirical can have contents and qualifications which are not empirical."[13]

There is a tension in the Kantian notion of the a priori between attributing to it too little, by insisting on the empirical character of our knowledge, and attributing to it too much, by

---

12
Ibid.

13
Ibid.

underlining its constitutive-formal function, such that, according to Kant, "we can know a priori of things only what we ourselves put into them."[14] On Sala's analysis, this tension can be overcome only by "drawing to its conclusion the Hinwendung zum Subjekt, which is the purpose of the transcendental analysis."[15] Benefiting from Kant's famous metaphor of the judge, Sala clarifies what this complete anthropologische Wendung would reveal.

The evaluation of a given criminal case is confided to a judge because he possesses juridical science, which enables him to pose precise questions to the witnesses. He promotes the data provided by the witnesses to the level of understanding and then, by reflection on all pertinent factors from the standpoint of his juridical science, to evidence sufficient to give him knowledge of a juridically determined fact, which is precisely what he set out to know.

The a priori of the judge is his juridical knowledge. But rather than saying with Kant that he has "put into" the juridically determined fact, it is more accurate to say that he has drawn something else from himself and put it into the data. This something else consists of his questions, through which alone he has come to know the facts.

Now, from the standpoint of Lonergan's cognitional theory, the juridical knowledge of the judge would be a particular specification

---

14
  Ibid., p. 5.

15
  Ibid.

of a "basic Vorverständnis, the same for all, by which every man, in knowing under this or that aspect, knows always being."[16] This basic Vorverständnis is not any knowledge of objects, of nature or of the human world, but the presence of the subject to himself, consciousness, in its immanent orientation toward the universe to be known. This orientation is the a priori in the basic sense; particular a priori's such as the judge's juridical science, are constituted a posteriori, "within the cultural components of the environment in which one is born and raised, and through the personal experiences which constitute the life of the individual in its unicity. The first a priori on the other hand is a priori in an absolute sense."[17]

While it is in virtue of his particular a priori that the judge is able to pose his specific questions, we are all able to ask the question about what is in virtue of the basic a priori. While Kant maintains that we can know a priori of things only what we ourselves put into them, it is more correct to say, "what we ourselves ask about them." The basic a priori, consciousness in its orientation to the universe to be known, is not itself a category of any kind; rather it renders possible every determination of whatever is known, every category. The questions for understanding are the operators moving the object as datum to the object as understood; the questions for reflection are the operators moving the object as

16
  Ibid., p. 7.

17
  Ibid., p. 8.

understood to the object as known. "The human spirit shows at the same time a total poverty and a total capability of discerning and judging by itself everything on the scale of truth."[18] Consciousness, the basic _a priori_, is normative of the entire cognitional process. The primordial question is the principle of the cognitional process, giving rise to specific single questions; at the same time, it penetrates the whole process, regulates everything, renders every single act meaningful.[19]

> Our radical questioning then is a dynamism towards knowledge, a dynamism intelligently and rationally conscious. The same dynamism has an unlimited scope. It is because of its character of intelligent and rational consciousness and of its unlimitedness that Lonergan names our pure desire to know the notion of its objective: being. The characters found in the object of this intention, when it is realized in a manner faithful to its immanent norms, are anticipated by the subject itself, which is not content with the data alone, but when confronted by them poses questions in order to understand and to reflect.[20]

The two kinds of questions establish a structure for knowledge, so that it moves from experience through understanding to judgment. "The many acts which the introspective analysis brings into light dispose themselves on three essentially different levels, each one adding a new and quite distinct dimension both to knowledge as immanent activity and to the thing known, until we reach on the one hand

---

18
  Ibid., p. 9.

19
  Ibid., p. 13.

20
  Ibid.

rational judgment and on the other the proportioned object."[21]
Our cognitive activities thus have different relations to the object.
This variable relation is determined, not by intuition but by our
desire to know, our intention of being.

The scope toward which our intention of being, as primordial
question, tends is unrestricted. The way in which we tend to the
object is unconditional. This unrestrictedness and unconditionality
are interdependent. Being is "the correlative of an unrestricted
intention capable of tending toward its own object without any qualification or condition."[22]

Such a notion, however, implies the intelligibility of being,
the rationality of the real. These notions, according to Sala, are
missing in Kant. "Man understands, conceives, and according to a
certain sense of the word, judges; he performs all these activities
in a manner coherent with their immanent norms. But for all that,
what does he know of reality? Nothing. The intelligent and rational
fulfillment of the cognitive dynamism is not [for Kant] the means of
knowing reality."[23] The reality called Noumenon is "something absolutely beyond our intelligent inquiry and our critical reflection."[24]

21
  Ibid.

22
  Ibid., p. 14.

23
  Ibid., p. 15.

24
  Ibid.

For a rational notion of the real, on the other hand, the intellect would have to grasp a new content not given through intuition, the intelligible of the sensible grasped in the sensible. "The Verstand thinks, or carries to the concept, or subsumes under the concept the object of sense, in so far as it adds to it an object which is not sensible."[25] "Instead of the Intuition Principle we must say that the sense intuition has its own content, the understanding of the Verstand has its own content, and, going beyond the binary structure, that the judgment of the Vernunft has its own content. . . . Each cognitive act gives its partial object. It is the task of the entire structure which is summed up in the rational judgment to give the proper object of knowledge: being."[26] In Kant's assumption, however, the intellectual contributions of Verstand and Vernunft refer to reality only through the sensible intuition. In fact, Vernunft, as tendency toward the unconditioned, will be doubly mediated, through both intuition and understanding. On the other hand, in Lonergan's account, there is an immediate relationship to reality as intended, in the intention of being, and to reality as attained, in the judgment; and there is a mediate relation to reality in understanding and conceiving.

Sala now considers each of the elements in knowledge—sensibility, Verstand, and Vernunft—according to its a priori element in each system of thought under investigation. This enables

---

25
   Ibid., pp. 15f.

26
   Ibid., p. 16.

him to distinguish sharply between an operational-heuristic a priori and a content-objective a priori at each of the stages in the process of knowledge. Both of these notions are found in Kant, thus indicating an inconsistency. Only the operational-heuristic notion is found in Lonergan. As Sala will find valid the operational-heuristic a priori accounted for in Lonergan's Insight, and invalid the content-objective a priori in Kant's Critique of Pure Reason, so I am seeking for an elucidation of the symbolic a priori that is continuous with the operational-heuristic a priori governing cognitional process, a notion that does not reflect the Kantianism of the content-objective a priori sometimes found in Jung's writings. This reflected Kantianism is connected, I believe, with Jung's reified "collective unconscious" and with the mystifying connotations of the recent discussions of the mundus imaginalis.

First, then, sensibility. The forms of space and time are considered by Kant both as systems of relationship among the contents of experience (operational-heuristic) and as containing contents of their own independent of the a posteriori content of experience and capable of being considered in this independence (content-objective). The operative-heuristic notion states that the a priori is the law of sensitive receptive operativity in relation to sense impressions. Space and time are nothing if we prescind from the operativity of the senses when confronted with sense data. The sense representation conforms to the constitution of the sensing subject.

There is also a twofold presentation of the a priori of understanding in the Critique of Pure Reason. The operational-heuristic a priori lies in the categories considered purely and simply as functions of the synthetic unity, functions of a judgment without content. By their synthetic activity exercised upon the contents of sensibility, they bring sense knowledge up to the level of human knowledge. As subjective forms of the unity of understanding, they are not objective contents but "the ability of the Verstand to add an intelligible content to the sense object by operating a synthesis upon it."[27] The Verstand is a spontaneity, an original synthetic capacity. Sala maintains that Kant does not extend far enough his analysis of this synthetic capacity of intelligent consciousness, not so much because the categories are fixed at twelve--a common criticism of Kantian scholars--but because they are regarded in too formalistic and logical a manner, in that Kant's discussion of them is infected also with a content-objective notion of the a priori. "Actually the spontaneity of the Verstand cannot be pigeon-holed into any set of concepts. Every concept, no matter how general, is a posteriori; but the operative intelligibility of the Verstand, owing to which it is an intelligent intelligible, is a priori. The concept is the product of this intelligibility, never the norm of its operation."[28]

Kant's content-objective conception of the categories highlights the rigidity of his notion of the a priori of understanding. This a priori is an addition by the cognitive faculty to the raw

_____

27
  Ibid., p. 25.

28
  Ibid., p. 26.

material of the sense impressions, an addition in the form of an
objective content.

> The entire problematic of the application of the pure concepts
> of the understanding to a corresponding intuition makes sense
> only because the pure concept of understanding is a content to
> be applied. Likewise the description of the a priori as of
> something which lies ready in the mind or in the Verstand
> obviously indicates it to be an object. Further, the affir-
> mation that the a posteriori, the empirical intuition, is only
> the occasion or the opportunity for the mind to draw forth
> from itself the formal a priori elements which it already
> possesses, points in the same direction, for, as regards a
> heuristic a priori the given is much more than mere occasion.[29]

Kant's own inconsistency on this point makes it difficult to
interpret his doctrine. But the Transcendental Deduction of the Pure
Concepts of the Understanding denies that objects can be given in
intuition independently of functions of the understanding.

> The appearances which enter our field of consciousness are
> already fruits of the synthetic activity of the Verstand, which
> works upon the appearances through the imagination. This is
> the final word of the Kantian critique. . . . The unifying
> moments of the pure concepts of understanding, as well as of
> the pure intuitions, are the result of the synthetic unity of
> consciousness which operates from the very beginning of the
> cognitive process, and finds progressively in the a posteriori
> datum what it has put there itself and thus goes ahead creating
> on the different levels of the structure the conditions of pos-
> sibility of objectively valid knowledge.[30]

Thus even the empirical itself is actually a consequence of the synthetic activity of the imagination. On Sala's interpretation, this
represents an attempt to find a substitute for the act of understanding
in the sensible. It makes the final direction of Kant's epistemology
to be "toward a totally thetic knowledge." That is to say:

29
   Ibid., p. 28.

30
   Ibid., p. 30.

The a priori either posits or is itself constitutive of the reality which it makes us know. . . . Upon this thetic activity which extends to the Anschauung depends the ontological status of known reality. The obscurity, the tortuousness, and even the incoherence of the [Critique of Pure Reason] are owing to the aim of recovering empiricist realism within this idealist perspective. What we consider to be the final word of [the Critique of Pure Reason], whenever it is said and as soon as it is said, comes to be corrected and reinterpreted within the empiricist perspective--in a swinging movement which shows in itself no criterion for settling in any one definitive position.[31]

We move now to the a priori of the Vernunft. There is a tendency in the human mind to the unconditioned, a tendency which for Kant necessarily forces us to transcend the limits of experience and thus of objectively valid knowledge. There are two aspects of the unconditioned, constituting two modes of the a priori functioning of the Vernunft. The unconditioned is either the totality of conditions or it is the absolute simpliciter.

Thus there is an operative-heuristic a priori of reason, rationality on the part of the subject, which requires and seeks unconditionality on the side of the objective content presented by experience and understanding. For Kant, this exigency is satisfied only by an indefinite regressive discursus, an infinite regress of prosyllogisms, which never attains the unconditioned; the latter is rather the infinite series in its totality. "There is no sense according to which it can be said that [the unconditioned] is also at each link of the chain."[32]

---

[31] Ibid., pp. 31f.

[32] Ibid., p. 33B.

The a priori of reason for Lonergan, on the other hand, is the same exigency of consciousness for the unconditioned, but it operates by means of the question for reflection, Is it so? "Such a question expresses the insatisfaction [sic] of our mind in respect to any representation whatever which does not bear the mark of absoluteness, i.e., which is not of the same value as our dynamic orientation, which is unrestricted and therefore unconditioned."[33] The function of the a priori in respect to judgment lies not only in the fact that judgment gives the answer to our tendency to the unconditioned, but also and much more in the fact that this tendency to the unconditioned "constitutes the operativity of the subject according to which it acts on every level."[34]

Neither of the two modes of the unconditioned in Kant's Transcendental Dialectic--the totality of the conditions and the absolute simpliciter--is able to acquire objective reference and thus become constitutive of our knowledge. There are also two modes of the unconditioned in Insight: the formally unconditioned, which has no conditions whatever, and the virtually unconditioned, which has conditions which are, however, fulfilled. The virtually unconditioned, according to Lonergan, can enter into the constituting of our knowledge; the unconditioned as the totality of conditions, according to Kant, cannot. What is the difference between them?

33
  Ibid., p. 34.

34
  Ibid., p. 36.

For Kant, reason tends toward the absolute totality of one
unified system, for the universe is conceived as one system of
natural events deterministically connected. But if the universe is
not a pattern of internal relations, such that no aspect of it can
be known in isolation from any and all other aspects of it, if the
universe is not explanatory system whose single aspects are totally
determined by their internal relations with all other aspects, if the
existents and occurrences of the universe diverge non-systematically
from pure intelligibility such that statistical knowledge is true
knowledge and the universe a universe of facts, then a judgment is a
limited commitment. As Lonergan ways, "So far from resting on knowledge of the universe, it is to the effect that, no matter what the
rest of the universe may prove to be, at least this is so."[35] A
true judgment affirms a single unconditioned which has a finite number of conditions which are, in fact, fulfilled. Sala summarizes:

> The Kantian Unbedingtes is the comprehensive coherence which
> embraces the entire universe and towards which we tend by
> asking questions for intelligence. There is no doubt that
> in this sense the unconditioned has a purely normative func-
> tion in our knowledge. In fact what we grasp with the under-
> standing is always a partial intelligibility, which therefore
> is not unconditioned; in itself, by its nature of intelligi-
> bility, it implies merely the possibility of being, not being
> simpliciter. But our cognitional structure shows another kind
> of questions, those for reflection, which turn precisely upon
> those intelligibilities which embrace a limited sphere of the
> universe. Now the reflexive inquiry subsequent upon these
> questions is capable of attaining an unconditioned which is
> the result of a conditioned (expressed by the concept) with
> the fulfillment of its conditions. It is the virtually uncon-
> ditioned or de facto absolute.[36]

35
   Bernard Lonergan, Insight, p. 344.

36
   Giovanni Sala, op. cit., p. 38.

The peculiar contribution of judgment to the process of knowledge is thus the absolute positing of synthesis, the knowledge of what in fact is so.

> A mental synthesis which has the character of absoluteness is a true synthesis, and the true is the 'medium in quo ens cognoscitur.' The true meaning mediates reality for man. To speak of an absolute positing of a synthesis is not to speak of perception alone, nor of perception plus concept, but rather of an act which is empirical, intelligent, and rational. There is only one way of safeguarding the role which the senses as well as the concept play in our knowledge of reality and that is to recognize that both intuition and concept are constitutive of that absolute motivation through which the cognitional process passes from thinking to judging.[37]

This process seeks self-transcendence, which is found neither in experience nor in intelligibility, but only in judgment, where "the relativity to the subject is identical with the transcendence in respect to the same subject and in respect to any restrictive qualification whatever, because in this case, and only in this case, the subject is defined as a tendency to the transcendent."[38] The content of a true judgment is not relative to me.

> To ask whether we know being is the same as to ask whether we are capable of a representation whose character, formally as representation, is unconditionality. Our answer is yes, since we saw that the cognitive process is capable of representing the virtually unconditioned, by thinking of a conditioned and fulfilling its conditions. The delicate point is, how is the content of our representation absolute? And our answer is, not by the direct way of formal content, but by the indirect way of the virtually unconditioned.[39]

37
  Ibid., p. 42.

38
  Ibid., p. 43.

39
  Ibid., p. 44.

Thus functions the a priori of human consciousness as quest of the
unconditioned. The reflective recognition that the affirmation of
the virtually unconditioned, and this alone, brings about the transcendence of human knowledge is what is meant by "intellectual conversion." It is a conversion "from the animal extraversion with
which our psychic life first develops and which perseveres as a valid
function throughout our entire human life, to the intellectuality and
rationality constitutive of our spirit, recognized and accepted, as
the immanent norm of our knowledge of the universe of being."[40]

Ultimately, then, on this analysis, the a priori of human
subjectivity is man's intrinsic endowment of meaning, "the dynamism,
intelligently and rationally conscious, which lies at the source of
the cognitive process, and thoroughly penetrates it, setting up the
principles normative of the different phases of the structure in which
it is realized."[41] Such an analysis eliminates a content-objective a
priori. "It does not seem to us that an attentive analysis of knowledge, particularly in its character of receptivity and development
confirms the a priori as a knowledge of an object, or of a partial
object, which lies ready in the mind."[42]

But, as we have emphasized throughout this paper, the proper
analysis of human subjectivity extends beyond scientific knowledge to

---

40
  Ibid.

41
  Ibid., p. 46.

42
  Ibid.

every other field and even reveals that the operative-heuristic
intelligible which we are <u>creates</u>, <u>constitutes</u> the meaning of man
and his world. At this point, that of the existential subject, and
not at the point of the objective knowledge of nature, we can restore
the Kantian thetic conception of the <u>a priori</u>.

> As regards the human world, the affirmation that objects must
> conform to our knowledge, i.e., to our intentionality or to
> our capacity of giving a meaning, or that we know of things
> only what we ourselves put into them, must be taken literally.
> Here truly the spirit gives the law to reality, raising nature
> to the ontological level of human reality. Here knowledge of
> reality is essentially interpretation, that is, knowledge of
> the meaning understood and realized by others from the horizon
> of their own meaning.[43]

Such interpretation is an <u>evaluative hermeneutic</u>. That is to say:

> The expansion of consciousness to the rational level is the
> ultimate as for the cognitive activity, but not as for the
> conscious activity of man. Our a priori is not only a dynamism
> which demands the truth of knowing in order to attain being, but
> also, beyond that, the consistency between knowing and doing in
> order to constitute the authentic human living on the basis of
> a true meaning.[44]

After this lengthy summary, and with this final constitutive
operation of consciousness in the forefront of our minds, we must turn
to Jung and seek light on the status of what he calls the archetypes.
Jung never seems to have attained to a sufficiently clear distinction
between these two modes of understanding the <u>a priori</u> element at the
symbolic level--the operative-heuristic and the content-objective <u>a
priori</u>. It is obvious, nonetheless, that he wrestled strenuously with
this precise problem. It will be our task to refine his notion so as

---

[43]
   <u>Ibid</u>., p. 46.

[44]
   <u>Ibid</u>., pp. 46f.

to render it continuous with Lonergan's treatment of the cognitive
and existential subject.

The Psychic A Priori

In one essay, Jung speaks of the archetypes as "autonomous
elements of the unconscious psyche which were there before any in-
vention was thought of." They are representations of the unalterable
structure of "a psychic world whose 'reality' is attested by the
determining effects it has upon the conscious mind."[45] This description is vague. What is unalterable, the structure or the representations, the structure or the psychic world itself?

In another volume, Jung's description would seem to indicate
that it is the representations of the psychic world itself, its contents, that are unalterable: "Within the limits of psychic experience, the collective unconscious takes the place of the Platonic realm
of eternal ideas. Instead of these models giving form to created
things, the collective unconscious, through its archetypes, provides
the a priori condition for the assignment of meaning."[46] Yet even
here there is a vagueness, for what is explicitly called a priori is
a condition of significance. But in the same volume there is reference
to "primordial images" which "can rise up anywhere at any time quite
spontaneously, without the least evidence of any external tradition,"[47]

45
    C. G. Jung, "Phenomenology of the Spirit in Fairytales,"
p. 250, par. 451.

46
    C. G. Jung, Mysterium Coniunctionis, p. 87, par. 101.

47
    Ibid., p. 88, par. 103.

and these primordial images are called "<u>symptoms</u> of the uniformity
of <u>Homo</u> <u>sapiens</u>."[48]

In his commentary on "The Secret of the Golden Flower,"
Jung speaks of the collective unconscious as "a common substratum
transcending all differences in culture and consciousness," comparable to the common anatomy of the human body through all racial
differences. He tells us that this common substratum consists not
merely of contents which can become conscious, but of "latent predispositions towards identical reactions." Thus the collective unconscious is "simply the psychic expression of the identity of brain
structure irrespective of all racial differences. This explains the
analogy, sometimes even identity, between the various myth motifs and
symbols, and the possibility of human communication in general. The
various lines of psychic development start from one common stock
whose roots reach back into the most distant past. This also accounts
for the psychological parallelisms with animals."[49] Jung goes on to
present the psychological meaning of this physiological "common stock."

In purely psychological terms this means that mankind has common
instincts of ideation and action. All conscious ideation and
action have developed on the basis of these unconscious archetypal patterns and always remain dependent on them. This is
especially the case when consciousness has not attained any high
degree of clarity, when in all its functions it is more dependent on the instincts than on the conscious will, more governed
by affect than by rational judgment.[50]

48
  <u>Ibid.</u>, p. xiii.

49
  C. G. Jung, <u>Alchemical Studies</u>, pp. 11f., par. 11.

50
  <u>Ibid.</u>

Thus, as long as circumstances do not arise that call for higher
moral effort, a "primitive state of psychic health" is assured.
When these patterns are assimilated by a higher and wider consciousness, however, an autonomy from the old "gods" develops; they are
recognized as "nothing other than those mighty, primoridal images
that hitherto have held our consciousness in thrall."[51]

There is still no clear distinction between structure and
content. The confusion is a bit less, however, in "Psychological
Aspects of the Mother Archetype."[52] At first, it appears that Jung
will clearly opt for a direction in which we would prefer not to go,
for he places his discussion in a context of what he calls a "rebirth
of the Platonic spirit" prepared, paradoxically, by Kant's destruction
of naive metaphysics. But then he immediately focuses his attention
on a priori structure. "There is an a priori factor in all human
activities, namely the inborn, preconscious and unconscious individual
structure of the psyche."[53] This structure consists of patterns of
functioning which Jung calls "images." The term "image" now designates a form of activity in a given situation. These patterns are
primordial in that they are peculiar to the whole human species. The
products of dream and fantasy render these patterns visible, "and it
is here that the concept of the archetype finds its specific

51
  Ibid.

52
  C. G. Jung, The Archetypes and the Collective Unconscious,
pp. 73-100.

53
  Ibid., p. 77, par. 151.

application."[54] While there is still some confusion in Jung's ex-
position, it is clear that what is a priori consists at least of
"living predispositions . . . that preform and continually influence
our thoughts and feelings and actions."[55] And according to the
formulation of this essay, at least, it is mistaken to think of
these dispositions on the analogy of "unconscious ideas." Most clear
and explicit of all is the following statement: "Archetypes are not
determined as regards their content, but only as regards their form
and then only to a very limited degree. A primordial image is determined as to its content only when it has become conscious and is
therefore filled out with the material of conscious experience. . . .
The archetype in itself is empty and purely formal, nothing but a
facultas praeformandi, a possibility of representation which is given
a priori."[56] Jung distinguishes between the archetype as such and its
representations in images and ideas. The representations are "varied
structures which all point back to one essentially 'irrepresentable'
basic form. The latter is characterized by certain formal elements
and by certain fundamental meanings, although these can be grasped
only approximately. . . . Everything archetypal which is perceived
by consciousness seems to represent a set of variations on a ground

---

54
    Ibid., p. 78, par. 153.

55
    Ibid., p. 79, par. 154.

56
    Ibid., p. 79, par. 155.

theme."[57]

The way to remove the abiding confusion between two different notions of the symbolic a priori in Jung's writings, it seems, is by clarifying this ground theme. The ground theme is the emergence or failure of emergence of the authentic existential subject as free and responsible constitutive agent of the human world. The basic a priori which is man's consciousness determines the theme. It is an intention of intelligibility, truth, and value, and it is to be realized only in self-transcending cognitional and existential subjectivity. This basic a priori is operative-heuristic. As such, it promotes human experience to human understanding by means of questions for intelligence, and human understanding to truth by means of questions for reflection. This same a priori dynamism promotes truth into action in a thetic manner, for the action is constitutive of the human world. The promotion of truth into action consistent with truth occurs through questions for deliberation. The primordial apprehension of the data for these questions occurs in feelings. These feelings structure various patterns of experience. These patterns of experience are imaginally or archetypally meaningful. The archetypal images revealed in dreams, then, promote both neural and psychic process, which permeates the various patterns of experience, to the status of a recognizable and intelligible narrative. The narrative has to do with the ground theme. When the patterns of experience have been released from their more or less customary muteness through symbolic images, they

---

57
Ibid.

can be interpreted. When the interpretation is affirmed to be true, the images have functioned helpfully in the process of bringing the existential subject to genuine self-knowledge. The archetypal function is part and parcel of the basic a priori which is man's consciousness.

This account is faithful to the process of analysis. With the aid of an analyst, I interpret the symbols of my dreams; I affirm the meaning interpreted; I thus come to a knowledge of my present condition, situation, and possibilities, through the illumination of "how I find myself" afforded by the symbolic images. The word "possibilities" is important. The image is an aid, not only to what we might call a symptomatic hermeneutic, but also to an evaluative hermeneutic. As Jung rightly insists, the image is creative. Psychotherapy aims not only at self-knowledge but also, beyond the affirmation of an interpretation as true, at the constitution and transformation of the subject and his world through authentic praxis. At this point the knowledge gained in the affirmation of a dream interpretation as true becomes thetic knowledge. What am I going to do about it? The interpretation of the image ought not to be affirmed as true, is not correctly so affirmed, unless it includes an interpretation of the creative possibilities revealed in the image. Genuine dream interpretation thus consists in the attentive reception of the dream as exploratory of the dispositional aspect of immediacy in its temporal constitution; in the understanding of what is thus laid open; in the judgment that the understanding is accurate; and in the responsible appropriation and negotiation of this self-knowledge in the

ongoing transformation of the human world and in the constitution
of myself as a free and responsible subject. The ultimate intentionality of authentic psychotherapy is coextensive with the total sweep
of the conscious intentionality of human subjectivity which is man's
basic a priori. The psychotherapeutic function is to conscript psyche
into the single transcendental dynamism of human consciousness toward
the authenticity of self-transcendence. This function is rendered
capable of being executed because the archetypal spontaneity of the
psyche directly pertains to and is part and parcel of this single
transcendental dynamism. The execution of this function is, as we
have seen, dialectical, for there is also a resistance factor in the
psyche parallel to the tendencies to bias on the part of cognitional
and volitional subjectivity. But the genuine intention of authentic
psychic self-appropriation is to enable one to achieve the capacity to
discover the symbolic meanings through which his world is both mediated
and potentially constituted at any given time, the symbolic meanings
through which his own story unfolds, so as to facilitate the development of the story as a reflection of the ground theme of human existence. The contents of the images are a posteriori, even when they
are found commonly across cultural, racial, and historical barriers.
Their operative-heuristic function is a priori, and it is what determines their ground theme, the emergence of the existential subject as
originative value. The common features found, it would seem, universally, reflect the structure of the ground theme, which in every case
is the primordial struggle between the dynamism to truth and value on
one side and the flight from genuine humanity on the other.

There is a sense, then, in which it is quite legitimate to speak of a symbolic a priori. Nonetheless, I prefer to use the expression, the archetypal function, so as to discourage the possibility of the content-objective understanding of the psyche still too prevalent in the writings of Jung.

CHAPTER V

PSYCHE AND INTENTIONALITY

In this chapter, I wish to present a more detailed understanding of the sublation of psyche into the dynamism of intentionality. We have already seen that the mediation of cognitive and
dispositional immediacy issues in second immediacy; that symbols
structure and reflect dispositional immediacy and thus that a
release of the symbolic function aids the mediation of dispositional
immediacy; that this is a dialectical process whose principal pro-
tagonists are intentionality and psyche; that this dialectic is
necessitated by a further dialectic within psyche itself; and that
psychic process is continuous with intentionality process because of
the operative-heuristic a priori function of symbols as operators,
so that the sublations which structure the emergence of intelligent,
rational, and responsible consciousness are complemented by a sublation raising dreaming consciousness to existential significance.
Now we must detail further the relationship between psyche and intentionality, by speaking, first, of the therapeutic context; secondly,
of psychic energy; thirdly, of the mutual qualifications of intentionality and psyche; fourthly, of psychic conversion; and fifthly,
of the psychic and the psychoid.

The Therapeutic Context

The sublation of the imaginal by existential subjectivity
is achieved in a psychotherapeutic context, in the general case.
It is effected in a cooperative-intersubjective milieu, with the aid
of a professional guide to lead one to the discovery and negotiation
of the archetypal function. Thus, for Gerhard Adler, the actual
interviews with an analyst play the decisive part in establishing
familiarity with the archetypal function as a permanent conscious
capacity on the part of an individual. "A great deal of impressive
unconscious material may be thrown up by the unconscious without
ever being 'realized;' the concreteness of the relationship, of the
encounter with an 'opposite,' plays an integral part in the assimilation of unconscious imagery, which otherwise may remain mere unuti-
lized raw material."[1]

Is the analytic situation needed? Adler comments:

This process can, and does, take place outside and without
analysis. But it is such a difficult process, full of pitfalls
at every step, that analysis seems often the only way. Simi-
larly, in the East there is also the possibility of achieving
by one's own effort insight into the nature of Brahman and into
its essential unity with the individual Atman; this is, however,
a rare alternative to the general way of achieving such insight
with the help of a guru.[2]

---

[1]
Gerhard Adler, The Living Symbol, p. 8. A number of the
quotations in this chapter will contain terminology which I have
tried to replace with what I believe to be more accurage language.
An effort must be made to read these quotations with my suggested
changes in mind.

[2]
Ibid.

We might also use the analogy of the experience of making the Ignatian _Spiritual Exercises_ with and without a competent director. In this case, the danger of self-delusion, of simply reinforcing one's religious inauthenticity, is so great that the attempt to proceed without competent direction, no matter what the extent of one's experience in prayer, is at best highly suspect. So too, it would seem, a guide to the attainment of familiarity with the complexity of the archetypal function is necessary until one has reached the point of quick and accurate access to the process of the ongoing appropriation of dreams. When this point is reached, I believe, the analysis is to be terminated. Otherwise one runs the risk of courting in a psychic fashion what Ivan Illych has called "iatrogenic disease."[3]

Particularly persistent in the analytic process is the almost inveterate habit of failing to realize that, in the general case, _the figures revealed in dreams are aspects of the dreaming subject._ This habitual failure is, I suspect, not unrelated to the extraversion responsible for the cognitive myth that the real is a subdivision of the "already out there now." Furthermore, it entails the subsequent tendency to view dreams as thermometers rather than barometers, as explanatory rather than exploratory, as referring to space before time and to the specific before the generic. An uncritical engagement in

---

[3] Ivan Illych, _Medical Nemesis: The Expropriation of Health_ (Cidoc Cuaderno, No. 89, 1974). The termination of the analysis is not the end of the psychic journey. In one sense, the latter never ends, in that one is certain to continue to have dreams as long as one lives. In another sense, though, it does end in the discovery of the soul beyond psychology which is the movement into the realm of transcendence.

the analytic process could very easily mire one further in myth and, depending on the atmospheric pressure, can eventuate in either temporary or permanent psychosis. Psychosis is a restoration to one's roots in the rhythms and processes of nature, but in such a way that nothing remains but the roots, entangling one another and eventually choking each other's avenue to differentiated consciousness. The return to the roots must be in terms of time rather than space, the interior rather than the exterior, the generic rather than the specific, and with reference to the self-transcendence of the existential subject in the constitution of the real world of men. For such a process to be successful, in the general case, it is helpful that one be warned by the admonitions of one well aware of these differences.

This is not to say that there are not dreams which are directly prophetic of external situations which may have either a great deal or seemingly very little to do with one's own responsibility as constitutive agent of the human world. Thus Bishop Joseph Lanyi of Grosswardein, Hungary, dreamed of the assassination of Archduke Ferdinand of Austria several hours before the event took place. He was awakened by the dream and immediately drew a picture of the event of which he dreamed. The picture corresponded almost point by point to the details of the assassination.[4] Needless to say, such dreams are the exception and indicate the limited range of our scientific knowledge of the sphere of being I have called the imaginal. But even those dreams which are prophetic of as yet unfamiliar places, people, and existential situations

---

[4] Edward C. Whitmont, The Symbolic Quest (New York: C. G. Jung Foundation, 1969), pp. 54f.

in one's own life, while not symbolically over-determined in the
same sense as most of the dreams which we can remember, and thus
while quite specific, are only appropriated by intentional consciousness to the extent that they are understood as bearing upon
interiority, the temporal, the generic, and one's stance vis-a-vis
the hierarchy of values.

The psychotherapeutic context must also respect the archeological-teleological unity-in-tension of the concrete symbol insis-
ted on by Ricoeur in his critique of Freud. The psychotherapeutic
context will thus be closer to that suggested by Jung than to that
inspired by Freud, for Jung was more aware of this tension within
symbolic process. The analytic process is reductive in the same way
that the hermeneutic of suspicion is an intrinsic and integral part
of the dialectical interpretation of symbols, and thus in the same
way that extreme iconoclasm belongs to the restoration of meaning.
The analytic process should further a gradually emerging pattern of
inner order, a continuous process of integration, a sense-giving
factor in the psyche,[5] but it must do so in part by mercilessly destroying the mythic reenactment of symbols in terms of immediate
belief, by moving their intentionality from the exterior, spatial,
specific, and human, to the interior, temporal, generic, and religious, from the explanatory to the exploratory.

This notion of the analytic process is more readily available
in Jung's writings than in those of Freud. These two pioneers of the

----

5
  Gerhard Adler, op. cit., p. 4.

psychotherapeutic revolution are not to be viewed simply as opposed
to one another, however, with Freud concerned only with reduction
and Jung solely with teleological orientation. While Ricoeur has
indicated the teleological moment implicit in Freudian analysis,
Jung speaks of a reductive moment in the analysis which he proposes.
This reductive moment "breaks down all inappropriate symbol-formations
and reduces them to their natural elements,"[6] while the synthetic
moment would consist in the integration and appropriation of the
archetypal spontaneity of one's psyche. As Adler says, "Indeed, it
is possible to lose sight of the fact that there are analyses in which
the therapeutic goal appears to be reached almost exclusively by a
process of _symbolical transformation_."[7] Jung comments on the complementarity of reduction and teleology in this transformative process:

> In psychology as in biology we cannot afford to overlook or
> underestimate [the] question of origins, although the answer
> usually tells nothing about the functional meaning. For this
> reason biology should never forget the question of purpose, for
> only by answering that can we get at the meaning of a phenomenon.
> . . . There are a number of pathological phenomena which only
> give up their meaning when we inquire into their purpose. And
> where we are concerned with the normal phenomena of life, this
> question of purpose takes undisputed precedence. . . .
> To supplement the causal approach by a final one therefore
> enables us to arrive at more meaningful interpretations not only
> in medical psychology, where we are concerned with individual
> fantasies originating in the unconscious, but also in the case

6
C. G. Jung, "On Psychic Energy," in _The Structure and
Dynamics of the Psyche_, p. 49, par. 93.

7
Gerhard Adler, _op. cit._, p. 3. On Jung and Freud, see
Bernard Lonergan, _Method in Theology_, pp. 67f., and especially foot-
note 4 on p. 68.

of collective fantasies, that is, myths and fairytales.[8]

There is another major difference between Freud and Jung which decisively calls for favoring Jung, namely his recognition of archetypes. For many people, Jung maintains, religious symbols have lost their numinosity, their thrilling power. The compensating primordial images which appear in dreams are for Jung wrongly reduced by Freud to purely personal experiences in much the same way as the alchemists misplaced them onto chemical substances.

> Both of them act as though they knew to what known quantities the meaning of their symbols could be reduced. . . . The result of this reduction . . . is not very satisfactory--so little, in fact, that Freud saw himself obliged to go back as far as possible into the past. In so doing he finally hit upon an uncommonly numinous idea, the archetype of incest. He thus found something that to some extent expressed the real meaning and purpose of symbol production, which is to bring about an awareness of those primordial images that belong to all men and can therefore lead the individual out of his isolation.

But Freud failed to realize the ulterior meaning of this insight and "succumbed to the numinous effect of the primordial image he had discovered." That is, he allowed himself to become a victim of what I have called myth by personalizing the archetype in the Oedipal complex and historicizing it in the murder of the primal father.[9] He made the symbol explanatory and etiological rather than exploratory and hermeneutic.

8
C. G. Jung, "On the Psychology of the Trickster Figure," in The Archetypes and the Collective Unconscious, pp. 260 and 266, pars. 465 and 476.

9
C. G. Jung, "The Philosophical Tree," Alchemical Studies, pp. 301f., par. 396.

On Jung's view, then, Freud missed the nature of the symbol. Freud's method consists in collecting a series of clues pointing to an unconscious background and interpreting this material in such a way as to reconstruct a set of elementary instinctual processes. Freud referred to these conscious clues as symbols but in reality they function for him as no more than signs or symptoms of "already there" subliminal processes.

> The true symbol differs essentially from this, and should be understood as an expression of an intuitive idea that cannot yet be formulated in any other or better way. When Plato, for instance, puts the whole problem of the theory of knowledge in his parable of the cave, or when Christ expresses the idea of the Kingdom of Heaven in parables, these are genuine and true symbols, that is, attempts to express something for which no verbal concept yet exists. If we were to interpret Plato's metaphor in Freudian terms we would naturally arrive at the uterus, and would have proved that even a mind like Plato's was still stuck on a primitive level of infantile sexuality. But we would have completely overlooked what Plato actually created out of the primitive determinants of his philosophical ideas, we would have missed the essential point and merely discovered that he had infantile sexual fantasies like any other mortal.[10]

Jung is not denying a partial validity to the Freudian therapeutic method, however. Pathological psychic formations must be broken down, so as to prepare the way for normal, healthy adaptation. But Jung denies the adequacy of Freud's method, and highlights its unsatisfactoriness by pointing to the poverty of Freud's critique of culture. When the Freudian point of view is applied, for example, to a work of art, it

---

[10]
C. G. Jung, "On the Relations of Analytical Psychology to Poetry," in The Spirit in Man, Art, and Literature, Collected Works vol. 15 (Princeton: Bollingen Series XX, 1966), p. 70, par. 105.

> . . . strips the work of art of its shimmering robes and
> exposes the nakedness and drabness of <u>Homo sapiens</u>, to which
> species the poet and artist also belong. The golden gleam
> of artistic creation . . . is extinguished as soon as we
> apply to it the same corrosive method which we use in ana-
> lyzing the fantasies of hysteria. The results are no doubt
> very interesting and may perhaps have the same kind of scien-
> tific value as, for instance, a post-mortem examination of
> Nietzsche, which might conceivably show us the particular
> atypical form of paralysis from which he died. But what
> would this have to do with <u>Zarathustra</u>? Whatever its sub-
> terranean background may have been, is it not a whole world
> in itself, beyond the human all-too-human imperfections,
> beyond the world of migraine and cerebral atrophy?[11]

It is the exclusiveness of Freudian reductionism, then, to

which Jung objects. "Freud's only interest is where things come

from, never where they are going. . . . Many psychological facts

have explanations entirely different from those based on the <u>faux pas</u>

of a <u>chronique scandaleuse</u>."[12]

The validity of Freudian method for Jung lies primarily in

its appropriateness to the historical situation in which it emerged.

Freud

> . . . preaches those truths which it is of paramount importance
> that the neurotic of the early twentieth century should under-
> stand because he is an unconscious victim of late Victorian
> psychology. Psychoanalysis destroys the false values in him
> personally by cauterizing away the rottenness of the dead cen-
> tury. . . . But in so far as a neurosis is not an illness spe-
> cific to the Victorian era but enjoys a wide distribution in
> time and space, and is therefore found among people who are not
> in need of any special sexual enlightenment or the destruction
> of harmful assumptions in this respect, a theory of neurosis or
> of dreams which is based on a Victorian prejudice is at most of
> secondary importance. . . . Freud has not penetrated into [the]

11
  <u>Ibid</u>., p. 69, par. 103.

12
  C. G. Jung, "Sigmund Freud in His Historical Setting," in
<u>ibid</u>., pp. 37f., par. 54.

deeper layer which is common to all men. He could not have
done so without being untrue to his historical task. And
this task he has fulfilled--a task enough for a whole life's
work, and fully deserving the fame it has won.[13]

In terms of our present analysis, we might say that Freud's
exclusivistic reductionism is due to a propensity to interpret
dream images in a content-objective rather than operative-heuristic
way. Causal exclusivism is parallel with a tendency to view "unconscious" processes as causing distorted content-images which
influence conscious life, culture and religion. An operative-heuristic notion, on the other hand, is by definition bound to teleology.

Psychic Energy

What seems to be at stake in this discussion is the nature
of psychic energy. Jung distinguishes between a mechanistic, purely
causal standpoint and an energic, final standpoint. The assumption
of the latter is that "some kind of energy underlies the changes in
phenomena, that it maintains itself as a constant throughout these
changes and finally leads to entropy, a condition of general equili-
brium," which can be called its direction or goal. This energic
standpoint is for Jung "an indispensable explanatory principle,"
functioning as "the logical reverse of the principle of causality."[14]

Now such a standpoint is valid for Jung only if some kind of
"quantitative estimate" of psychic energy is possible. Jung finds

---

13
  Ibid., pp. 39f., pars. 56, 57, and 59.

14
  C. G. Jung, "On Psychic Energy," pp. 3-5, pars. 2-4.

one source of such "quantitative estimates" in an individual's conscious system of values. "Values are quantitative estimates of energy."[15] Thus, we can determine the relative strength of our evaluations by weighing them against one another in terms of different intensities of value in relation to similar qualities or objects. But--a caution very pertinent to our present discussion-- such a process has minimal applicability once we realize how much of our orientation to the world is undifferentiated or, in Jung's terms, in relation to unconscious value intensities. Here another point of departure is required, one that will allow some indirect estimate.

Jung maintains that his early studies in word association showed the existence of groupings of psychic elements around feeling-toned contents or complexes, whose psychological significance is frequently "unconscious." Each complex has a nucleus consisting, first, of an experientially and environmentally determined factor and, second, of an innate and dispositional factor in the individual. The feeling-toned complex is a "value quantity." An indirect estimate of this quantity is possible, based on the constellating power of its nuclear element, which can be estimated in terms of the relative number of constellations it effects, the relative frequency and intensity of the reactions indicating a complex, and the intensity of the accompanying affects. The symbolic images of dreams are ciphers to such an estimate.

---

[15]
Ibid., p. 9, par. 4.

Psychic energy for Jung is a specific part of a broader energy called life energy or libido. The main principle governing an understanding of its functioning is the principle of the conservation of energy, especially as considered under the rubric of the principle of equivalence: "For a given quantity of energy expended or consumed in bringing about a certain condition, an equal quantity of the same or another form of energy will appear elsewhere."[16] Freud has clearly shown the psychological applicability of this principle in his account of repressions and their consequent substitute formations. But for Jung, while libido never leaves one structure, e.g., the sexual, to pass over into another, without taking the character of the old structure over into the new, the idea of psychic development demands the possibility of change in various systems of energy capable of theoretically unlimited interchangeability and modulation under the principle of equivalence. In other words a theory of psychic development demands the teleological point of view, according to which causes are also means to an end. The theory of the symbol is the key to this teleological point of view.

From a purely causal point of view, the whole edifice of civilization becomes a mere substitute for the impossibility of incest. But the teleological point of view takes seriously the difference, for example, between the personal mother and the mother-imago and regards regression to the latter as a means of finding the memory associations by means of which further development can take place--e.g., from a

----

[16]
Ibid., p. 18, par. 34.

sexual system into an intellectual or spiritual system. Thus, "what to the causal view is fact to the final view is symbol, and vice versa. . . . The symbolic interpretation of causes by means of the energic standpoint is necessary for the differentiation of the psyche, since unless the facts are symbolically interpreted, the causes remain immutable substances which go on operating continuously. . . . Cause alone does not make development possible. For the psyche the reductio ad causam is the very reverse of development; it binds the libido to the elementary facts."[17]

Thus, when psychic development has occurred it is because the causes have been (operatively and heuristically) transformed into "symbolical expressions for the way that lies ahead. The exclusive importance of the cause . . . thus disappears and emerges again in the symbol, whose power of attraction represents the equivalent quantum of libido."[18] In the context of our previous discussion of mystery and myth, a reenactment of the symbol through immediate belief is a reduction of the symbol to a cause, while the reenactment through sympathetic imagination holds fast to the symbolic quality and follows its direction toward development. The attitude of mystery alone is in accord with the principle of equivalence, which for Jung is the basic law of psychic energy.

---

[17] Ibid., p. 24, pars. 45f.

[18] Ibid., p. 24, par. 46.

The direction of psychic energy's symbolic process is towards entropy, an equalization of differences or a unity of opposites. Thus, Jung's alchemically inspired understanding of a unity of opposites cumulatively yielding a new attitude whose stability is the greater in proportion to the magnitude of the initial differences, is an expression of the teleological point of view.

> The greater the tension between the pairs of opposites, the greater will be the energy that comes from them; and the greater the energy, the stronger will be its constellating, attracting power. This increased power of attraction corresponds to a wider range of constellated psychic material, and the further this range extends, the less chance is there of subsequent disturbances which might arise from friction with material not previously constellated. For this reason an attitude that has been formed out of a far-reaching process of equalization is an especially lasting one.[19]

Jung refers to the process of the transformation of energy as "the canalization of libido," a phrase which refers to the "transfer of psychic intensities or values from one content to another."[20] Culture results from and then further enables the conversion of natural instincts into other dynamic forms productive of work. Instinctual energy is channeled into an analogue of its natural object. "Just as a power-station imitates a waterfall and thereby gains possession of its energy, so the psychic mechanism [the symbol] imitates the instinct and is thereby enabled to apply its energy for special purposes."[21]

19
  Ibid., p. 26, par. 49.

20
  Ibid., p. 41, par. 79.

21
  Ibid., p. 42, par. 83.

It is only a small part of our total psychic energy that can
be thus diverted from its natural flow, a relative surplus of energy
not used to sustain the regular course of life. It is the symbol
that makes this deflection of excess libido possible. An energy-
converting symbol is called by Jung a "libido analogue."[22] It "can
give equivalent expression to the libido and canalize it into a form
different from the original one."[23] These symbols have never been
devised consciously, but have always been produced spontaneously.
Most of the symbols used throughout history for the conversion of
psychic energy probably derive directly from dreams. Today we are
witnessing a recrudescence of such individual symbol-formations parallel to the fading away of those religious forms which tended to suppress
individual symbol-formation as a matter of central significance for life.

Reductive psychoanalysis is called for, then, when one's psychic
libido flows off unconsciously along too low a gradient. This is the
moment which "breaks down all inappropriate symbol-formations and reduces them to their natural elements,"[24] restoring the natural flow of
life-energy. But another gradient than the merely natural one will be
sought for one's excess libido. "When the unsuitable structures have
been reduced and the natural course of things is restored, so that
there is some possibility of the patient living a normal life, the

---

22
   Ibid., p. 48, par. 92.

23
   Ibid.

24
   Ibid., p. 49, par. 93.

reductive process should not be continued further. Instead, symbol-formation should be reinforced in a synthetic direction until a more favourable gradient for the excess libido is found."[25] "Reversion to nature must therefore be followed by a synthetic reconstruction of the symbol"[26] in a spiritual, cultural, and religious direction.

> Freudian theory consists in a causal explanation of the psychology of instinct. From this standpoint the spiritual principle is bound to appear only as an appendage, a by-product of the instincts. Since its inhibiting and restrictive power cannot be denied, it is traced back to the influence of education, moral authorities, convention, and tradition. These authorities in their turn derive their power, according to the theory, from repression in the manner of a vicious circle. The spiritual principle is not recognized as an equivalent counterpart of the instincts.[27]

When useless symbols are broken down by reduction and life is returned to its natural course, a damming up of libido occurs. This condition can be the beginning of an individual religion, which is the way to further development.

> . . . an advance always begins with individuation, that is to say with the individual, conscious of his isolation, cutting a new path through hitherto untrodden territory. To do this he must first return to the fundamental facts of his own being, irrespective of all authority and tradition, and allow himself to become conscious of his distinctiveness. If he succeeds in giving collective validity to his widened consciousness, he creates a

---

25
 Ibid., p. 50, par. 94. Jung is here expressing his understanding and conviction of what I would call the intention of truth and value, of self-transcendence, within the psyche itself.

26
 Ibid., p. 50, par. 95.

27
 Ibid., p. 55, par. 104.

tension of opposites that provides the stimulation which culture needs for its further progress.[28]

The transformation of energy from biological forms to cultural forms,
aside from the forced sublimations of convention and collective religion, is always an individual one and is achieved by means of the
symbol.

James Hillman goes so far as to say, correctly I believe,
that Jung's psychology is a psychology of creativity. For Jung the
creative is the essence of man. In addition to the "instincts" of
hunger, sexuality, activity, and reflection, there is the "instinct
of creativity," the quintessentia. "His major concern in both his
therapy and his writing was with the manifestations and vicissitudes
of the creative instinct and with disentangling it from the other
four. Consequently, we are led to state that Jungian psychology is
based primarily upon the creative instinct and in turn to infer that
Jungian psychology is primarily a creative psychology."[29] Thus, "his
insistence upon finality in regard to the libido, upon the final point
of view toward all psychic phenomena and upon the prospective interpretation of the dream--all have as basis a creative psychology."[30]
On our analysis, then, Jung's concern with an archeology of the subject is within a broader dialectical and operative-heuristic context
concerned with the fulfillment of psychic infrastructure in its

---

28
   Ibid., p. 59, par. 111.

29
   James Hillman, The Myth of Analysis, pp. 33f.

30
   Ibid., p. 35.

incorporation into the dynamism of intentionality.

Intentionality and Psyche

We are offering here, though, not Jungian psychology, but a new interpretation of what psychotherapy can become. My specific points of difference with Jung have already been indicated, and those that are epistemological have, I believe, been at least partly settled. Let me add simply that by "inappropriate symbol-formations" I mean those formations which sponsor a reenactment of the symbol through immediate belief or an acceptance of the symbol as explanatory, and which orient the subject immediately to the exterior, the spatial, the specific, and the human. The process of symbolic transformation would involve the turn to the interior, the temporal, the generic, and the transcendent.

In addition, though, I am insisting that the process of intentional self-appropriation toward which Lonergan leads one should be regarded as the first and indispensable moment in a total mediation of immediacy within the context of method. The appropriation of one's cognitional being through the aid of Insight is the first stage of a more inclusive process. When joined with Lonergan's later analysis of the existential subject, it is the stage of the discrimination of spirit, of active mind, of logos, word, idea, intellect, principle, abstraction, meaning, ratio, nous, animus. A second stage is that of the cultivation of soul. It is the stage of psyche, mythos, image, symbol, atmosphere, feeling, relation, earth, nature, rhythm, anima. The end point in this stage is the experience of the Crucified as symbol of the Self. A third stage then follows, beyond logos and

psyche, reason and imagination, _animus_ and _anima_, beyond common
sense, theory, and interiority. It is the progressive discovery
of the realm of transcendence. It is the religious journey under
the cloud of unknowing. It is the agapic stage of the surrender
of discriminated spirit and cultivated soul to the _mysterium_ _tre-
mendum_ _et_ _fascinans_. The movement of self-appropriation in the
context of method should pass through these stages in this order,
for the cultivation of soul without the discrimination of spirit is
the romantic agony, and religion without psyche is rootless. In
contrast, the process of self-appropriation I am suggesting would
provide, as I will argue in the next chapter, the inclusive horizon
for the theological enterprise in our emerging epoch and the key to
dialectic and foundations as functional specialties within both the
scienza _nuova_ in general and theology in particular. When method
takes the step into the domain of psyche, when self-appropriation
becomes appropriation first of intentionality and then of psyche,
the foundations of theology consist of a patterned set of judgments
of cognitional fact and of value cumulatively heading toward the
full position on the human subject.

Nonetheless, intelligence, reason, and intentionality can
also be understood archetypally from the standpoint of the psyche.
The psyche seems to insist on this input, as a matter of fact. Not
only does Jung speak of a "thinking function," but he adds that a
change has come over our consideration of understanding and reason
since Kant's _Critique of Pure Reason_, a change which for me is valid
irrespective of whether one accepts Kantian epistemology, a change

which reflects the dynamic thrust of the _anthropologische Wendung_ toward radicalization. Understanding and reason are no longer regarded as independent processes subject only to the eternal laws of logic. Rather, they are "co-ordinated with the personality and subordinate to it." This means the addition of a "personal equation" in every intellectual investigation.

> We no longer ask, "Has this or that been seen, heard, handled, weighed, counted, thought, and found to be logical?" We ask instead, "Who saw, heard, or thought?" . . . Today we are convinced that in all fields of knowledge psychological premises exist which exert a decisive influence upon the choice of material, the method of investigation, the nature of the conclusions, and the formulation of hypotheses and theories. . . . Not only our philosophers, but our own predilections in philosophy, and even what we are fond of calling our "best" truths are affected, if not dangerously undermined, by this recognition of a personal premise. . . . Can it be possible that a man only thinks or says or does what he himself _is_?[31]

Thus not only does the destruction of the cognitional myth that the real is a subdivision of the "already out there now" also aid one toward the dissolution of the affective dimensions of this myth and thus toward turning from inappropriate symbolic formations to appropriate symbolic formations, from myth to mystery, so that the specifically psychic part of the total process of self-appropriation is greatly aided to the extent that one is self-consciously attentive, intelligent, reasonable, and responsible; but we must also attend to the reciprocal dynamics of these two movements. _Befindlichkeit_ is meaningful independently of any representative

---

[31]
C. G. Jung, "On the Psychology of the Mother Archetype," pp. 76f., par. 150.

conceptual meaning.[32] While self-appropriation begins with the
appropriation of one's cognitional process, such an appropriation
is itself a therapeutic contribution, and as such helps the construction of a more inclusive semantics of human desire. Not only
does it determine the movement from logos to methodos but it also
foreshadows the movement of method into and through psyche. This
latter movement affects method's understanding of itself, makes it
accept humbly the archetypal significance which psyche insists it
bears. For the conclusion of this moment is a kind of coniunctio
in second immediacy of animus and anima, of the two interlocking
and equiprimordial constitutive ways of being Dasein.

It might be helpful to understand the point we are here making
if we turn to Jung's notion of four psychological functions: thinking,
feeling, sensation, and intuition.[33] In normal psychological development, aided by no such reflective technique as psychotherapy or cognitional analysis, only one of these functions is truly successfully
differentiated. This Jung refers to as an individual's superior
function. Depending on whether an individual's orientation is extra-
verted or introverted, this function determines one's personality
type. Now, one or two of the other functions may be partially
differentiated, and, to this extent, aid the superior function. The
latter is one's most reliable function, the one most amenable to his

32
Eugene Gendlin, op. cit., p. 96.

33
C. G. Jung, Psychological Types, Collected Works, vol. 6
(Princeton: Bollingen Series XX, 1971).

conscious intentions. The fourth, inferior function, around which one's "shadow" is constellated, proves to be inaccessible to conscious willing. Thus even the differentiated functions have only partially freed themselves from the undifferentiated, for the psyche is one. The three more or less differentiated functions are confronted by the fourth, totally undifferentiated function. The latter disturbs the former, to the extent that the worst enemy of the superior function is in truth another aspect of the same psyche to which it itself belongs. "Like the devil who delights in disguising himself as an angel of light, the inferior function secretly and mischievously influences the superior function most of all, just as the latter represses the former most strongly."[34]

This whole matter would be better understood within a context more sensitive to intentionality and its differentiation from the psyche. Jung tends to swallow all the functions into the psyche and frequently speaks as though man were _only_ a psychic being. Lonergan's Insight is an aid to the differentiation of what Jung is reaching for in his notions of the thinking function and the intuitive function. The existence of other influences is acknowledged by Lonergan, either aiding or disturbing insightful and reasonable performance. But these latter influences are not the principal concern of Insight and so they are not described in such a way as significantly to further their differentiation. It may well be that Insight's

---

[34] C. G. Jung, "Phenomenology of the Spirit in Fairytales," p. 238, par. 431.

appeal to date has been largely to those whose normal development
has issued in a differentiation of what Jung calls the thinking
function as one's superior function. But even the further and more
self-conscious differentiation aided by Insight will not free the
thinking function from the deleterious interference of what is undifferentiated (which is likely, in this case, to be one's feeling
function). Further self-appropriation is called for and it is the
task of authentic psychotherapy, as understood within this context,
to get "all systems going" in a harmonious unity through the cumulative reconciliation of opposites.

On the other hand, for one whose normal psychological development has seen the differentiation of another function, psychic
wholeness will demand the differentiation also of the thinking
function, which, in this instance, is liable to be the function most
neglected. May I be so bold as to suggest that a complete therapeutic process could do no better, for such a purpose, than to stress
intentionality and even to encourage cognitional self-appropriation
as aided by Insight? For in such an instance, perhaps what is ther-
apeutically most important is the mediation of active mind, of
spirit, logos, word, idea, intellect, principle, abstraction, meaning,
ratio, nous--of animus as archetype of intentionality.

Psychic Conversion

The conscious capacity for the sublation of the imaginal is
effected by a conversion on the part of the existential subject. This
conversion I call psychic conversion. Psychic conversion is inte-
grally related to the religious, moral, and intellectual conversions

specified by Lonergan as qualifying authentic human subjectivity.

Lonergan first began to thematize conversion in his search for renewed foundations of theology. In a lecture in 1967, he describes the new context of theology in terms of the demise of the classical mediation of meaning and the struggle of modern culture for a new maieutic, only to conclude that this new context demands that theology be placed on a new foundation, one distinct from the citation of Scripture and the enunciation of revealed doctrines characteristic of the foundation of the old dogmatic theology. What was this new foundation to be?

Lonergan drew his first clue from the notion of method, considered as "a normative pattern that related to one another the cognitional operations that recur in scientific investigations."[35] The stress in this notion of method is on the personal experience of the operations and of their dynamic and normative relations to one another. If a scientist were to locate his operations and their relations in his own experience, maintained Lonergan, he would come to know himself as scientist. And, since the subject as scientist is the foundation of science, he would come into possession of the foundations of his science.

Of what use is such a clue to one seeking a new foundation for theology? Lonergan says: "It illustrates by an example what might be meant by a foundation that lies not in sets of verbal

35
Bernard Lonergan, "Theology in its New Context," Theology of Renewal, Vol. I (Montreal: Palm, 1968), p. 43.

propositions named first principles, but in a particular, concrete, dynamic reality generating knowledge of particular, concrete, dynamic realities."[36]

Lonergan then draws a second clue from the phenomenon of conversion, which is fundamental to religious living. Conversion, he says, "is not merely a change or even a development; rather, it is a radical transformation on which follows, on all levels of living, an interlocked series of changes and developments. What hitherto was unnoticed becomes vivid and present. What had been of no concern becomes a matter of high import."[37] Conversion of course has many degrees of depth of realization. But in any case of genuine conversion, "the convert apprehends differently, values differently, relates differently because he has become different. The new apprehension is not so much a new statement or a new set of statements, but rather new meanings that attach to almost any statement. It is not new values so much as a transvaluation of values."[38] Conversion is also possible as a change that is not only individual and personal but also communal and historical; and when viewed as an ongoing process, at once personal, communal, and historical, it coincides, Lonergan says, with living religion.[39]

---

[36] Ibid., p. 44.

[37] Ibid.

[38] Ibid., pp. 44f.

[39] Ibid., p. 45.

Now, if theology is reflection on religion, and if conversion is fundamental to religious living, then not only will theology also be reflection on conversion, but reflection on conversion will provide theology with its foundations. "Just as reflection on the operations of the scientist brings to light the real foundation of the sciences, so too reflection on the ongoing process of conversion may bring to light the real foundation of a renewed theology."[40] Such is the basic argument establishing what is, in fact, a revolutionary recasting of the foundations of theology.

For the moment, however, my concern is not theology but conversion. The notion is significantly developed in Method in Theology, where conversion is differentiated into its religious, moral, and intellectual varieties. I am maintaining that the emergence of the capacity to disengage the symbolic constitution of the feelings in which the primordial apprehension of values occurs satisfies Lonergan's notion of conversion but also that it is something other than the three conversions of which he speaks. As any other conversion, it has many facets. As any other conversion, it is ever precarious. As any other conversion, it is a radical transformation of subjectivity influencing all the levels of one's living and transvaluing one's values. As any other conversion, it is "not so much a new statement or a new set of statements, but rather new meanings that attach to almost any statement."[41] As any other conversion, it too can become communal,

---

40
 Ibid.

41
 Ibid., p. 44.

so that there are formed formal and informal communities of men
and women encouraging one another in the pursuit of further understanding and practical implementation of what they have experienced.
Finally, as any other conversion, it undergoes a personal and ar-
duous history of development, setback, and renewal. Its eventual
outcome, most likely only asymptotically approached, is symbolically described by Jung as the termination of a state of imprison-
ment through a cumulative unity of opposites,[42] or as a resolution
of the contradictoriness of "the unconscious" and consciousness
(read: of psyche and intentionality) in a nuptial coniunctio,[43] or
as the birth of the hero issuing "from something humble and forgotten."[44] But, like any other conversion, psychic conversion is not
the goal but the beginning. As religious conversion is not the
mystic's cloud of unknowing, as moral conversion is not moral perfection, as intellectual conversion is not methodological craftsman-
ship, so psychic conversion is not unified affectivity or total integration with intentionality or immediate release from psychic im-
prisonment. It is, at the beginning, no more than the obscure
understanding of the nourishing potential of the psyche to maintain
the vitality of conscious living by a continuous influx of energy;

------

[42]
C. G. Jung, Mysterium Coniunctionis, p. 65, par. 66.

[43]
Ibid., p. 81, par. 88.

[44]
C. G. Jung, "Concerning Rebirth," The Archetypes and the
Collective Unconscious, p. 141, par. 248.

the hint that one's psychic being can be transformed so as to aid one in the quest for individual authenticity; the suspicion that coming to terms with one's dreams will profoundly change one's ego by ousting it from its central and dominating position in one's conscious living, by shifting the birthplace of meaning gradually but progressively to a deeper center which is simultaneously a totality, the Self.[45] Slowly one comes to discover the ambiguity of the psyche and to affirm the arduousness of the task to which one has committed oneself. Slowly one learns that the point is what is interior, temporal, generic, and indeed religious, and not what is exterior, spatial, specific, and human. Slowly a system of internal communication is established between intentionality and psyche. Slowly one learns the habit of disengaging the archtypal significance of one's feeling-toned responses to situations, people, and objects. Slowly one learns to distinguish symbols which further one's orientation to truth and value from those which mire one in myth and ego-centered satisfactions. One becomes attentive in a new way to the data of sense and the data of consciousness. One is aided by this new symbolic consciousness in his efforts to be intelligent, reasonable, and responsible in his everyday living and in his pursuit of truth and value. Some of the concrete areas of one's own inattentiveness, obtuseness, silliness, and irresponsibility are revealed one by one, and can be named and quasi-personified. They are complexes with a quasi-personality of their own. When personified, they

---

45
C. G. Jung, "On the Nature of the Psyche," pp. 223f., par. 430.

can be engaged in active imagination, in imaginative dialogue where one must listen as well as speak. The dialogue relativizes the ego and thus frees the complexes from rigidity. Some of them can then even be befriended and transformed. When thus paid attention to and in a sense, compromised with, they prove to be sources of conscious energy one never before knew were at his disposal. Such is psychic conversion. In itself it is not a matter of falling in love with God or of shifting the criterion of one's choices from satisfactions to values or of reflectively recognizing that knowing is not looking but the affirmation of the virtually unconditioned. It is not religious conversion or moral conversion or intellectual conversion. It _is_ conversion, but it is something other than these. In the next chapter I shall describe its relation with these other conversions. For the moment, I am satisfied with establishing its uniqueness, with putting it on the map.

The Psychic and the Psychoid

Psychic conversion heads toward what Jung, in his own vocabulary, calls "the achievement of a synthesis of conscious and unconscious, and the realization of the archetype's effects upon the conscious contents."[46] Such an achievement represents the "climax of a concentrated spiritual and psychic effort, in so far as this is undertaken consciously and of set purpose."[47]

---

[46] _Ibid._, p. 210, par. 413.

[47] _Ibid._

The achievement is described as a movement from psychic dissociation to psychic integration. Psychic dissociation arises from the conditional nature of the link between psychic processes. Not only are there the rare cases of split personality or double consciousness, but much more frequently we find smaller fragments of the personality which have been broken off from the larger psychic totality to form autonomous complexes. The original state of the psyche contains very loosely knit processes and "it often takes only a little to shatter the unity of consciousness so laboriously built up in the course of development and to resolve it back into its original elements."[48]

A dissociated element or "secondary subject" owes its separation to one of two definite causes.

> In the one case, there is an originally conscious content that became subliminal because it was repressed on account of its incompatible nature: in the other case, the secondary subject consists essentially in a process that never entered into consciousness at all because no possibilities exist there of apperceiving it. That is to say, ego-consciousness cannot accept it for lack of understanding, and in consequence it remains for the most part subliminal, although, from the energy point of view, it is quite capable of becoming conscious.[49]

On Jung's account, as opposed to Freud, the latter case, which is not pathological, is the most frequent.

Both kinds of undifferentiated material have an effect on consciousness and manifest themselves first in symptoms which are in

---

[48]
Ibid., p. 174, par. 365.

[49]
Ibid., pp. 174f., par. 366.

in part semiotic rather than symbolic. That is, to a certain extent
we are to identify their causes rather than follow their direction.
But these symptoms are in part also symbolic, since they are "the
indirect representatives of unconscious states or processes whose
nature can be only imperfectly inferred and realized from the contents that appear in consciousness."[50] To the extent that we cannot
strictly identify causes, we may explore through sympathetic imagination the direction opened up by these manifestations, which then
play a symbolic role.

The sphere of these complexes is called "the psychic." It
is an intermediate sphere with an upper and a lower threshold, both
of which mark its differentiation from what Jung calls "the psychoid."
"The psychic" is the sphere uncovered when "the disturbances emanating
from the unconscious, the effects of spontaneous manifestations, of
dreams, fantasies, and complexes, [are] successfully integrated into
consciousness by the interpretative method."[51] The lower threshold
of the psychic is the boundary between the compulsive functioning,
the all-or-non reaction, of physiological drives, and the more or less
emancipated functioning of energy which is capable of more extensive
and varied application. The upper threshold marks the boundary where
the intrinsic energy of the function ceases altogether to be oriented
by original instinct and attains a spiritual form. It is the sphere

---

50
Ibid., p. 175, par. 366.

51
Ibid., p. 178, par. 370.

between these two more or less flexible boundaries that is called
the psychic.[52] It is the sphere affected by psychic conversion.
Within this sphere, psychic functions can be voluntarily modified
in a number of ways. While the differentiation of psychic function
from physiological compulsion is indispensable for the maintenance
and promotion of human life, such psychic flexibility or disposable
energy increases the possibility of collision and produces dissoci-
ations which jeopardize the unity of consciousness.

There are then for Jung three systems: instinct, psyche,
and spirit. The first and the third are autonomous and cannot be
voluntarily coerced. But between them is a sphere of disposable
energy based on, but relatively free from, specific instinctual compulsion and capable of either harmony or disharmony with the outer
limits of instinct and spirit. Psychic conversion may be understood
as the gaining of the capacity of intentional consciousness to integrate this flexible psychic system and even to effect a cumulative
harmony with instinct and spirit, in such a way that "all systems
are working" and working more or less in harmony. It is a self-
appropriation of the psychic system on the part of the existential
subject, an appropriation based on the dialectic of the symbol and
its more than purely personalistic intentionality.

Thus, when undifferentiated feeling-toned complexes are
attended to, they can be transformed. "They slough off their mythological envelope, and, by entering into the adaptive process going

---

52
    Ibid., pp. 181f., par. 377.

forward in consciousness, they personalize and rationalize themselves to the point where dialectical discussion becomes possible."[53] When not integrated, and with increasing dissociation, undifferentiated psychic process approximates the underlying instinctual pattern of "autonomous non-susceptibility to influence, all-or-none reaction."[54] This analysis of Jung's thus corroborates our notion of a dialectic within the psyche itself. For Jung, the cumulative harmony of all three systems is possible because of the archetypes. While they represent the authentic element of spirit, and while "archetype and instinct are the most polar opposites imaginable," yet archetype and instinct "belong together as correspondences, which is not to say that the one is derivable from the other, but that they subsist side by side as reflections in our own minds of the opposition that underlies all psychic energy."[55]

These opposites of instinct and spirit are "never incommensurables; if they were they could never unite. All contrariety notwithstanding, they do show a constant propensity to union."[56] The symbol, appropriately dealt with by existential consciousness, is the function of their unification, precisely because of its archeological-

---

53
  Ibid., p. 187, par. 385.

54
  Ibid.

55
  Ibid., p. 206, par. 406.

56
  Ibid., p. 207, par. 406.

teleological unity-in-tension. The moral significance of the opposites is found not in either taken singly, but depends on conscious
integration and negotiation of symbolic processes--i.e., attentive,
intelligent, reasonable, responsible, cooperative-intersubjective
discrimination. Conscious confrontation with a representative of
an instinct or with an archetype is "an ethical problem of the first
magnitude."[57] Jung provides a helpful example:

> A poorly developed consciousness . . ., which because of massed
> projections is inordinately impressed by concrete or apparently
> concrete things and states, will naturally see in the instinc-
> tual drives the source of all reality. It remains blissfully
> unaware of the spirituality of such a philosophical surmise,
> and is convinced that with this opinion it has established the
> essential instinctuality of all psychic processes. Conversely,
> a consciousness that finds itself in opposition to the instincts
> can, in consequence of the enormous influence then exerted by
> the archetypes, so subordinate instinct to spirit that the most
> grotesque 'spiritual' combinations may arise out of what are
> undoubtedly biological happenings. Here the instinctuality of
> the fanaticism needed for such an operation is ignored.[58]

It is the capacity of the existential subject for a symbolic dialectical disengagement of psychic process that will see one between these
symbolic counterpositions to a genuine harmony of instinct and spirit
in incarnate authentic subjectivity. This perhaps is one way of
phrasing the finality of the event I call psychic conversion.

I close this chapter by repeating in a new context something
I have said before. Jung's notion of individuation as a cumulative
process of the reconciliation of opposites under the guidance of

---

57
   Ibid., p. 208, par. 410.

58
   Ibid., p. 207, par. 407.

responsible consciousness and with the aid of a professional guide, is an extraordinarily accurate and fruitful one. Furthermore, Jung's insistence that neither of the polar extremes of instinct or spirit is in itself good or evil, that moral significance attaches rather to the process of reconciliation, is correct. Nonetheless, there _is_ a problem of evil. Jung's researches help us enormously in rejecting a falsely spiritualistic tendency to locate the root of evil in instinct. But Jung did not adequately understand the problem of evil, and his psychology cannot handle it. What is worse, however, is the tendency of his psychology to _try_ to handle it on the analogy of the process of the unity of opposites which determines the therapeutic dialectic. The divine and only solution to the problem of evil radically affects and transforms the psyche, but not by making it the locus where good and evil, grace and sin, embrace. Perhaps this tendency alone in Jung's psychology is sufficient to render intelligible the accusation of gnosticism to which he is subject. Psychology is not the source of answers to the ultimate problem of man, and it never will be. With sufficient understanding of the limited range of its concern, depth psychology can be conscripted into the far more extensive collaboration of man with God in working out the solution to the problem of evil in concrete circumstances. But when it insists on originating the solution, it joins the ranks of the contributors to the problem, and is ever so subtly co-opted by the counterphilosophies which deny the ulterior finality of existential subjectivity.

CHAPTER VI

PSYCHE AND THEOLOGY

In the Introduction to this work, I stated a twofold aim. My intention was, first, to contribute to our understanding of the existential subject by using Lonergan's thought to help me generate categories appropriate to a methodological understanding of depth psychology; and, secondly, to use this latter understanding to fill out my notion of the foundations of theology. The first intention has been fulfilled, and I turn now to the second. I must clarify the relation of the psyche both to foundational reality and to the functional specialty, foundations. I discuss first foundational reality in _Insight_ and in the later Lonergan; second, psyche and foundational reality; third, the functional specialties of dialectic and foundations; and fourth, psyche and foundations.

Foundational Reality:

The Early Lonergan and the Later Lonergan

A discussion of foundations in _Insight_ occurs within the context of an attempt to outline a method of metaphysics. This problem is raised by Lonergan immediately after the establishing of what he calls the basic positions: the position on the subject in Chapter 11, the position on the real in Chapter 12, and the position on objectivity in Chapter 13. The problem is raised in the following terms:

while these three basic positions are accounted for in terms of the
intellectual pattern of experience, human consciousness is polymorphic, and thus other patterns of experience may give rise to
different views concerning the human subject, the real, and objectivity. The intellectual pattern of experience is not the only
pattern of experience, nor has Lonergan ever expressly argued that
it is the privileged pattern of experience. Human experience can
also be patterned in biological, dramatic, practical, aesthetic, artistic, and mystical modes. Furthermore, though:

> These patterns alternate; they blend or mix; they can interfere,
> conflict, lose their way, break down. The intellectual pattern
> of experience is supposed and expressed by our account of self-
> affirmation, of being, and of objectivity. But no man is born
> in that pattern; no one reaches it easily; no one remains in it
> permanently; and when some other pattern is dominant, then the
> self of our self-affirmation seems quite different from one's
> actual self, the universe of being seems as unreal as Plato's
> noetic heaven, and objectivity spontaneously becomes a matter
> of meeting persons and dealing with things that are "really out
> there."[1]

Thus:

> Against the objectivity that is based on intelligent inquiry
> and critical reflection, there stands the unquestioning orien-
> tation of extroverted biological consciousness and its uncriti-
> cal survival not only in dramatic and practical living but also
> in much of philosophic thought. Against the concrete universe
> of being, of all that can be intelligently grasped and reason-
> ably affirmed, there stands in a prior completeness the world
> of sense, in which the "real" and the "apparent" are subdivi-
> sions within a vitally anticipated "already out there now."
> Against the self-affirmation of a consciousness that at once
> is empirical, intellectual, and rational, there stands the na-
> tive bewilderment of the existential subject, revolted by mere
> animality, unsure of his way through the maze of philosophies,
> trying to live without a known purpose, suffering despite an

---

[1] Bernard Lonergan, _Insight_, p. 385.

unmotivated will, threatened with inevitable death and, before death, with disease and even insanity.[2]

Lonergan maintains that a philosophy of philosophies can be developed, according to which "the many contradictory, disparate philosophies can all be contributions to the clarification of some basic but polymorphic fact," i.e., human consciousness.[3] It is toward this philosophy of philosophies that his four chapters on metaphysics head. These philosophies share a twofold unity: they originate in inquiring intelligence and reflecting reasonableness, and they ambition truth. This twofold unity "is the ground for finding in any given philosophy a significance that can extend beyond the philosopher's horizon and, even in a manner he did not expect, pertain to the permanent development of the human mind."[4] It is in the mind of any given philosopher that contradictory contributions attain their complex unity. This unity is heuristically structured by the principle that the positions invite development and the counter-positions reversal.

It is in explicating this principle that Lonergan discusses foundations. He distinguishes between the basis of any philosophy, which lies in its cognitional theory, and the expansion of that philosophy in its pronouncements on metaphysical, ethical, and

---

2
Ibid.

3
Ibid., pp. 386f.

4
Ibid., p. 387.

theological issues. In the basis, he distinguishes further between
two aspects: the <u>determination</u> of cognitional theory in an appeal
to the data of consciousness and to the historical development of
human knowledge, and the inevitable inclusion in one's <u>formulation</u>
of cognitional theory, of one's judgments on basic issues in philosophy. That is to say, first, that one will arrive at one's cognitional theory by an analysis of the data of one's own conscious
knowing performance and by an appeal to the discovery and development of mind; and, secondly, that one cannot articulate his cognitional theory without committing himself in advance on certain basic
philosophic questions.

It is with respect to these philosophic commitments necessarily immanent in the formulation of cognitional theory that there
arises for Lonergan in the first instance the notions of position
and counter-position. The philosophic issues concerning which one
must take a stand in the formulation of cognitional theory concern
reality, the subject, and objectivity. What determines whether one's
basic philosophic commitments are positions open to development or
counter-positions inviting reversal is their agreement or discre-
pancy with the judgments concerning reality, the subject, and objectivity expressed, respectively, in the twelfth, eleventh and
thirteenth chapters of <u>Insight</u>.

> . . . the inevitable philosophic component, immanent in the
> formulation of cognitional theory, will be either a basic
> position or else a basic counter-position.
>   It will be a basic position,
>   (1) if the real is the concrete universe of being and not
> a subdivision of the "already out there now;"
>   (2) if the subject becomes known when it affirms itself
> intelligently and reasonably and so is not known yet in any

prior "existential" state; and
  (3) if objectivity is conceived as a consequence of intelligent inquiry and critical reflection, and not as a property
of vital anticipation, extroversion, and satisfaction.
  On the other hand, it will be a basic counter-position if
it contradicts one or more of the basic positions.
  . . . Any philosophic pronouncement on any epistemological,
metaphysical, ethical, or theological issue will be named a
position if it is coherent with the basic positions on the
real, on knowing, and on objectivity; and it will be named a
counter-position if it is coherent with one or more of the
basic counter-positions.[5]

The second of these basic positions needs a brief clarifi-

cation. The subject becomes known when it affirms itself intelli-

gently and reasonably. Now, <u>nothing</u> is known unless it is intelli-

gently grasped and reasonably affirmed. The self-affirmation inevi-

tably included in the basis of one's philosophy, however, is the

intelligent and reasonable affirmation of one's own intelligence and

reasonableness. It is the judgment, "I am a knower," where knowledge

is the compound of experience, understanding, and judgment. Thus the

basic position on the subject in <u>Insight</u> is the position on the knowing

subject. The self-knowledge of the subject is true if it is based in

his intelligent grasp and reasonable affirmation of his own intelli-

gence and reasonableness. This affirmation, along with positions on

the real and objectivity, are the positions which constitute the

foundations or basis (to use the term employed in <u>Insight</u>) of meta-

physics, ethics, and philosophical theology.

In the terminology of the post-1965 Lonergan--I take

"Dimensions of Meaning" as signalling the transition to the "later

---

5
  <u>Ibid.</u>, pp. 387f.

Lonergan"--these positions are attained as a result of a basic philosophic conversion, which Lonergan calls intellectual conversion. But
now, intellectual conversion is seen usually, though not necessarily,
to follow upon and to be conditioned by the conversions which he calls
religious and moral. We have seen in Chapter One what Lonergan means
by religious and moral conversion. In the general case, religious
conversion occurs first, and gives rise to moral conversion, in that
it is on the basis of one's religious experience that one is moved to
self-transcendence in one's actions. Intellectual conversion, in the
general case, is consequent upon and conditioned by religious and moral
conversion, in that there is a realism implicit in one's religious and
moral self-transcendence which conditions the recognition of the
realism of knowing that is intellectual conversion. On the other hand,
the latter conversion is that which Lonergan prefers to explicate first,
since this articulation helps him to say what is meant by the self-
transcendence of moral goodness and of authentic religion.

> I should urge that religious conversion, moral conversion, and
> intellectual conversion are three quite different things. In an
> order of exposition I would prefer to explain first intellectual,
> then moral, then religious conversion. In the order of occurrence
> I would expect religious commonly but not necessarily to precede
> moral and both religious and moral to precede intellectual. In-
> tellectual conversion, I think, is very rare.[6]

This developed understanding of conversion is concomitant with the
emergence of a distinct notion of the good. Thus, in the 1968 lecture
The Subject, as we have seen, a primacy is assigned to the subject

---

[6]
"Bernard Lonergan Responds," in Philip McShane, ed.,
Foundations of Theology (South Bend: Notre Dame University Press, 1972)
pp. 233f.

trying to be good, to the existential subject. Nothing that was
accorded the cognitional subject in _Insight_ is denied him in the
later works. But the basic position on the subject would seem to
be more than the basic position on knowing, for the subject as deciding, deliberating, evaluating is granted a primacy. The basic
position on the subject would now seem to be a compound position,
consisting not only of judgments of cognitional fact, but also of
judgments of value. Furthermore, if the intellectual conversion
which issues in the basic positions which are foundational for philosophy is somehow consequent upon religious and moral conversion, then
the foundations of one's metaphysics, ethics, and theology would seem
to lie in the objectification of all three conversions in this patterned set of judgments concerning the subject as cognitional and as
existential. Such is the crucial significance of the emergence of a
distinct notion of the good. My present concern is not with the
very serious question of what this means philosophically and especially for metaphysics, but with what it means for theology. At the
present moment, the jury in my own mind is still out on the question
of whether it is valid for Lonergan to proceed to a metaphysics on
the foundations laid in _Insight_. But it is a fact that he does _not_
proceed to a theology on these foundations alone. The foundations
of theology include but go far beyond _Insight_'s basic positions on
knowing, the real, and objectivity. And they transcend these positions not by denying them in the least, but by affirming that the
position on knowing is not the full position on the human subject.
The authentic human subject is the subject who is self-transcending

in his knowing, his doing, and his religion. This subject is the foundational reality of theology. The functional specialty, foundations, consists in an objectification of self-transcending subjectivity in its cognitional and existential dimensions. The subject's intelligent and reasonable affirmation of his own intelligence and reasonableness may be the beginning of a foundational position on the subject, so that Lonergan prefers to discuss intellectual conversion before moral and religious conversion; but it is not the full position on the subject. This is quite clear from Lonergan's recent writings. It is not simply my interpretation of Lonergan, but rather necessarily is included in Lonergan's affirmation of the primacy of the subject as existential. Foundational reality consists not only of a subject who intelligently and reasonably affirms his own intelligence and reasonableness, but also of an existential subject for whom the criterion of decision has been shifted from the satisfactions spontaneously desired by biological extraversion to the values prized by a consciousness which is not only intelligent and reasonable but also responsible, and finally of a religious subject in love with an otherworldly mysterium tremendum et fascinans. The intentionality of human consciousness itself, the primordial infrastructure of human subjectivity, is a dynamism heading toward self-transcendence in knowing, morality, and religion. The subject whose conscious performance is in accord with this dynamism is foundational reality. The objectification of this dynamism in a patterned set of judgments of cognitional fact and of value constitutes the foundations of theology.

This development settles for me what has been a very persistent problem ever since my first reading of Insight. Human experience is variously patterned. As we have seen, Lonergan discusses its various patterns. In Insight, he highlights its intellectual pattern for, as he has said, his purpose was a study not of human life but of human understanding.[7] But the overall impression conveyed by Insight--an impression which will, of course, find no verification in Lonergan's explicit utterance but which is nonetheless communicated--is that the intellectual pattern of experience is the privileged pattern of experience. But with the emergence of a distinct idea of the good, cognitional analysis becomes intentionality analysis. Then, what is privileged is not some one pattern of experience but a self-transcendence that can be attained in any of several patterns of experience--in the dramatic pattern of experience of common sense, in the aesthetic and artistic patterns of experience, in the mystical pattern of experience, and of course in the intellectual pattern of experience. Lonergan is probably quite correct that this self-transcendence is best grasped in a discussion of the intellectual pattern of experience operative in knowing, and thus probably quite justified in his preference to discuss intellectual conversion before moral and religious conversion. But the emergence of the distinct notion of the good in Lonergan's later writings, when sufficiently appreciated for its radical importance in his development, decisively changes the atmosphere and shifts the balance present in

---

[7] See Philip McShane, ed., Language, Truth, and Meaning, p. 310.

his thought taken as a whole. As self-transcending subjectivity
defines human authenticity, so Lonergan's thought as a whole is not
primarily cognitional theory but an elucidation of the drama of
the emergence of the authentic subject. It is a basic semantics of
human desire. Such is, I believe, the most accurate interpretation
and assessment of his achievement.

Psyche and Foundational Reality

For the author of Insight, counter-positions invite reversal
because they are incoherent, not with one another, but with the activities of grasping them intelligently and affirming them reasonably.
Thus they prompt the intelligent and reasonable inquirer to introduce
coherence. The activities themselves of intelligent grasping and
reasonable affirmation contain the basic positions on the real, on
knowing, and on objectivity. But if the position on the subject is
not coincident with the self-affirmation of the knower, with the
position on knowing, can it be said that the activities of intelligent
grasping and reasonable affirmation of one's own intelligence and
reasonableness contain the basic position on the subject? Or does
that basic position find enunciation only when judgments of cognitional fact are joined with judgments of value? If the latter is the
case, and if judgments of value are mediated with judgments of fact
by feelings, then does not the basic position on the subject demand
not only the functioning of intelligence and reasonableness grasping
and affirming intelligence and reasonableness, and not only a satisfactory transcendental analysis of the human good, but also a set of
judgments detailing the authentic development of feelings? If the

story of the development and aberration of feelings or of dispositional immediacy can be told by disengaging the spontaneous symbols
produced in dreams, if the habit of such disengagement is mediated
to the subject by psychic conversion, if conversion is foundational
reality, if the objectification of conversion is the functional
specialty, foundations, then is psychic conversion not an aspect of
foundational reality and will not an objectification of psychic
conversion constitute a genuine aspect of foundations? There are
counter-positions on the real, on knowing, and on objectivity that
are incoherent with the activities of intelligent grasping and
reasonable affirmation. But there are also counter-positions on the
subject that are incoherent, not specifically with these activities
alone, but with the emergence of the authentic existential subject.
Only in this latter incoherence are they suspected of being counter-
positions, for they are apprehended as articulations of counter-values
in the feelings of the existential subject striving for self-transcendence, and they are judged to be such in the same subject's judgments
of value. They are incoherent, not specifically with the self-transcendence intended in the unfolding of the desire to know, but with
the self-transcendence toward which the primordial infrastructure of
human subjectivity as a whole is headed. The subject who contains
implicitly the full position on the subject is not the intelligent and
reasonable subject, but the experiencing, intelligent, reasonable,
responsible, religious subject. In fact, we would even have to say
that, if one is looking for the full position on the human subject by
scrutinizing only one's intelligence and reasonableness, one is heading

for the articulation of a counter-position. One is the victim of
an intellectualist bias too easily confirmed by the writings of
the early Lonergan in those readers whose spontaneous subjective
development has been characterized by a preference for the super-
iority of what Jung has called the thinking function. I cannot
emphasize too much that the emergence of the notion of the good as
distinct from, though not contradictory to, the intelligent and
reasonable in the writings of the post-1965 Lonergan decisively
shifts the atmosphere--yes, the archetypal significance--of his work
as a whole. Human authenticity is a matter of self-transcendence.
Self-transcendence can be achieved in one's knowing, in one's free
and responsible constitution of the human world, and in one's religious
living as a participation in the divine solution to the problem of
evil. The struggle between the dynamism for self-transcendence and
the flight from authenticity is the archetypal struggle which provides
the ground theme unifying the various aspects of this achievement.
The articulation of this struggle in an objectification of conversion
constitutes a semantics of human desire.

This ground theme itself is invested with a symbolic or archetypal significance. Not only does intentionality in its dynamic thrust
for self-transcendence have the potential of conscripting psyche into
its service through the dialectical disengagement of the intention of
truth and value present in psyche, but psyche insists on stamping the
entire drama with its own characteristic mark by giving it an archetypal representation, by releasing in dreams the ciphers of the present status of the drama, by indicating to the existential subject

how it stands between the totality of consciousness as primordial infrastructure intending self-transcendence and the subject's explicit self-understanding in his intention of or flight from truth and value. The articulation of the story of these ciphers, the disengagement of their systematically intelligible pattern in a dialectical hermeneutic phenomenology of the psyche would constitute a transcendental aesthetic. This aesthetic would, I wager, follow Jung's phenomenology of the psyche quite closely until one comes to the farthest reaches of the psyche, which also constitute its center. There the dialectic becomes that of good and evil, grace and sin, and at that point dialectic itself breaks down. Just as a dialectical analysis of human progress and decline is not adequate for meeting the problem of evil, so dialectical reconciliation of opposites is not the process for engaging this ultimate psychic struggle. Intentionality and the psyche it has conscripted into its adventure must at this point surrender to the gift of God's love poured forth in our hearts by the Holy Spirit who has been given to us. The symbol of this surrender, the embodiment of the Self at these far reaches of the psyche, is the Crucified. The transcendental aesthetic issues in kerygma, manifestation, proclamation in the return to the fullness of language simply heard and understood, in the return to the homeland of one's own life from the journey to the mountaintop and the sojourn in the forest. This is the second naiveté intended by Paul Ricoeur. It is mediated by the process of self-appropriation in its entirety, by the objectification of the primordial infrastructure of cognitional and existential subjectivity in a two-fold mediation of immediacy by meaning.

Psychic conversion, as religious and moral conversion, is an event which normally takes place outside and independently of method. But I must now attempt to articulate a better understanding of its role within method, by stating its relation to the three conversions specified by Lonergan as constituting the authentic subjectivity which is foundational reality. We have already seen that, in the order of occurrence, religious conversion generally precedes moral conversion, and both religious and moral conversion generally precede intellectual conversion. But that is not the complete story of their existential interrelationships. For in Method in Theology, Lonergan tells us that subsequent to the occurrence of these events, intellectual conversion is sublated by moral conversion, and that both intellectual conversion and moral conversion are sublated by religious conversion.[8] It is within the context of these sublations that I understand the foundational significance of psychic conversion. Lonergan understands sublation along the lines suggested by Karl Rahner, and not in a fashion inspired by Hegel. Sublation, then, is in no sense a negating or nihilating of what is sublated. Rather, "what sublates goes beyond what is sublated, introduces something new and distinct, puts everything on a new basis, yet so far from interfering with the sublated or destroying it, on the contrary needs it, includes it, preserves all its proper features and properties, and carries them forward to a fuller realization within a richer context."[9] Thus, the

---

[8] Bernard Lonergan, Method in Theology, pp. 241-243.

[9] Ibid., p. 241.

achievement of a familiarity with the self-transcending capacities
of human knowing that is intellectual conversion is needed, included,
preserved, elevated to a new level, and carried forward to more
precise specification by the self-transcending capacities of the
existential subject in the free and responsible constitution of the
human world. And the same happens to each of these in the movement
of deepening one's commitment to collaboration with God in the divine
solution to the problem of evil. While intellectual conversion may be
the rarest of the conversions, it is not the final answer, for it is
not the solution to man's ultimate problem. It is a facet of the
collaboration of some in working out the concrete and specific details
of the solution. But there is no way in which one can claim that
Lonergan proposes a sublation of religion into knowing, of religious
conversion into intellectual conversion, or of the divine solution to
the problem of evil into a human understanding of human understanding.
This Hegelian trap is avoided at every step in the writings of both
the early and the later Lonergan. In the later formulation, what happens to the subject in the specifically philosophic conversion which
provides him with familiarity with the self-transcending capacities
of human judgment is taken up by the more extensive dynamic orientation to self-transcendence in human responsibility and human openness to the gift of God's love. How does psychic conversion affect
this double movement of sublation?

First, let me state that psychic conversion does not occur
necessarily either before or after the three conversions spoken of by
Lonergan. It is the emergence of a capacity to disengage the symbolic

constitution of immediacy. It can conceivably occur with or without religious faith, with or without the existential self-transcendence usually consequent upon religious faith. It obviously occurs quite frequently without even the suspicion that there may be something like a philosophic conversion through which one comes to affirm what one is doing when one is knowing, why that is knowing, and what one knows when one does that. Since its finality is determined by the ground theme of the emergence of the self-transcending existential subject, it is highly doubtful whether it can be carried to any fruitful conclusion without at least moral resolve and something resembling religious faith and trust in God. But in itself it is an independent event, and I would not want to state where it usually occurs in the temporal sequence of the conversions. My concern is rather with its role in method, and thus with its function in the interrelationship of all the conversions through sublation.

The orientation of intentionality toward self-transcendence in knowing, doing, and religion includes an exigence for psychic self-appropriation. The precise room for the methodological understanding of this exigence is provided by the emergence of a distinct notion of the good in the writings of the later Lonergan. As the good is apprehended in feelings and as feelings are symbolically certifiable, so psychic conversion is an aid to the discrimination of one's stance regarding the good. The story of one's own personal engagement in the drama of the existential subject is enabled to be told by psychic conversion. Thus, I locate psychic conversion methodologically as facilitating the sublation of intellectual conversion by moral conversion and of both by religious conversion; as facilitating the richer context within which one's familiarity with the self-transcending capacity of human judgment is carried forward by the self-transcending capacity of human action, and the still richer context within which both of these are carried forward by the soul beyond both cognitional analysis and psychology, the soul in love with God, the soul moving toward the God wrapped in the cloud of unknowing. Psychic converwion functions in aid of the self-appropriation of the existential subject. It enables such a subject to narrate the drama of his own struggle against the flight from authenticity. This drama is primal. It is archetypal. It is the ground theme of human history and of personal life. It is the story of one's salvation or of one's loss. It is the story of the human good writ large in the pages of history, the story of the progress or decline of groups, of cultures, of nations and polities, of civilization, of the world. While it is the story of man from his origins to the present day, of myth through logic to the recapitulation of both logic and myth in method, it is ontogenetically reproduced in the individual story of contemporary men and women as they struggle for release from the flight from authenticity or succumb to that flight at the expense of their humanity. The gate that leads to life is a narrow gate, as we are well aware. Familiarity with the psyche can be brought to aid one in the recognition of the contours of that gate, of its distinctiveness from the avenues to destruction, and of the path along which one is walking oneself. As there are philosophies which deny the self-transcending finality of human knowing and doing, so there are psychologies which deny the moral and religious significance of psychotherapy. It is only within the context of a thoroughgoing intentionality analysis that depth psychology can discover its own inner meaning and finality. Depth psychology cannot answer the question, what is man?, for an objectification of the transcendental infrastructure of human subjectivity will include far more than a knowledge of the human psyche. But depth psychology can contribute to the answer to the question, who am I?, when the psychic journey is undertaken as an aid to the quest for self-transcendence on the part of the existential subject; and it can figure in a transcendental anthropology when the psychic journey itself is objectified as a transcendental aesthetic with a place of its own within the overarching context of transcendental method.

I have related psychic conversion to moral conversion and religious conversion within the context of the sublations affirmed by Lonergan. I have said little of its relation to intellectual conversion. I have spoken of its moral and religious finality, but I have not yet indicated how it aids in the sublation of intellectual conversion into this ulterior dynamism of human intentionality. To that question I must now turn. My comments are offered within the context of the contention that, with the emergence of a distinct notion of the good, Lonergan's thought in its entirety is no longer primarily cognitional analysis but rather intentionality analysis, that the full position on the subject is not the position on knowing but a patterned set of judgments of cognitional fact and of value, and that the privileged domain of human subjectivity is not the intellectual pattern of experience but self-transcendence in one's knowing, doing, and religion.

In its full sweep intellectual conversion is the mediation of immediacy which occurs when one answers correctly and in order the three critical questions. The answer to the first question, what am I doing when I am knowing?, reveals the dynamic structure, promoted by questioning, of human cognitional process. The answer to the second question, why is that knowing?, reveals that structure to be transcendental and in principle not subject to revision. The answer to the third question, what do I know when I do that?, is that what I know when I faithfully pursue the process is what I intended to know when I began the process: what is, being, the real, the true. Concomitant with answering these questions is the elimination of the cognitional myth that the real is a subdivision of the already out there now and that it is to be known by looking.

What I wish to emphasize is that an objectification of intellectual conversion plays a role within an articulated semantics of human desire, for intellectual conversion, when sublated by existential subjectivity, has a distinctly therapeutic value. It is a step, and perhaps methodologically the first step, in the displacement of the origin and home of meaning and value away from naive consciousness. It is a contribution to the movement of subjectivity toward the deeper center, the Self. It is a shift in the center of human significance away from the near-animal extraversion of untutored consciousness and toward the infolding of human desire in a unified and self-appropriated subjectivity. It achieves this shift by rendering a thematization of something that was previously quite undifferentiated, the dynamic structure-in-process of the subject's orientation to truth. It is a self-conscious appropriation of what otherwise is left inarticulate. The three critical questions are an aspect of the exigence for appropriation in terms of interiority that has given rise to the third epoch in human conscious evolution. In its deepest significance, this exigence is existential. It is an exigence to heal the rift between the self as conscious and the self as known. It is an exigence for self-knowledge and one of its dimensions calls for an understanding of one's own understanding.

I have called intentionality analysis as articulated by Lonergan the appropriation of _logos_. As such it is the thematization of the emergence of _logos_ from _mythos_. This description is particularly apt for Lonergan's cognitional analysis. The emergence of _logos_ from _mythos_ involved a release and liberation of human consciousness from the domination of the maternal imagination, from the hegemony of psyche. It was the announcement of intentionality that psyche is not the horizon of Being, that the transcendental time-structure of imagination may be the form of inner sense and the institution of _Befindlichkeit_ in its primordiality, unity, and totality, but that the transcendental imagination does not constitute intentionality as a whole. It was the heroic severing of the umbilical cord which binds mind to maternal imagination. It was archetypally represented in the drama of Orestes. It was the condition of the possibility of the systematic control of meaning which found its first secure triumph in the Socratic maieutic and expended itself in needless exhaustion in the Hegelian dialectic. It is repeated in the ontogenetic development of the conscious subject who is the heir of Western philosophy and science. The answers to the critical questions thematize for that subject the cognitional significance of the manifesto of _logos_. They render cognitional subjectivity present to itself by thematizing the heroic achievement which some two thousand years have brought to maturity.

The drama of Orestes, however, reflects the fact that, while intentionality may in a self-inflated fashion proclaim that it is now done with psyche, psyche is by no means done with intentionality. There is an existential crisis which results from the heroic victory of intentionality, from its rightful proclamation of hegemony, from its defiance of the pretended totalitarianism of the imagination. Orestes is pursued in a frightful fashion by the darkest powers of the psyche. He is finally vindicated by the combined judgment of the reasonable citizens who represent the positive aspect of his triumph and by the embodiment of psyche as wisdom in the goddess Athena. The judgment of vindication must be a combined judgment. Psyche must have its say in the final outcome, a decisive say. And what were the darkest powers of psychic nature must be _persuaded_ by psyche as wisdom to take up their abode in the depths of the earth upon which the city of reasonable men is built, and to lend their powerful support to the advance of cultured humanity. They cannot be disposed of or escaped from. They can be transformed by persuasion. But they will never go away.

The appropriation of _logos_, then, must give way to the appropriation of _mythos_, to the transformation by dialectical persuasion of these otherwise chaotic powers. The answering of the critical

questions is only the beginning of a far more extensive process
demanded by the existential situation of a consciousness which has
brought to some kind of conclusion the demands of its systematic
differentiation. If this existential crisis is left unattended, it
will bring catastrophe to the city of reasonable men, to the scientific
community, to the economy, to the polity, to the nations, to the
world. It is the same crisis that is manifested cognitively in the
split between theoretically differentiated consciousness and common
sense. But its existential ciphers are far more dramatic. It is the
lonely isolation of the hero from all that has nourished him. It is
his self-chosen separation from the primal ground of his being. It
is the alienation of the light from the darkness out of which it violently broke forth, but without which it cannot remain light.
Lonergan's articulation of the necessary victory of _logos_ over the
uroboric dragon of myth is the methodologically primary step toward
the healing of an existential crisis which threatens civilization
with destruction. But it is only a beginning. It clarifies what has
happened, thematizes what has occurred. But it does not heal the
crisis. _Logos_ still remains isolated, cut off from the rhythms and
processes of nature, separated from psyche, alienated from the original darkness which both nourished it and threatened to smother it,
guilty over the primal murder of an ambiguously life-giving power.
With Lonergan's help, we now know what we have done in overcoming the
gods and claiming a rightful autonomy. But we still do not know how
to achieve a differentiated reconciliation with psychic darkness. For
a time, we even suspect that all such reconciliation is regression, a

cancelling of the victory of _logos_, a repudiation of a bitterly won
autonomy. But then we are told that intellectual conversion needs
to be sublated by moral and religious conversion, and that the
first step in an understanding of moral conversion is a thematization
of the primordial apprehension of values in symbolically charged
feelings. Perhaps we are on the way, on a road which leads simultaneously to a vindication of the decision of _logos_ in favor of understanding and truth, and to a transformation of those dark and strange
powers which have been overruled by this decision but as yet by no
means pacified and conscripted into its ulterior orientation. Self-
appropriating _logos_ can utilize its own newly discovered resources
in the intelligent hermeneutic, reasonable affirmation, and responsible
transformation of those imaginal roots out of which these very powers
of intelligent grasping, reasonable affirmation, and responsible constitutive subjectivity have violently wrested their birthright. This
is the psychic, moral, and religious imperative now manifest in the
epochal shift of the control of meaning whose overarching contours
have been erected by Lonergan. It is also the first really secure
step in the sublation of intellectual conversion by moral conversion.

Dialectic and Foundations

The foundations of theology lie in an objectification of conversion, in a reflective thematization of the movement of conversion
in its origins, its developments, its purposes, its achievements, and
its failures.[10] Such foundations articulate the _horizon_ within which

---

10
    Ibid., p. 131.

the meaning of any doctrinal or theological statement can be understood.

Perspectives and Horizons

Lonergan distinguishes between perspective and horizon. Perspectives are perhaps best understood in the context of the progress
of both historical research and history itself. Historical research
may to all intents and purposes regard a given investigation as complete. But then new sources of information are discovered which call
for the rewriting of history. "Archeological investigations of the
ancient Near East complement Old Testament study, the caves of Qumran
have yielded documents with a bearing on New Testament studies, while
the unpublished writings found at Kenoboskion restrain pronouncements
on Gnosticism."[11] Furthermore, as history itself goes forward, earlier
events are placed in new perspectives by later ones. "The outcome of
a battle fixes the perspective in which the successive stages of the
battle are viewed; military victory in a war reveals the significance
of the successive battles that were fought; the social and cultural
consequences of the victory and the defeat are the measure of the
effects of the war. So, in general, history is an ongoing process.
As the process advances, the context within which events are to be
understood keeps enlarging. As the context enlarges, perspectives
shift."[12]

---

[11]
Ibid., p. 192.

[12]
Ibid.

Shifting perspectives are not contradictory, and thus they

do not invalidate previous work.

> New documents fill out the picture, they illuminate what before
> was obscure; they shift perspectives; they refute what was ven-
> turesome or speculative; they do not simply dissolve the whole
> network of questions and answers that made the original set of
> data massive evidence for the earlier account. Again, history
> is an ongoing process, and so the historical context keeps en-
> larging. But the effects of this enlargement are neither uni-
> versal nor uniform. For persons and events have their place in
> history through one or more contexts, and these contexts may be
> narrow and brief or broad and enduring with any variety of in-
> termediaries. Only as much as a context is still open, or can
> be opened or extended, do later events throw new light on
> earlier persons, events, processes. As Karl Heussi put it, it
> is easier to understand Frederick Wilhelm III of Prussia than
> to understand Schleiermacher and, while Nero will always be Nero,
> we cannot as yet say the same for Luther.[13]

A horizon is something other than a context or perspective.

The latter is a prior understanding derived, say, from historical

sources. The former is derived from elsewhere. To hold for the mo-

ment to the historian, a horizon reflects one or several basic options

reflected in preconceptions about what must have happened or at least

about what could not have happened. A horizon is constituted of basic

convictions about man and the world, and these convictions are derived

from one's upbringing, education, and cultural milieu. It is the

notion of horizon, rather than that of perspective, which accounts for

histories that are, not more or less comprehensive, but irreconcilable.

To change one's horizon is a quite different and far more radical pro-

cedure than to change or enlarge one's perspective. While perspectival

differences result from the complexity of data, differences of horizon

---

[13]
  Ibid., pp. 192f.

originate in an explicit or implicit cognitional theory, an ethical
stance, and a religious outlook. They can be overcome only by the
radical transformations effected in intellectual, moral, and religious conversion. There is a functional specialty called dialectic
which brings precisely these radical conflicts into the light and objectifies the differences in subjectivity that account for them.
Interestingly enough from our present perspective, dialectic and
foundations are the two functional specialties correlated with the
fourth level of intentional consciousness, the level highlighted in
Lonergan's later writings because of the emergence of a distinct
notion of the good, the level of existential subjectivity. On my
present interpretation, just as it is the emergence of the distinct
notion of the good that accounts for the possibility of these two
functional specialties, so it is these two functional specialties which
contain the key to understanding Method in Theology.

Dialectic

Foundations as a functional specialty is best understood, I
believe, from the understanding of dialectic. First, then, not all
differences in horizon are dialectical. Within a given cultural framework, people from any different backgrounds and with many different
occupations and fields of competence will recognize the need in that
culture for the competencies of the others. In this sense their
different horizons, determined by the different worlds in which they
live, will also either include the horizons of the others or at least
complement them. "Singly they are not self-sufficient, and together
they represent the motivations and the knowledge needed for the

functioning of a communal world. Such horizons are complementary."[14]

Furthermore, different horizons may be related genetically as suc-

cessive stages in a process of development. Horizons are dialectically

opposed when "what in one is found intelligible, in another is unintel-

ligible. What for one is true, for another is false. What for one is

good, for another is evil."[15] Moreover:

> . . . the other's horizon, at least in part, is attributed to
> wishful thinking, to an acceptance of myth, to ignorance or
> fallacy, to blindness or illusion, to backwardness or imma-
> turity, to infidelity, to bad will, to a refusal of God's grace.
> Such a rejection of the other may be passionate, and then the
> suggestion that openness is desirable will make one furious.
> But again rejection may have the firmness of ice without any
> trace of passion or even any show of feeling, except perhaps a
> wan smile. Both astrology and genocide are beyond the pale, but
> the former is ridiculed, the latter is execrated.[16]

Any given horizon is a "structured resultant of past achieve-

ment and, as well, both the condition and the limitation of further

development. . . . Horizons then are the sweep of our interests and of

our knowledge; they are the fertile source of further knowledge and

care; but they also are the boundaries that limit our capacities for

assimilating more than we already have attained."[17]

From the French Jesuit moral philosopher Joseph de Finance,

Lonergan draws the distinction between an exercise of freedom within

---

14
  Ibid., p. 236.

15
  Ibid.

16
  Ibid., pp. 236f.

17
  Ibid., p. 237.

a given horizon, horizontal freedom, and the exercise of freedom by which we move from one horizon to another, vertical freedom. The exercise of vertical freedom is twofold. Either one moves from one horizon to another in a continuous fashion, so that "the new horizon, though notably deeper and broader and richer, none the less is consonant with the old and a development out of its potentialities;"[18] or one moves by way of an about-face, by repudiating the characteristic features of the old horizon, by beginning a new sequence that reveals ever deeper and broader and richer dimensions. The latter exercise of vertical freedom is consequent upon a conversion, an intellectual conversion, a moral conversion, or a religious conversion. Each of the conversions is a modality of self-transcendence. "Intellectual conversion is to truth attained by cognitional self-transcendence. Moral conversion is to values apprehended, affirmed, and realized by a real self-transcendence. Religious conversion is to a total being-in-love as the efficacious ground of all self-transcendence, whether in the pursuit of truth, or in the realization of human values, or in the orientation man adopts to the universe, its ground, and its goal."[19] We have already seen Lonergan's account of the occurrence and sublation of these conversions.

If conversion is an about-face in terms of self-transcendence, there is also an about-face in the direction of inauthenticity. Such

---

18
 Ibid.

19
 Ibid., p. 241.

an about-face is termed a breakdown. Lonergan's account of breakdown

is interesting, and I choose to present here a lengthy quotation.

> What has been built up so slowly and so laboriously by the indi-
> vidual, the society, the culture, can collapse. Cognitional
> self-transcendence is neither an easy notion to grasp nor a
> readily accessible datum of consciousness to be verified. Values
> have a certain esoteric imperiousness, but can they keep out-
> weighing carnal pleasure, wealth, power? Religion undoubtedly
> had its day, but is not that day over? Is it not illusory com-
> fort for weaker souls, an opium distributed by the rich to quiet
> the poor, a mythical projection of man's own excellence into the
> sky?
> Initially not all but some religion is pronounced illusory,
> not all but some moral precept is rejected as ineffective and use-
> less, not all truth but some type of metaphysics is dismissed as
> mere talk. The negations may be true, and then they represent an
> effort to offset decline. But also they may be false, and then
> they are the beginning of decline. In the latter case some part
> of cultural achievement is being destroyed. It will cease being a
> familiar component in cultural experience. It will recede into a
> forgotten past for historians, perhaps, to rediscover and recon-
> struct. Moreover, this elimination of a genuine part of the cul-
> ture means that a previous whole has been mutilated, that some
> balance has been upset, that the remainder will become distorted
> in an effort to compensate. Further, such elimination, mutilation,
> distortion will, of course, be admired as the forward march of pro-
> gress, while the evident ills they bring forth are to be remedied,
> not by a return to a misguided past, but by more elimination, mu-
> tilation, distortion. Once a process of dissolution has begun, it
> is screened by self-deception and it is perpetuated by consis-
> tency. But that does not mean that it is confined to some single
> uniform course. Different nations, different classes of society,
> different age-groups can select different parts of past achieve-
> ment for elimination, different mutilations to be effected, dif-
> ferent distortions to be provoked. Increasing dissolution will
> then be matched by increasing division, incomprehension, suspicion,
> distrust, hostility, hatred, violence. The body social is torn a-
> part in many ways, and its cultural soul has been rendered inca-
> pable of reasonable convictions and responsible commitments.
> For convictions and commitments rest on judgments of fact and
> judgments of value. Such judgments, in turn, rest largely on
> beliefs. Few, indeed, are the people that, pressed on almost any
> point, must not shortly have recourse to what they have believed.
> Now such recourse can be efficacious only when believers present a
> solid front, only when intellectual, moral, and religious skeptics
> are a small and, as yet, uninfluential minority. But their num-
> bers can increase, their influence can mount, their voices can
> take over the book market, the educational system, the mass media.
> Then believing begins to work not for but against intellectual,

moral, and religious self-transcendence. What had been an uphill but universally respected course collapses into the peculiarity of an outdated minority.[20]

The functional specialty, dialectic, then, has a twofold task. Its first task is evaluative. There is a functional specialty called interpretation, whose task is to understand the _Sache_ of a text, its words, its author, and oneself; to judge the accuracy of one's understanding; and to determine the best way of expressing what one has understood. There is also a functional specialty called history, whose job is to determine the facts about what was going forward in the various movements being studied. Now, besides a hermeneutic which understands, there is also a hermeneutic which evaluates the constitutive and effective force of the meanings one has understood. And besides a history which determines facts, there is a history which evaluates achievements in terms of good and evil. Regarding the latter, Lonergan quotes the eminent historian Carl Becker: "The value of history is . . . not scientific but moral: by liberating the mind, by deepening the sympathies, by fortifying the will, it enables us to control, not society, but ourselves--a much more important thing; it prepares us to live more humanely in the present and to meet rather than to foretell the future."[21] Evaluative hermeneutic, evaluative history, and the promotion of the specialized research needed for them are one task of dialectic.

20
   Ibid., pp. 243f.

21
   Ibid., p. 245, quoting from Charlotte Smith, _Carl Becker: On History and the Climate of Opinion_ (Ithaca: Cornell, 1956), p. 117.

The second task of dialectic may be called horizon-encounter. We have already seen that dialectic deals with differences of horizon rather than differences of perspective, and with those differences of horizon which depend on opposed and radical convictions concerning the intellectual, moral, and religious infrastructure of human subjectivity. The only remedy to such differences is conversion. When such differences are involved in history, the discovery of new data will not remedy them, for the new data are just as susceptible of opposed readings as the old data. Regarding interpretation, there is a different self to be understood if one is convinced of the intellectual, moral, and religious capacities for self-transcendence from the self that is understood if one implicitly or explicitly rejects such self-transcendence. Such opposed self-understandings give rise to different understandings of the Sache of a text, of its words, of its author, and of the manner of expressing what one has understood. Regarding research, one's horizon determines what one will regard as appropriate data for hermeneutic and history. "One easily finds what fits into one's horizon. One has very little ability to notice what one has never understood or conceived. No less than interpretation and history, the preliminary special research can reveal differences of horizon."[22] Dialectic, then, is a matter of meeting the persons one is studying in history and interpretation, appreciating the values they represent, criticizing their defects, and letting oneself be

---

22
Ibid., p. 247.

challenged radically in the process, thus putting one's own self-understanding and horizon to the test.[23] Of particular relevance to our present concern is the observation that "such response is all the fuller, all the more discriminating, the better a man one is, the more refined one's sensibility, the more delicate one's feelings."[24]

Dialectic, then, is the completion of the phase of theology which mediates the past. It is a necessary complement to research, interpretation, and history, for while these latter respectively provide data, clarify what the data means, and narrate what was going forward, it is not their task to promote horizon encounter. But interpretation and history need such encounter, for hermeneutic depends on one's self-understanding and history as written depends on one's horizon.

The existence of dialectically opposed horizons gives rise to an enormous problem.

> All three types of conversion may be lacking; any one may be present, or any two, or all three. Even prescinding from differences in the thoroughness of the conversion, there are eight radically differing types. Moreover, every investigation is conducted from within some horizon. This remains true even if one does not know one operates from within a horizon, or even if one assumes that one makes no assumptions. Whether they are explicitly acknowledged or not, dialectically opposed horizons lead to opposed value judgments, opposed accounts of historical movements, opposed interpretations of authors, and different

---

23
 Ibid.

24
 Ibid., p. 245.

selections of relevant data in special research.[25]
Dialectic, as a functional specialty within theology, is confronted
with the formidable task of meeting these problems head on.

Two precepts govern the process of dialectic. Those statements compatible with intellectual, moral, and religious conversion
are to be furthered and developed; those statements incompatible with
intellectual, moral, and religious conversion are to be reversed.
The development of the compatible statements occurs through integrating them with fresh data and further discovery. The reversal of
the incompatible statements occurs by expeditiously excising from
these statements the elements incompatible with conversion. While
these two precepts determine the heuristic structure of dialectic,
though, the actual process is obviously far more complicated. Researches, interpretations, and histories, events, statements, and
movements have to be assembled. Then they have to be evaluated.
There follows the task of comparing them, so as to mark out affinities and oppositions. Then the dialectician must try to reduce
the affinities and oppositions to an underlying root, determine
which of these underlying sources depend on dialectically opposed
horizons, and finally select only these as the material to which he
devotes his energies under the guidance of the two heuristic principles. The different results achieved by different dialecticians,
furthermore, have to be clarified, and this clarification takes
place through a threefold objectification of horizon. First, each

---

25
   Ibid., pp. 247f.

investigator distinguishes between those statements compatible with any or all of the conversions and those statements found to be incompatible. Secondly, each investigator indicates the view that would result from the development of compatible statements and from the reversal of incompatible statements. Thirdly, each investigator takes these results as themselves materials to be operated on, to be assembled, evaluated, compared, reduced, classified, selected; that is, each investigator proceeds to the task of developing positions and reversing counter-positions.

Now, if the dialectician is operating from the basis of the conversions, his development of statements compatible with the conversions and his reversal of statements incompatible with them will result in what Lonergan calls "an idealized version of the past, something better than was the reality."[26] I take this to mean that he will find challenges to conversion everywhere. Moreover, he will find himself in agreement with all other dialecticians operating from the same foundation and supported in part by those operating from the foundation of one or two of the conversions. On the other hand, a dialectician not operating from the foundation of conversion would end up mistaking counter-positions for positions and positions for counter-positions, and developing counter-positions while reversing positions. The result would be that he would present, not an idealized version of the past, but a representation of it as worse than it really was. I think here, for example, of Leslie Dewart's presentation

---

26
Ibid., p. 251.

of the deleterious infection of the Christian message by the concerns
of Greek philosophy.[27] That the problem is real enough does not indicate that it is so blithely to be treated as nothing but a catastrophe. At any rate, while the dialecticians operating from the
foundations provided by intellectual, moral, and religious conversion
will find themselves in agreement with one another, dialectic carried
out without such foundations can produce a further dialectic in seven
different ways. For there will be dialecticians without any experience of conversion, those with the experience of only one of the
three conversions, and those lacking the experience of only one of
the three conversions. Those who present an idealized view of the
past will agree with one another in their idealization, while those
who represent the past as worse than it really was can disagree with
one another in seven dialectically opposed ways. Theoretically, then,
dialectic can be performed in eight radically different manners. The
problem is not only complicated; it is radical.

> It is only through the movement towards cognitional and moral
> self-transcendence, in which the theologian overcomes his own
> conflicts, that he can hope to discern the ambivalence at work
> in others and the measure in which they resolved their prob-
> lems. Only through such discernment can he hope to appreciate
> all that has been intelligent, true, and good in the past even
> in the lives and the thought of opponents. Only through such
> discernment can he come to acknowledge all that was misinformed,
> misunderstood, mistaken, evil even in those with whom he is
> allied. Further, however, this action is reciprocal. Just as
> it is one's own self-transcendence that enables one to know
> others accurately and to judge them fairly, so inversely it is

---

27
    Leslie Dewart, The Future of Belief (New York: Herder and
Herder, 1966).

through knowledge and appreciation of others that we come to know ourselves and to fill out and refine our apprehension of values.

Inasmuch, then, as investigators assemble, complete, compare, reduce, classify, select, they bring to light the dialectical oppositions that existed in the past. Inasmuch as they pronounce one view a position and its opposite a counterposition and then go on to develop the positions and reverse the counter-positions, they are providing one another with the evidence for a judgment on their personal achievement of self-transcendence. They reveal the selves that did the research, offered the interpretations, studied the history, passed the judgments of value.

Such an objectification of subjectivity is in the style of the crucial experiment. While it will not be automatically efficacious, it will provide the openminded, the serious, the sincere with the occasion to ask themselves some basic questions, first, about others but eventually, even about themselves. It will make conversion a topic and thereby promote it. Results will not be sudden or startling, for conversion commonly is a slow process of maturation. It is finding out for oneself and in oneself what it is to be intelligent, to be reasonable, to be responsible, to love. Dialectic contributes to that end by pointing out ultimate differences, by offering the example of others that differ radically from oneself, by providing the occasion for a reflection, a self-scrutiny, that can lead to a new understanding of oneself and one's destiny.[28]

Foundations

It is dialectic, then, which brings to light the key to

Method in Theology, for "the basic idea of the method we are trying

to develop takes its stand on discovering what human authenticity is

and showing how to appeal to it. It is not an infallible method, for

men are easily unauthentic, but it is a powerful method, for man's

deepest need and most prized achievement is authenticity."[29] While

dialectic is the functional specialty which makes this basic idea a

---

28
   Bernard Lonergan, Method in Theology, pp. 252f.

29
   Ibid., p. 254.

topic, a question which affects the theologian as theologian, foundations is the functional specialty which thematizes this question. The first question dealt with in the foundations of theology is, What is human authenticity? The answer to this question provides theology with its foundations. Moreover, an individual theologian's answer to this question reveals the foundations of the theology of which he is the author.

Foundational Reality and the Functional Specialties

Besides the phase of theology which mediates the past, the phase of research, interpretation, history, and dialectic, there is the phase in which the theologian articulates his own positions, joins them together systematically, relates them to the sciences, to philosophy, and to history, and participates in the collaboration through which what one judges to be true is communicated to different members of different classes in different cultures. The foundations of theology are, for Lonergan, more specifically the foundations of this second or mediated phase of theology, of doctrines, systematics, and communications. The foundational reality, conversion, will be operative in research, interpretation, history, and dialectic, but it will not be a prerequisite for engaging in these functional specialties. Its operation will be implicit, in that "it does not constitute an explicit, established, universally recognized criterion of proper procedure in these specialties." Even with respect to dialectic, conversion is not necessary for lining up opposed positions, for revealing the polymorphism of human consciousness reflected in opposed interpretations and histories, "the deep and unreconcilable oppositions on religious, moral, and intellectual issues."[30] Conversion indeed functions in taking sides, but the sides are taken not by the dialectician as such but by the converted or unconverted person. The sides are taken in "a decision about whom and what you are for and, again, whom and what you are against. It is a decision illuminated by the manifold possibilities exhibited in dialectic. It is a fully conscious decision about one's horizon, one's outlook, one's world-view. It deliberately selects the framework, in which doctrines have their meaning, in which systematics reconciles, in which communications are effective."[31] Foundational reality is a deliberate decision in favor of "total surrender to the demands of the human spirit: be attentive, be intelligent, be reasonable, be responsible, be in love."[32] It is consciousness become conscience which constitutes the foundational reality. Such constitution is anything but the arbitrary drifting into one or another contemporary horizon that marks the unauthentic person. Nor is it a purely private affair based on nothing but intensely personal experience.

> While individuals contribute elements to horizons, it is only within the social group that the elements accumulate and it is only with century-old traditions that notable developments occur. To know that conversion is religious, moral, and intellectual, to discern between authentic and unauthentic conversion, to recognize the difference in their fruits--by their fruits you shall know them--all call for a high seriousness

---

30
  Ibid., p. 268.

31
  Ibid.

32
  Ibid.

and a mature wisdom that a social group does not easily attain or maintain.

It follows that conversion involves more than a change of horizon. It can mean that one begins to belong to a different social group or, if one's group remains the same, that one begins to belong to it in a new way. Again, the group will bear witness to its founder or founders whence originated and are preserved its high seriousness and mature wisdom. Finally, the witness it bears will be efficacious in the measure that the group is dedicated not to its own interests but to the welfare of mankind. But how the group is constituted, who was the founder to whom it bears witness, what are the services it renders to mankind, these are questions not for the fifth functional specialty, foundations, but for the sixth, doctrines.[33]

The foundations of the mediated phase of theology will consist in an objectification of this deliberate decision about one's horizon. What will be paramount for the foundations of a theology that is an ongoing, developing process, will not be a set of logically first propositions, but the immanent and operative set of norms guiding each forward step, ensuring the acceptance and development of positions and the rejection and reversal of counter-positions. The sole and ever precarious guarantee of such process lies in the three conversions. It is provided only if "investigators have attained intellectual conversion to renounce the myriad of false philosophies, moral conversion to keep themselves free of individual, group, and general bias, and religious conversion so that in fact each loves the Lord his God with his whole heart and his whole soul and all his mind and all his strength."[34] Such a foundation will not provide the premises for deducing all desirable conclusions. It is not a set of

---

33
  Ibid., p. 269.

34
  Ibid., p. 270.

propositions uttered by a theologian but "a fundamental and momentous change in the human reality that a theologian is. It operates, not by the simple process of drawing inferences from premises, but by changing the reality (his own) that the interpreter has to understand if he is going to understand others, by changing the horizon within which the historian attempts to make the past intelligible, by changing the basic judgments of fact and of value that are found to be not positions but counter-positions."[35]

While the attainment or nonattainment of converted foundational reality will not affect the methods followed in research, interpretation, history, and dialectic, the foundational question is of more than minimal importance to these functional specialties.

> One's interpretation of others is affected by one's understanding of oneself, and the converted have a self to understand that is quite different from the self that the unconverted have to understand. Again, the history one writes depends on the horizon within which one is attempting to understand the past; the converted and the unconverted have radically different horizons; and so they will write different histories. Such different histories, different interpretations, and their underlying styles in research become the center of attention in dialectic. There they will be reduced to their roots. But the reduction itself will only reveal the converted with one set of roots and the unconverted with a number of different sets. Conversion is a matter of moving from one set of roots to another. It is a process that does not occur in the marketplace. It is a process that may be occasioned by scientific inquiry. But it occurs only inasmuch as a man discovers what is unauthentic in himself and turns away from it, inasmuch as he discovers what the fulness of human authenticity can be and embraces it with his whole being.[36]

35
Ibid., pp. 270f.

36
Ibid., p. 271.

Foundational Reality and Pluralism

The manifestation of conversion in deeds and words depends on the degree of differentiation of consciousness in the converted subject. Thus the same fundamental stance of faith is expressed in a pluralism of forms and in a multiplicity of theologies. Lonergan distinguishes six differentiations of consciousness: common sense, theory, interiority, scholarship, art, and transcendence. "Any realm becomes differentiated from the others when it develops its own language, its own distinct mode of apprehension, and its own cultural, social, or professional group speaking in that fashion and apprehending in that manner."[37] The mathematically possible combinations of these differentiations are thirty-two in number. Moreover, each of them can be incipient or mature or receding.

> In a devout life one can discern the forerunner of mystical experience, in the art lover the beginnings of creativity, in a wisdom literature the foreshadow of philosophic theory, in the antiquarian the makings of a scholar, in psychological introspection the materials of interiorly differentiated consciousness. But what has been achieved need not be perpetuated. The heroic spirituality of a religious leader may be followed by the routine piety of his later followers. Artistic genius can yield place to artistic humbug. The differentiated consciousness of a Plato or Aristotle can enrich a later humanism though the cutting edge of genuine theory does not live on. High scholarship can settle down to amassing unrelated details. Modern philosophy can migrate from theoretically to interiorly differentiated consciousness but it can also revert to the undifferentiated consciousness of the Presocratics and of the analysts of ordinary language.[38]

---

[37] Ibid., p. 272.

[38] Ibid., p. 275. Notice the aside to Heidegger.

Thus, besides the radical pluralism that is the dialectical resultant of the presence or absence of the conversions, there is the "more
benign yet still puzzling variety that has its root in the differentiation of human consciousness."[39] Lonergan discusses the varieties of
Christian theology in terms of these differentiations,[40] only to conclude that the theology dominated by theoretically differentiated
consciousness is at an end, that theology will no longer turn to metaphysics for guidance and help in clarifying its thought and making it
coherent, but that the new source of basic clarification will be found
in interiorly and religiously differentiated consciousness. The former differentiation will provide theology with its general categories,
those which it shares with other disciplines; the latter differentiation will provide it with its special categories, those proper to
theology as such. The theologian engaged in the functional specialty,
foundations, has the task of working out both general and special theological categories on the basis or foundation of the conversions.

Foundations and Categories

Such a basis or foundation is transcultural, not as it may be
formulated by a given author, but in the realities represented in the
formulations. "These realities are not the product of any culture but,
on the contrary, the principles that produce cultures, preserve them,

---

39
  Ibid., p. 276.

40
  Ibid., pp. 276-281.

develop them."[41] The base for general theological categories is transcendental method, that of special theological categories God's gift of his love. General and special theological categories will be themselves transcultural only to the extent that they refer to the inner core of this twofold base. "In their actual formulation they will be historically conditioned and so subject to correction, modification, complementation. Moreover, the more elaborate they become and the further they are removed from that inner core, the greater will be their precariousness."[42] Nonetheless, as a set of interlocking terms and relations they will have the utility of models. They will be useful in guiding investigations, in framing hypotheses, and in writing descriptions. They may provide the theologian with a basic sketch of what he finds to be the case or they may not; if they do not, the very discovery of their irrelevance may help him uncover the clues necessary for further work. They may provide an adequate language to enable the theologian to discuss known realities. They may greatly facilitate description and communication. To the extent that they are built up from the basic terms and relations provided by transcendental method and religious experience, their validity will be quite real. Only the individual theologian, however, can decide whether any model is to be taken as more than a model, whether in itself it can be taken as a hypothesis or a description.

41
  Ibid., p. 282.

42
  Ibid., p. 284.

How are theological categories derived? Lonergan discusses first the generation of general theological categories, those which theology shares with other disciplines. The base or foundation of these categories is the theologian himself in his structured subjectivity as an attending, inquiring, reflecting, deliberating subject, as an intention of truth and value; it is the theologian himself with the operations of experiencing, understanding, judging, and deciding which he has uncovered within himself; it is the structure of these operations in their dynamic relations promoting intentionality through the transcendental precepts, Be attentive, Be intelligent, Be reasonable, Be responsible; it is the subject as self-transcending, as one whose operations reveal objects, whose structured operations reveal compound objects and whose self-conscious operations reveal, not objects, but the subject himself. This basic set of terms and relations can be verified, not only in the theologian himself, but in the men and women of all ages; and in these men and women, not in isolation, but as living in social groups which through their development and decline generate history. Furthermore, this basic set of terms and relations can be differentiated in many different manners. Each of the different conscious operations occurs in biological, aesthetic, intellectual, dramatic, practical, and religious patterns of experience. There is a different quality of consciousness inherent in the different conscious operations, and there are different manners in which the operations themselves proceed toward their goals--the manner of common sense, that of the sciences, of interiority and philosophy, of prayer and theology. These different manners of proceeding give rise

to different realms of meaning. The operations proceed toward their
goals within different heuristic structures. There is a sharp contrast between the differentiated consciousness that shifts with ease
from one manner of operation in one world to another manner of
operation in another world, and the relatively or completely undifferentiated consciousness which is at home only in its local manner or
variety of common sense. There is another sharp contrast between
those that have or have not been converted religiously, morally, or
intellectually, and this contrast gives rise to dialectically opposed
positions and counter-positions, models, and categories.

These various manners of differentiation vastly enrich the
basic and initial nest of terms and relations found in the intention
of truth and value that is objectified in transcendental method. This
broadened basis alone is what has provided Lonergan with the materials
for a sophisticated discussion of the human good, of values and beliefs,
of meaning, and of religion. These analyses, along with others such as
the elaboration of models of change in scientific knowledge; the analysis of developmental process from global operations through differentiation to integration; the understanding of scientific revolutions on
the model of successive higher viewpoints, of the universe of propor-
tionate being as a process of emergent probability, of authenticity as
generating progress and unauthenticity as bringing about decline; the
understanding of the problem of evil as the introduction to the discussion of religion; the intention of a potential universal point of
view providing a general semantics for hermeneutic--all of these
analyses from _Insight_--are what provide theology with its general

categories. In every case, the categories are derived from the transcultural base provided by the objectification of the transcendental infrastructure of human subjectivity in its intention of intelligibility, truth, and value. In every case, what is truly transcultural is the infrastructure, not its objectification in method nor the formulation of the categories derived from it. Nonetheless, what Lonergan is saying basically can be summarized by stating that Insight and the first four chapters of Method in Theology provide examples of what is meant by speaking of general theological categories.

The derivation of special theological categories is quite different today from what it was in medieval theoretical theology. There the starting-point was a metaphysical psychology representing the order of nature and founding general theological categories, and a notion of sanctifying grace framed in terms of this metaphysical psychology and articulated in terms of supernatural entities. Now the starting-point is rather intentionality analysis and transcendental method as grounding general theological categories, and a dynamic state of being in love with God, a state manifested in inner and outer acts, as grounding special theological categories. The data on the foundation of these categories are the data on conversion and development. They will provide the functional specialty, foundations, with its first set of special theological categories. "There are needed studies of religious interiority: historical, phenomenological, psychological, sociological. There is needed in the theologian the spiritual development that will enable him both to enter into the experience of others and to frame the terms and relations that will express that experience."[43] A second set will be derived by moving from the subject to the community, to "the history of the salvation that is rooted in a being-in-love, and the function of this history in promoting the kingdom of God amongst men."[44] A third set is derived by moving from our loving to the loving source of our love. "The Christian tradition makes explicit our implicit intending of God in all our intending by speaking of the Spirit that is given to us, of the Son who redeemed us, of the Father who sent the Son and with the Son sends the Spirit, and of our future destiny when we shall know, not as in a glass darkly, but face to face."[45] A fourth set of categories will deal, not with authentic or inauthentic humanity, but with authentic or inauthentic Christianity, and a fifth set with the progress and decline which are generated respectively from these. "Not only is there the progress of mankind but also there is development and progress within Christianity itself; and as there is development, so too there is decline; and as there is decline, there also is the problem of undoing it, of overcoming evil with good not only in the world but also in the church."[46]

43
 Ibid., p. 290.

44
 Ibid., p. 291.

45
 Ibid.

46
 Ibid.

In general, then, "the derivation of the categories is a matter of the human and the Christian subject effecting self-appropriation and employing this heightened consciousness both as a basis for methodical control in doing theology and, as well, as an a priori whence he can understand other men, their social relations, their history, their religion, their rituals, their destiny."[47] The general theological categories function in any of the eight functional specialties. The use and acceptance of the special theological categories as referring to reality occurs in doctrines, systematics, and communications. The concern of foundations is "with the origins, the genesis, the present state, the possible developments and adaptations of the categories in which Christians understand themselves, communicate with one another, and preach the gospel to all nations."[48]

Psyche and Foundations

Foundations, then, would seem to have a twofold task: that of articulating the horizon within which theological categories can be understood, and that of deriving the categories which are appropriate to such a horizon. What is the relationship of my present work to this twofold task?

I have spoken of the first task in terms of framing a patterned set of judgments of cognitional fact and of value cumulatively heading toward the full position on the human subject. I have described my

---

47
  Ibid., p. 292.

48
  Ibid., p. 293.

own work as a contribution to this patterned set of judgments and thus to the full position on the subject. Implicit in this description is the claim that the present work is a complement to the work of Lonergan. My question now is whether it is a needed complement. Is psychic self-appropriation an intrinsic part of transcendental method? Is it a necessary feature of the objectification of the transcendental infrastructure of human subjectivity? Can it be dispensed with completely? Can it be politely treated as a useful auxiliary? Or is it demanded by the task set by Lonergan, the task of moving toward a viable control of meaning for a new epoch in the historical evolution of Western mind? The question is answered, I believe, already by the affirmation that the psyche is no accidental feature of the transcendental infrastructure of human subjectivity and that it does not achieve its integration with intentionality by some kind of higher integration introduced by knowledge, but only in the free and responsible decisions of the existential subject. The integration of psyche and intentionality, to be sure, is not the only task confronting the existential subject. It is a task that for the most part affects his effective freedom, and there is the more radical question which he must deal with at the level of his essential freedom. What do I want to make of myself? The integration of psyche with intentionality occurs in the framework of his answer to that question. But occur it must, if this more radical answer is to bear fruit in the effective constitution of himself and of his world.

Lonergan speaks of placing "abstractly apprehended cognitional activity within the concrete and sublating context of human

feeling and of moral deliberation, evaluation, and decision."[49]
Until cognitional activity, no matter how correctly apprehended, is
so placed, it remains abstract in its apprehension. The move toward
greater concreteness on the side of the subject demands this second
mediation of immediacy by meaning. Only such mediation brings transcendental method to its conclusion. I confess that my own experience
and my association and collaboration with others who have been profoundly affected by Lonergan's cognitional analysis have prompted me
to the conviction that this is no easy task, that it is at least as
complicated as comprehending cognitional activity, that equally sophisticated techniques are needed for its execution, and that without
it the movement brought into being by Lonergan is left incomplete,
and those influenced by this method are left the potential victims of
what I must call an intellectualist bias. The shift of the center of
attention in Lonergan's work from cognitional analysis to intentionality analysis, from the intellectual pattern of experience to self-
transcendence in all patterns of experience as the privileged domain
of human subjectivity, has not yet been sufficiently attended to. The
underlying assumption is still that intellectual conversion is the last
and the rarest of the conversions. But the exigence giving rise to a
new epoch in the evolution of human consciousness only begins to be
met in the philosophic conversion aided by Lonergan's cognitional analysis. The radical crisis is not cognitional but existential. It is the
crisis of the self as objectified becoming approximate to the self as

---

49
    Ibid., p. 275.

conscious. It is the exigence for a mediation of the transcendental infrastructure of the subject as subject that would issue in a second immediacy. This exigence is only initially met by the appropriation of _logos_. Psyche will never cease to have its say and to offer both its potential contribution and its potential threat to the unfolding of the transcendental dynamism toward self-transcendence. My suspicion is that something along the lines of the psychic self-appropriation proposed in this paper is, in the general case, quite necessary if the concrete sublation of appropriated cognitional activity within the context of human feeling and moral decision is to take place. My suspicion is, too, that something like a depth psychological analysis carried out according to the understanding here offered is a necessary contribution to the maieutic that _is_ the self-appropriating subject. It is my conviction, then, that an articulation of psychic conversion is a constituent feature of the patterned set of judgments of cognitional fact and of value cumulatively heading toward the full position on the human subject that constitutes the renewed foundations of theology.

There is a second task of foundations. It is that of deriving categories appropriate to the horizon articulated in the objectification of conversion. What is the relation of psychic self-appropriation to this foundational task?

All theological categories have an archetypal significance. The general theological categories are those derived from the transcendental base giving rise to the emergence of the authentic cognitional and existential subject. This emergence is archetypally significant.

It is the ground theme of the dialectic between intentionality and psyche. It is objectified in a semantics of human desire. Special theological categories are those proper to a theology which would mediate between the Christian religion and the role and significance of that religion within a given cultural context. The cultural context is a compound of stories reflecting the ground theme of the emergence of existential subjectivity. The Christian religion is the fruit of a collaboration between man and God in working out the solution to the radical problem of this emergence. Both are archetypally significant. As the emergence of the existential subject is the archetypal drama of human existence, so the Christian religion in its authenticity is the fruit of the divinely originated solution to that drama. As psyche will continue to have its say in the drama even when intentionality has proclaimed its relative autonomy from imagination, so at the farthest reaches of the psyche there stands the image of the Crucified, symbolizing the surrender to the Father in which alone the finality of the psyche as a constituent feature of human subjectivity is achieved. Psychic self-appropriation is a part of the objectification of the transcendental and transcultural base from which both general and special theological categories are derived. It affects the self-understanding in terms of which one mediates the past in interpretation, history, dialectic, and the special research generated by their concerns. And it gives rise to the generation of theological categories appropriate to the mediated phase of theology, the phase which takes its stand on self-appropriation and ventures to say what is so to the men and women of different strata and backgrounds in different cultures

of the world of today. It gives rise to the possibility of theological categories, doctrines or positions, and systems which are
legitimately symbolic or poetic or aesthetic. It makes it possible
that such categories, positions, and systems can be poetic without
ceasing to be explanatory, without ceasing to fix terms and relations
by one another, without falling into a theology which is little more
than the camouflaged narrative of a given theologian's autobiography,
a purely descriptive theology relating the things talked about only
to the dramatic subjectivity of the given theologian. A hermeneutic
and dialectical phenomenology of the psyche would be the objectification of psychic conversion that is a constituent feature of the
foundations of theology in terms of which appropriate explanatory
categories can be enunciated. What Ray L. Hart has called a systematic symbolics[50] is an ambition that is methodologically both
possible and desirable. But its valid methodological base is found,
I believe, only in the mediation of immediacy in which one discovers,
identifies, accepts one's submerged feelings, only in the kind of
depth psychological analysis rendered possible by psychotherapy.

Second immediacy will never achieve a total mediation of
primordial immediacy. Complete self-transparency is impossible short
of the ulterior finality of man in the vision of God. Only in seeing
God as he is will we know ourselves as we are. But there is a poetic
enjoyment of the truth about man and God that has been achieved in

---

[50] Ray L. Hart, Unfinished Man and the Imagination (New York:
Herder and Herder, 1968).

many cultures, at many times, within the framework of many differentiations of consciousness, and related to different combinations of
the various realms of meaning. The second mediation of immediacy by
meaning can function in aid of a recovery of this poetic enjoyment.
Methodologically it can function in aid of the second naiveté ambi-
tioned by Paul Ricoeur, the immediacy of the twice-born adult, in
which I "leave off all demands and listen."[51] It may well be, in
Eliot's words, that

> . . . the end of all our exploring
> Will be to arrive where we started
> And know the place for the first time.[52]

In that case, however, the end of all our exploring will be neither intellectual conversion nor even the far more complete mediation of <u>logos</u>
as intention of self-transcendence aided by the later Lonergan. The
mediated return to immediacy demands in addition the satisfaction of a
further exigence toward a second mediation of immediacy by meaning.
Moral and religious conversion can consciously and consistently sublate intellectual conversion only if they are aided by a further step
in the process of the appropriation of human interiority.

As this process of sublation goes forward, one will confirm
the suspicion, I believe, that the gift of God's love has been responsible for initiating and sustaining the whole process, that one's own
responsibility has been a cooperation with a fated call to a dreaded

---

51
Paul Ricoeur, <u>Freud and Philosophy</u>, p. 551.

52
T. S. Eliot, "Little Gidding."

holiness, with a "charged field of love and meaning, which at times has reached notable intensity, but more often has been 'ever unobtrusive, hidden, inviting each of us to join.'"[53] He will discover that he has been in love all along, experiencing something analogous to the ups and downs, the misunderstandings and reconciliations of every love relationship. While he may suspect and affirm this relationship all along or at least at intervals, the eye of faith becomes sharpened and its interpretations more sensitive as one learns to confess the extent to which he is loved with an otherworldly, all-embracing, completely gratuitous, and severely jealous love, and to experience the extent to which he can indeed be brought to leave off all demands and listen. Psychic conversion facilitates the sublation of one's commitment to truth into a commitment to all value, and the sublation of both into a state of surrender leaving the unified affectivity of love, joy, peace, patience, kindness, goodness, faithfulness, gentleness, and self-control concerning which there is no law. But this post-critical religious consciousness is quite different from the religious experience which may have initiated the entire process, for it is habitually focused in its immediacy on interiority, time, the generic, and the divine, rather than on exteriority, space, the specific, and the human. The clearing of the possibility of such religious consciousness and the elucidation of its experienced reality would be the first task of the foundations of a theology which would mediate a critically conscious and historically sophisticated cultural

---

53
  Bernard Lonergan, Method in Theology, p. 290.

matrix and the role and significance of living religion within that matrix. But such a consciousness is attained only in the third stage of the appropriation of interiority: not in the stage of the discrimination of spirit or _logos_ in intentionality analysis, nor in the stage of the cultivation of soul in psychological analysis, but in the stage of the self-surrender to the undertow on the part of discriminated spirit and cultivated soul. Then, in the language of the concerns of the new hermeneutic, "if theology is understood as language about God, it is to be asked to what extent its language is _from_ God."[54] God and ourselves will be, in a sense, together in the one sentence, for God will be thought and affirmed again in strict relation to "real life," to the world mediated by meaning in its experienced immediacy. When a transcendental aesthetic becomes a part of the foundations of theology, the ultimate religious and theological dialectic will occur in the dialogue of world religions, and it will revolve about the concrete figures of this ultimate dialectic: Gotama, Krsna, Lao-Tse, Confucius, Mohammed, Abraham and Moses, Jesus. Through this dialogue, perhaps as nowhere else, the common rootedness of the human side of all religion in the archetypal function will be recognized. Moreover, systematic theology can then become, in John Macquarrie's phrase, "a kind of phenomenology of faith."[55] But its basic terms and relations will be explanatory, because derived from the most thorough-

---

[54] Robert W. Funk, Language, Hermeneutic and Word of God, p. 68.

[55] John Macquarrie, An Existentialist Theology (London: SCM Press, 1955), p. 6.

going fidelity to the methodical exigence. Such fidelity, pursued to its limits, turns truth into poetry. As Vico declared all to begin with poetry, so perhaps there is a way of affirming that all ends with poetry: we end where we began, but we see the place as if for the first time. Perhaps even of the theologian, it may be said with Hölderlin and Heidegger:

Full of merit, and yet poetically, dwells
Man on this earth.[56]

---

[56]
Quoted by Heidegger in "Hölderlin and the Essence of Poetry," in Existence and Being, Douglas Scott, trans. (Chicago: Henry Regnery, 1949), p. 270.

BIBLIOGRAPHY

Adler, Gerhard. The Living Symbol: A Case Study of the Process of Individuation. Princeton: Bollingen, 1961.

Becker, Ernest. The Denial of Death. New York: The Free Press, 1973.

Campbell, Joseph. The Masks of God. Vol. I: Primitive Mythology. New York: Viking Press, 1970.

Crowe, F. E., ed., Collection: Papers by Bernard Lonergan. New York: Herder and Herder, 1967.

Dunne, John S. The Way of all the Earth. New York: Macmillan, 1972.

Edinger, Edward F. Ego and Archetype: Individuation and the Religious Function of the Psyche. New York: C. G. Jung Foundation, 1972.

Eliot, T. S. Four Quartets. New York: Harcourt, Brace and World, 1971.

Funk, Robert W. Language, Hermeneutic, and Word of God. New York: Harper and Row, 1966.

Gendlin, Eugene. Experiencing and the Creation of Meaning. Toronto: Free Press of Glencoe, 1962.

Hart, Ray L. Unfinished Man and the Imagination. New York: Herder and Herder, 1968.

Hegel, G. W. F. Sämtliche Werke, Bd. IV, Wissenschaft der Logik, Erster Teil: Die Objective Logik. Stuttgart: Frederick Fromann Verlag, 1965.

Heidegger, Martin. Being and Time. Translated by John Macquarrie and Edward Robinson. New York: Harper and Row, 1962.

_____. Kant und das Problem der Metaphysik. Frankfurt am Main: Klostermann, 1951.

Henderson, Joseph L. The Wisdom of the Serpent. New York: Braziller, 1963.

Hillman, James. The Myth of Analysis. Evanston: Northwestern University Press, 1972.

Ihde, Don. Hermeneutic Phenomenology: The Philosophy of Paul Ricoeur. Evanston: Northwestern University Press, 1971.

Illych, Ivan. Medical Nemesis: The Expropriation of Health. Cuernavaca: Cidoc Cuaderno, No. 89, 1974.

Jaffé, Aniela. The Myth of Meaning. Translated by R. F. C. Hull. New York: C. G. Jung Foundation, 1971.

Jung, C. G. Collected Works. 17 volumes. Translated by R. F. C. Hull. Princeton: Bollingen Series XX, 1953-1973.

_____. Letters, I: 1906-1950. Selected and edited by Gerhard Adler and Aniela Jaffé. Translated by R. F. C. Hull. Princeton: Bollingen Series XCV, 1973.

_____. ed., Man and His Symbols. New York: Dell, 1971.

_____. Memories, Dreams, Reflections. Recorded and edited by Aniela Jaffé. Translated by Richard and Clara Winston. New York: Vintage Books, 1961.

Lonergan, Bernard. The Subject. Milwaukee: Marquette University Press, 1968.

_____. Insight: A Study of Human Understanding. New York: Philosophical Library, 1957.

_____. Method in Theology. New York: Herder and Herder, 1972.

_____. Philosophy of God, and Theology. Philadelphia: Westminster, 1973.

Macquarrie, John. An Existentialist Theology. London: SCM Press, 1955.

McShane, Philip, ed. Foundations of Theology. Notre Dame: University of Notre Dame Press, 1972.

Neumann, Erich. Depth Psychology and a New Ethic. Translated by Eugene Rolfe. New York: C. G. Jung Foundation, 1969.

_____. The Origins and History of Consciousness. Translated by R. F. C. Hull. Princeton: Bollingen Series XLII, 1954.

Progoff, Ira. The Death and Rebirth of Psychology. New York: McGraw Hill Paperbacks, 1973.

_____. The Symbolic and the Real. New York: McGraw-Hill Paperbacks, 1973.

Ricoeur, Paul. Fallible Man. Translated by Charles Kelbley. Evanston: Northwestern University Press, 1965.

_____. Freud and Philosophy. Translated by Denis Savage. New Haven: Yale, 1970.

_____. The Symbolism of Evil. Translated by Emerson Buchanan. Boston: Beacon Press, 1969.

Sala, Giovanni. Das Apriori in der menschlichten Erkenntnis: Eine Studie über Kants Kritik der reinen Vernunft und Lonergans Insight. Meisenheim am Glan: Verlag Anton Hain, 1971.

Storr, Anthony. C. G. Jung. New York: Viking Press, 1973.

von Franz, Marie-Louise. Number and Time: Reflections Leading Toward a Unification of Depth Psychology and Physics. Translated by Andrea Dykes. Evanston: Northwestern University Press, 1974.

Weaver, Rix. The Old Wise Woman: A Study of Active Imagination. New York: C. G. Jung Foundation, 1973.

Whitehead, Alfred North. Process and Reality: An Essay in Cosmology. New York: Harper and Row, 1957.

Whitmont, Edward C. The Symbolic Quest. New York: C. G. Jung Foundation, 1969.

Articles

Corbin, Henri. "Mundus Imaginalis, or the Imaginary and the Imaginal," Spring: An Annual of Archetypal Psychology and Jungian Thought, 1972, pp. 1-19.

Durand, Gilbert. "Exploration of the Imaginal," Spring: An Annual of Archetypal Psychology and Jungian Thought, 1971, pp. 84-100.

Hillman, James. "Anima," Spring: An Annual of Archetypal Psychology and Jungian Thought, 1973, pp. 97-132; 1974, pp. 113-146.

Lawrence, Frederick. "Self-Knowledge in History in Gadamer and Lonergan," in Philip McShane, ed., Language, Truth, and Meaning. Notre Dame: University of Notre Dame Press, 1972.

Lonergan, Bernard. "Theology in its New Context," in L. K. Shook, ed., Theology of Renewal I. New York: Herder and Herder, 1968, pp. 34-46.

Sala, Giovanni. "The Notion of Apriori in Kant's Critique of Pure Reason and Lonergan's Insight." Unpublished paper delivered at International Lonergan Congress, 1970.

Woolger, Roger. "Against Imagination: The Via Negativa of Simone Weil," Spring: An Annual of Archetypal Psychology and Jungian Thought, 1973, pp. 256-273.

Unpublished Material

Crowe, Frederick E. "An Exploration of Lonergan's New Notion of Value." Unpublished lecture, 1974.

Lonergan, Bernard. "Insight Revisited," Paper for discussion at the thirty-fifth Annual Convention of the Jesuit Philosophical Association, College Jean-de-Brebeuf, Montreal, 1972.

_____. "Prolegomena to the Study of the Emerging Religious Consciousness of Our Time," unpublished lecture, Willowdale, Ontario, Canada, 1974.

Moore, Sebastian. Journey into a Crucifix. Milwaukee, 1974.

ABOUT THE AUTHOR

The author, born in New York City, has been a
member of the Society of Jesus since 1956. He attended St. Louis University, where he received A.B. and M.A.
degrees in philosophy, writing a Master's thesis on the
development of the notion of freedom in the thought of
St. Thomas Aquinas. For the past ten years, he has been
studying the thought of Bernard Lonergan, and for the
last five years relating Lonergan's work to the concerns
of depth psychology. In 1975, he received his Ph.D. degree
from Marquette University, Milwaukee. He was an assistant
professor of theology there until 1978, when he accepted
his present position as an assistant professor of theology
at Creighton University in Omaha, Nebraska. He has published
articles germane to the topic of the present book in Anglican
Theological Review, The Thomist, Journal of Religion, and
Thought, and has spoken on the topic of his research at the
Boston College Lonergan Workshops in 1974, 1976, and 1977.
His research for the present work took him to the Lonergan
Center at Regis College, Toronto, and to the C. G. Jung
Institute, Zürich, Switzerland.